GW00982724

PEWTER
OF GREAT BRITAIN

PEWTER
OF GREAT BRITAIN

CHRISTOPHER A. PEAL

with contributions by
P. Spencer Davies
C. J. M. Hull
D. A. Mundill
I. D. Robinson
J. L. Scott

JOHN GIFFORD · LONDON

First published 1983 by
John Gifford Ltd,
125 Charing Cross Road,
London WC2

SBN 0 7071 0635 4

Photoset and printed in Great Britain by
Photobooks (Bristol) Limited,
Barton Manor, St Philips, Bristol

Contents

Acknowledgements

Acknowledgements are like the Toast of the Guests, up to a point, for we try to thank everyone concerned. That is where the similarity ends, for I have no witty stories to throw in.

To our wives, whose company pewter has usurped—especially to Sheila who married not only me, but the house and its decor. To my colleague writers—Dr Peter Spencer Davies, for his Scottish chapter; Charles Hull, for 'The Company'; Derrick Mundill, for his continental pewter; Dr Ian Robinson, for the new angle on British pewter in the States; and Dr Jack Scott, for a brief summary of his researches on the hitherto much-neglected Britannia metal. Most have shot their own photographs, with Mr P. J. B. Johnson providing the Company's, and Mr Alan Anderson for Dr Scott's chapter.

Less directly, perhaps more important to the end result, are the researchers, writers and photographers of the past, particularly H. H. Cotterell, A. Sutherland Graeme and Ronald Michaelis. Then we must remember with nostalgia the late-night sessions with a handful of collectors. I recall particularly staying up long after meetings with 'John' Minchin, Bill Cooper, Ron Michaelis, Ken Bradshaw and Rod Campkin; and a continuous 24 hours, with only 5 hours sleep, with David Walter-Ellis. It is invidious where to cease mention. Many more collectors, home and abroad, have provided more than stimulus—in alphabetical order, Bill Blaney, Michael Boorer, Walter Buckell, Tom Campbell, Win Carter, John Douglas, Ken Gordon, Frank Holt, Ron Homer, Bill Kayhoe, Sandy Law, Hepburn Myrtle, Stanley Shemmell, Peter Starling, all especially come to mind. And many more. Not to forget the many unknowns who ask questions at talks or in letters, which sharpen the thoughts. To Peter Starling for his kindly trenchant reading of my typescript and captions.

Especially am I eternally grateful for membership of The Pewter Society, for all the happiness it has polished onto the subject. It is impossible to remember just who said or sparked off each thought. Outside the Society, credit to Maurice Stephenson, formerly editor of *Libra*, with his insatiable efforts to further information on standards, capacities, verifications and so on. Let us remember the several first class and very knowledgeable professional pewter men: the late Bert Isher, Richard Mundey, Charles Casimir, Peter Hornsby, Albert Bartram inter alia, with all of whom it is so easy to integrate in conversation, and to whose activities our collections owe so much. And to the Cotswolds for being what they are, and harbouring traditionally so much pewter.

Let us remember the many museums' curators and keepers (primarily the Victoria and Albert, the Museum of London and see Appendix I) who have let down both their hair and their drawbridges to help us all—churches, too. Mentioned last—to pack a punch at the end of the round—who has done more than the Worshipful Company of Pewterers? It *is* invidious to draw the line. Several notable knowledgeable people wish to be anonymous. I do hope no-one is overlooked. I must thank the Board of Trade (Weights and Measures Department) for permission to publish verification marks and numbers, B. T. Batsford Ltd for permission to show extracts from Cotterell's *Old Pewter, Its Makers and Marks* and the British Museum for the trade cards. Also the various book and magazine publishers who have asked me to write for them and on whose pages some of the illustrations in this book have appeared—*Antique Collecting, Antique Collector, Antique Dealer and Collector's Guide, Antique Finder, Apollo, The Connoisseur, Antique Collector Yearbook of Australasia, Antiques of America, Bulletin of The Pewter Collectors Club of America,* and *Journal of The Pewter Society.*

Finally to all who have contributed to the production of this book at Giffords, who have let me get on with it in my own way with tolerance and help. To the many, particularly the library of photographs of The Pewter Society, who have loaned me photographs for selection. To John Peal and David Tattersall for the great majority of photography, and also to D. Burton, R. Newing, M. Veasey and Tom Wilson. Also to Jarrold Colour Publications Ltd for permission to reproduce some of the full-colour shots of nineteenth-century pewter from their publication *Let's Collect British Pewter* (by this current author with drawings by Selwyn Taylor and Dave Shea).

Thank you, all of you, and many others.

The above acknowledgements were written by the late Christopher A. Peal at about the date of the beginning of his terminal illness. It is sad that he did not live to see the publication of this book, but he did see the galley proofs when he was in hospital. He was by then too ill to deal with them himself; if he could say so, he would wish me to thank most deeply his good friend Peter Starling, a fellow member of the Pewter Society, who took on posthumously the difficult task of proof-correcting and editing this his final work. I cannot be sufficiently grateful to Peter, and I hope that all readers and collectors will appreciate his labours on Chris's behalf.

Sheila K. Peal.

List of Illustrations

1. Introduction

'. . . you long for simple pewter' W. S. Gilbert

You might think that pewter is all just plain, simple. But, believe me, every piece has much to whisper to you, intimately, once you have gained its confidence. Some continental work is much more ornate, and 'pretty'—but in this book we are hardly concerned with work from abroad, except in one important chapter introducing it, helping to enable recognition.

You will never be poor as long as you have a collection: not that I support the investment collector. All abhor him, unless he puts as much knowledge back into the subject as he takes. Pewter is of unending interest, something to seek out, to look at, even if not to acquire, and on the journey one meets many of the people connected with it. Virtually every piece you see, whether in shops, museums or collections, even the mid-nineteenth-century piece, has some quality or information you can extract.

In a fire all stock and production material of the original edition of *British Pewter & Britannia Metal (BP & BM)* was destroyed. Perhaps the Almighty thought it was time to disseminate more up-to-date information, for there are many things in it which can be updated! Everyone knows that as soon as you go into print you are out of date, but let us be as close as possible. This is a phoenix of *BP & BM* much revised, greatly amplified, with many new photographs, from a diversity of sources very largely unpublished. In fact, a new book.

I have taken in a 'continental' chapter on the more likely types to be seen, so that you know what you are buying; or, if you wish to remain insular, you know what *not* to buy. The subject is vast, and there are few books available. Derrick Mundill is bi-lingual and so has access to the best of both worlds. There is a specialised chapter on Britannia by an author in the United States who broke new ground when studying in Sheffield in researching this vastly-scorned subject, and has prepared a book on British Britannia. Britannia has hitherto been shunned by collectors, but let us remember that before the Second World War early pewter was in good supply, and the cast was preferred to the spun and die-stamped. Alas, tons and tons of good Britannia was worth more as scrap than as products. Dr Scott has kindly produced an enticing chapter on the subject.

There is a chapter of great interest to American collectors by Ian Robinson on English pewter exported new, originally for use in the States. The Worshipful Company of Pewterers' librarian, Charles Hull, very kindly contributed a chapter, which makes the position of the Company through the ages more comprehensible.

Scottish pewter, too, is dealt with by a most knowledgeable collector in the subject which, particularly in regard to nineteenth-century pots, has been so disregarded. Do not most people, when considering Scottish, switch off after tappit hens, Edinburgh

1

and Glasgow measures, and very similar stately flagons and communion cups? I am delighted to have Dr Peter Spencer Davies contributing the chapter on Scottish pewter since he has been researching the subject for many years.

At the outset we must have a clear, common understanding of what we are talking about. 'Pewter' is tin alloyed with lead or other (grey) metal, and it includes the very fine ware of the later Middle Ages when it was alloyed with a small amount of copper. Equally 'pewter' is accepted as including Britannia metalware—items made from sheet form antimony-alloyed tin, but in the cold processes such as spinning. This constitutes a sub-class (the process having been expressly forbidden of old in the Pewterers Company rules), yet it comes under the umbrella title of pewter, and many collectors are pleased to acquire good specimens of Britannia ware. On its own, Britannia ware is a fascinating subject, almost more akin to silver than 'pewter'. The *traditional* pewter, no matter what alloy, was always cast.

So pewter has two meanings: (a) the family of tin alloys—with copper, lead, antimony (and additives); and specifically (b), items cast in these alloys. Likewise 'Britannia metal' has two meanings; primarily it is wares made by the cold processes of spinning, die-stamping and hand-forming; secondarily, referring to the antimony alloy used for those wares (but also this was used for nineteenth-century better-quality cast products). These dual definitions are important to grasp, and will explain and reconcile a divergence of view apparent in Dr Scott's most interesting chapter on Britannia. Recently the Pewter Society of Great Britain agreed the following description of Britannia metal: 'Britannia metal ware is understood by collectors as referring to items made of a pewter alloy containing antimony and is essentially manufactured from rolled sheet by cold forming and thus differs from pewter ware which is cast. Ancillary parts such as handles, feet and knobs may be cast and the items assembled by soldering.'

It was, apparently, never intended that pewter should contain silver; traces, if any, are due to its presence in the ore, and to remove it would have been very costly: its presence serves neither harmful nor beneficial purposes in the minute proportions which occur. 'Real silver pewter' used to be included in the sales talk of antique dealers; they were probably referring to the hard alloy used increasingly for fine ware in the eighteenth century, and more comprehensively in the nineteenth. This hard metal is tin alloyed with antimony (probably plus copper), with the total exclusion of lead. In the text I will refer to the alloys by the variant, for example, 'lead alloy', the ninety or ninety-five percent or so tin being understood.

The standards of alloying were simply and (although rather incomprehensibly) exactly laid down in our earliest surviving records, going back to the fourteenth and fifteenth centuries. Control and observation of the regulations were well maintained, for failure to comply soon entailed fines and seizure of faulty or sub-standard products. However, evasion and enterprise developed towards the latter part of the seventeenth century and long before the mid-nineteenth century the Worshipful Company of Pewterers, who were the controlling body, no longer had effective control.

In the nineteenth century manufacturers used different (qualities of) alloys, and in the last few years more thought has been applied to these. Analyses by modern methods are not destructive, but are very expensive—so not very much has been done. By the enterprise and co-operation of the Pewterers Company, sufficient *has* been done to throw a headlight on the road ahead, from analyses of some eighteenth century items, so that now we are adequately aware and can be tolerably sure of the basic

2

alloying agent. Specimens with copper alloy are now very rare. I have only one such plate (of c.1490) in my collection which demonstrates a quite different result from that of lead alloy—it is much harder, more resonant and apparently almost infinitely less susceptible to oxidation. Therefore we can deduce that copper was very seldom used after the mid-sixteenth century.

From then on lead was not the sole adulterant (with other useful traces too), for antimony had appeared in continental pewter in the sixteenth century, and had made its entrance into British pewter in the seventeenth century. Increasingly it was used conversely with lead through the eighteenth century. Interesting analyses have been carried out by the Tin Research Institute, and by Winterthur Museum.

To turn to Britannia metal briefly—this alloy was first produced in the eighteenth century, but it is now very unusual to find specimens of the cold-process ware earlier than about 1830. A separate chapter is devoted to this subject, which surely is recognised as 'collectable'. It was evolved for economy, better properties in use and capability of copying silver styles more closely. It comprised tin, approximately ninety-two percent, antimony six percent and copper two percent. This produced a harder alloy, which was practical in a much thinner gauge in sheet form and could be worked like the ornate styles of silver, yet still retain strength. One might say that Britannia metal is the spurned poor relation of pewter, although this Fitz-Pewter is sometimes very charming. In any case; it was the final death blow to its forbear. Cotterell, the first real authority, regrettably and with the purest intentions did a great disservice to unborn potential collectors, for in his writing he lost no opportunity to decry this medium (possibly intending to refer to the latter-century Electro-Plated Britannia metal products)—and so the very people who had an affinity for base metal were advised to weed out Britannia metal and be rid of it. Having inspired neither interest nor followers, Britannia has been ill-served by research and publications in Great Britain until now when it has taken an American—Dr Jack Scott, studying in this country—to recognise the potential, and we are fortunate to have a chapter by him, although his interpretation is stimulatingly at variance from ours.

In the original edition was written 'Why turn away from Britannia metal or Art Nouveau?'. How prophetic, only 8 years ago! But still good Britannia is hard to come by, even though the price has gone up five- to ten-fold. And Art Nouveau—some collect it in all media but others collect only Art Nouveau pewter. I believe that Liberty's of London have made efforts to keep a wide stock of the original and beautifully-made 'Tudric' products—their own brand. I suppose it is true of many subjects of collecting: if you like it, and can afford it, buy it; otherwise in two years you will regret it sorely.

There should be plenty of information for the experienced collector too. Since advocating collecting nineteenth-century pewter I have seen some very fine collections —one must consist of over a thousand pieces. I have been very happy to put together a good collection right across the range, but this is not so easy these days. So, if you have the inclination, put on your skis!

Never, I think, has there been so much good pewter—in collections; and perhaps even more encouraging are the frequent major sales. But I *do* feel that the provincial antique shop is an unpromising source. All seems to go via the major salerooms, and 'finds' are scarce—unless you seek some off-beat subject, and I hope you do. So much research is required, and therein lies the real interest. I should know, for I receive a large amount of correspondence. Until recently I was honorary secretary of a world-wide society, which has shown me the very great depth and spread of current interest in

3

this subject and what a very valuable contribution many of the 'unknowns' supply to the general fund of detailed information. Never was pewter in better heart except, perhaps, in the ordinary everywhere antique shop. Literature, demand, and therefore prices, have brought out so much pewter. But still, mark my word, there are bargains to be had, from bric-à-brac to specialised suppliers. No-one knows everything, so with diligence and possibly special requirements you may be lucky in your thirty-to-one specialisation.

To revert, there is a very great movement of pieces on the market, principally via the salerooms, at a price. So it behoves the potential purchaser to know what he faces. Are all parts true? Is it that wee bit apart which puts it in a class of its own? Is it a repro? Or a fake? I wonder how many fakes, if any, have been destroyed! There is only a small proportion of these but, if you are unskilled, do be careful of things which have 'stuck' in shops. There may be a reason why the runners, and trade, and other collectors have shunned the piece. You have much more money in your pocket than I had but then prices are much higher. I do regret almost everything I ever passed on—the exceptions being the 'naughty' ones which all embryo collectors cannot resist, and they are always most embarrassing to dispose of. Always at a loss—but watch out for the provincial sale!

Do not expect to find prices quoted in this book. To attempt to do so would be to render a very great disservice to collectors and the trade. It is a free market, and let it remain so. At sales sometimes two people go mad—from desire, jealousy or ignorance. I have seen examples of each when prices fetched were about three times higher than those expected, while other prices were lower. One can soon establish, by observation, the normal price of nineteenth-century pewter. But it is very foolish to lay down prices of rarities—however much individuals would like to have them quoted. With any such rarity, and a comparatively narrow market, two or three large sales could very possibly depress prices. Stock on the market, economic conditions both in this country and elsewhere, condition of items, embellishments such as engraving, marks, doubts about the entirety or authenticity, will all have a very strong effect on prices. If you see prices 'quoted', you can only view them with great caution.

So, prices vary. If you go to a shop in an out-of-the-way place, you can usually expect to pay less than in a glamorous area on the American tour route—but it does not always work out logically. A dealer will sometimes price up to what he thinks he might get, or perhaps he has paid too much for the piece. From certain major salerooms one can buy lists of prices fetched, subsequent to a sale. Conversation with experienced collectors may elicit some idea of values, or one can visit specialised dealers.

Taken all round, prices have gone forward horrifyingly, at least so it seems to some of us who cannot readily keep up with inflation. Now that the subject is so well established on such a wide base it is only reasonable that prices will continue to go ahead similarly; this has a very pleasant corollary—it is a very short time before you can expect to see your money back on a piece, should you wish to sell; and at the previous rate, it would be only very few years before you had beaten the rising cost of living index.

Everyone wants an author to be authoritative, to be given facts with certainty, but narrow dating of pieces and styles must usually be subject to a little tolerance. For example, one must take into account the span of use of a maker's mark, or how long before a style was adopted provincially. The chapter on marks will amplify and clarify the reasons for some uncertainties.

So, realising I do not know everything, here is a survey, aided by some extremely competent assistants. A word of warning—you should not accept the written word as the last word. One of my favourite tags is—'The more you know, the more you know you don't know'. How true, and how humble I am, in the face of the new rising stars. There is room all round for so much more research, probably *c.* 1700 onwards, the later, the more! So there is plenty of scope for anyone to make a name for himself. I only hope that there are serious contenders in action right now!

Let us run through a very brief history. Pewter was evolved by the Romans in Britain in the third and fourth centuries, and they made a remarkably-wide range of sophisticated wares. It then disappeared until the eleventh century, in which there is record of church use. Twelfth-, thirteenth- and fourteenth-century graves of monks

1   A typical example of a Romano-British plate, amongst the earliest pewter. Usage was as a stand for an ewer. *c.*350 AD. Dia. 15¼in.

when disturbed, disclose sepulchral chalices. Without doubt there was by that time considerable manufacture of widespread domestic pieces. Ordinances of 1348 establish the standard alloy, and make it clear that pewter manufacture was a recognised craft. A little more than a century later the London pewterers were granted a charter, and the industry was thriving in other centres. Records relate to a wide range of products but we cannot identify what they were; very few examples, except spoons, survive. The records give much information concerning the sixteenth century and, although rare, there are a fair number of plates still in existence, but almost no hollow-ware.

The seventeenth century was the 'golden age', and many examples of domestic ware of the latter half are now in collections, and also church flagons spanning the whole

2 The golden age—a representative group of fine pieces of *c*.1660–1700.

century. Competition from other media—and perhaps too many tradesmen—caused a recession and undermined the Pewterers Company. In the eighteenth century styles became longer lived, the Company lost control, and towards the end Britannia metal appeared.

In the nineteenth century a big impetus was caused by the implementing of Imperial Measure—but only for pub tankards and measures to which use pewter manufacture was more or less confined. But there *was* a lot being manufactured, over a very wide range of products—much for medical use in the Crimean War, for instance. By now Britannia metal had taken over domestic use.

In the first decade of the twentieth century two exhibitions were staged and the first books appeared. Awareness and collectability were created and the Society of Pewter Collectors was founded in 1918. Reproductions and fakes appeared in the 1920s and Cotterell's monumental work, *Old Pewter, Its Makers and Marks (OP)* was published in 1929. Finally, in the early 1930s pubs were no longer allowed to serve beer in pewter unless asked to do so. Presumably this was for hygiene reasons, but it may also have been due to the easy denting of lead pewter, with the consequent slight diminishing of contents. I think that the last item in lead pewter must have been the loggerheads inkpots, commonly mounted on a large pewter flange, which were still in use in post offices in the 1960s. The last functional use of lead pewter has ceased.

I am often asked if drinking from pewter is dangerous. Modern pewter is made from the lead-free alloy which constitutes the alloy of Britannia metal. It is, I suppose, possible that if you let your beer lie in lead pewter, the slight acidity might attack the metal. The answer is easy—drink up! In the case of tea—well, the teapots you are likely to be using are of Britannia base, and are completely harmless. So, either way, drink up, serve your friends (not your enemies) with home brew in your nineteenth-century pots—earlier if they are to hand. Pewter pots and home brew are wonderfully harmonious.

To build any collection entails an enormous expenditure of concentration and effort— preferably a time-and-patience effort rather than buying big too soon. So many other media are of numerous, widely-distributed items, well known by types and marked prices. For instance, silver is commonplace compared with pewter. Pewter of various types and ages is scarce—very scarce—and even more so in relation to demand. It is most rewarding to one's ego to recognise and buy such items at a reasonable price. Pewter is something you live with, in intimacy; not put behind glass windows, but ready always to be handled. If you have an affinity for metals then pewter is a most satisfying medium, and almost subconsciously you are aware of its part-personal ownership, its association with the past generally, and whether it evokes Pickwick or Pepys is only a matter of degree. It looks, feels, and is old. Pewter is a sufficiently off-beat subject to keep its adherents not too numerous, to enable the collector to be individualistic.

Like all collecting it results in constant awareness—seeking sources, parallels, information, museums, friends, churches, collections and shops. Maybe you will want to trace the maker, and where he lived, and generally conduct further research on the individual and his environment. Cotterell in his *OP* gives ample lead in this connection, yet there is a wealth still to do in order to understand more about the subject as a whole. This research has been continued. *More Pewter Marks (MPM)* is a different conception from being a working book, with as many marks again as *OP* and containing the gathered notes, rubbings, drawings and facts which so many collectors have rendered in the last 50 years. The response was so immediate and great, that its extensive *Addenda* (one third of the size of *MPM*) was published within a year, containing many more marks, and many marriages of *MPM* marks with makers. They were a wonderful example of the observation and co-operation of collectors past, old or rising, here and all over America and Australia. Identifications, new marks, still turn up, but in this subject we can never know all the makers of 400–500 years ago—unless science comes up with some method of evoking names from products! Methods of recording are mentioned in the chapter on marks.

There is a great excitement in tracing makers' marks—perhaps to find that they are unrecorded, or perhaps to add more to existing knowledge. Present collectors are but custodians of historical items. They must be conscientious custodians. They have had the fun of the chase. Its conclusion has led to the satisfaction of the increased knowledge. So those with collections should pay back into the kitty of overall knowledge all the research and information which can be extracted. Particularly now is this very important, while there are still some large collections and houses of suitable size; because how very much easier it is to compare and observe many pieces together than to have to travel, rely on the post or work from photographs. If you visit you cannot take very much and inevitably some necessary piece is left at home. Please, all those with collections, share out your knowledge verbally, written or pictorially. It is the due to both past, present and, even more important, the future. As homes and collections diminish in size, so will the ease of comparison. Perhaps that is why I press on although I am not a professional writer. You readers can do so much more and better, especially for pewter made during the last 200 or 250 years.

In the home it is not easy to display pewter in quantity with modern stark decor. Obviously a dresser, shelf or mantelpiece is excellent and all are suitable positions, but be prepared . . . you may start off with one or two pieces but with a little reading, increased enthusiasm, a surge of searching, and some luck, you become an ardent devotee and your collection grows. For a tolerant companion in the house—something basic and homely, with its soft gleam broken up by a myriad of dents and irregularities, yet not fragile—what medium is more peaceful? Now so many books are written on antiques and so much knowledge is disseminated by magazines, press, television, lectures and exhibitions, would-be collectors and the trade are more widely educated and to a higher standard. Prices are higher and more uniform. This has brought more out on the market and into circulation through recognition. The holder perhaps sees his collection change from intimate brothers and sisters to haughty glamour pieces, almost remote from the touch, even to be banished to the bank.

When your search has at last led you to a find, factors to consider are age, rarity, demand, condition, authenticity, price. Be bold from knowledge, not rash with optimism. How often one finds a collector who has impatiently rushed his fences— spent more money than sense—and has bought a fake, made-up piece or reproduction. One sees it so often, and I have done it myself, when more keen than knowledgeable. So often desire is greater than discretion. To collect for pleasure and investment, you must balance desire with knowledge, discrimination and money available. It is this latter factor being so out of gear with experience which has led over-confident lone-wolf collectors to waste away resources on fakes, or half-fakes. Why is it that an ignoramus of a subject so often seems to think that the piece he buys is *the* find of the year? This is the hazard of brashly stepping out of his sphere. It does not mean to say that with taste

3   Those were the days, when one could come across flagons like
this in ordinary antique shops. Note the hammered body. Maker,
John Emes, *c.* 1685. 8in to lip. *OP* and *MPM* 1566.

and background you cannot make a killing. I did not really know what my first piece of good pewter was, but fortunately had enough experience of oxide and general form to have found an exceptionally rare type of seventeenth-century flagon. Later I bought a fake glamorous candlestick, a reproduction tappit hen and, later still, a faked horned headdress spoon—the first and the last of these from high-class, well-known shops (now gone). The fact that neither shop should have possessed, offered or purveyed such goods (and very fully priced) is beside the point. The responsibility is the purchaser's. He must be the judge—and judges are wise, experienced and observant men!

The chapter head quotes ' long for simple pewter', 'Simple' pewter All is fascinating, with so much to disclose if you ask it the right questions. You can tell a girl how pretty she is, and she will not argue convincingly. You have to live with pewter to appreciate it to the full, to learn all it has to tell you about itself and about its brothers and sisters. One longs for pewter for the British simplicity of line and its subtlety of design, and the weight of its curves.

Do not forget, which we are inclined to do, that American ancestors are from many European countries, and in the field of pewter they range not only from England, Scotland and Ireland, but also from Germany and Sweden to which, naturally, Dutch and French pewter has flowed. So the chapter on continental pewter may also be of good use. Particularly, though, in the last 10 years, the attractions of British pewter have become apparent, and many an American collector has turned his pewter eye towards this country's wares.

If you are impatient to get to grips with detail by all means do some leap-frogging. Turn to the chapters you want—but do come back! You may have some possessions, and only want to know how to clean them. May I invite you to seek more detail as to the date and background of your mugs or plates. For this reason there are some early action chapters, for example, cleaning and marks. However, inspecting the background in all connections is a short cut to many years of expensive and hard-won experience and, perhaps, lost opportunities. It may be asked by new and future collectors, why waste time delving into facts which are purely archaeological and archivistic? They are *not*. You never know when you may meet something.

Several times over the years I have found pieces unwanted by other people, collectors too, who have not seen their potential or rarity value, simply because the collectors were sheep and had applied no imagination, no flexibility, to their buying. Yet here were items of far greater rarity, unrecognised, only because they *were* rare, and had not been illustrated. Far too many collectors only want to collect to a 'published catalogue': what is illustrated is respectable. Well, these collectors do serve a useful purpose by preserving standard types, but they never get any further.

Latterly, I am delighted to say, there has been a swing the other way particularly amongst the younger collectors. Perhaps because of price, perhaps because of a greater catholicity of selection, perhaps because of a greater wish to go out on a limb (and therefore not shun the unknown), a greater proportion of these un-illustrated pieces has been rescued. Later in this book I hope you may see some things which will arouse a sense of adventure, of seeking and striking out. Never despair; you too will see pieces, but not when you look for them, for they appear when you least expect them, quite possibly in the shop of a specialised dealer who may not have recognised the significant differences He may have bought it for rarity, but his clientele were sheep. Perhaps he has only just bought it. Perhaps he kept it for you?

Since *BP & BM* was published there has been an enormous surge in demand, particularly in nineteenth century ware. What was commonplace is scarcely seen

4 A measure of unknown use, spurned by some
collectors because they had not the reassurance
of seeing similar pieces illustrated. Develop your
own confidence. *c*.1710.

now, and costs accordingly. Prices will advance further still, faster than inflation. No-one wants money—cash—now. Anything is better than paper money. Yet antiques are no *guarantee*. Some years ago silver had a recession. Was not oak in the doldrums fifteen years ago? Pewter may go off the boil, but its following is far too broad now for prices to drift much. The Stock Market has not been very glamorous; certainly it has not been a pensioner's delight. In the time that pewter has shown a profit against inflation, the Stock Market is only about one-third of its old spending power. Pewter pays no dividends, but it does yield plenty of interest; and if necessary, it is very readily marketable. And it is legitimate to see that your money is wisely spent, with no harm done.

The format of this book follows *BP & BM* in that the advisable general subjects are dealt with first, including the Company, before going on to English pewter (by periods, not categories of wares) through Scottish to pewter exported originally *for use* in antiquity. This will help Americans to recognise British ware originally used there, and to distinguish it from pewter made (possibly by some of the very same immigrant makers) in the States. It will also throw a new light on some of our makers and their products. A Briton, Ian Robinson is a very keen resident collector in that exact area of the States where much imported ware has been found; because of his location his research and findings have been comparatively easy and logical.

Appendix I is a directory of 'where to see'. I do not claim it to be comprehensive and some displays may have been unintentionally omitted. There has been no qualifying standard, and many more museums have a few, sometimes very rare, pieces to show. Others may have large collections, but not on display. With the modern policy of changing displays it would be well to check before making a journey specially to see a 'rested' display. Sometimes there are short-term exhibitions.

Appendix II consists of a short bibliography of books particularly recommended. Some may be out of print or hard to get. Some are on the point of publication. There is also a list of magazine articles which, although by no means comprehensive, includes the more useful ones. If these are not on the shelf, reference libraries are most helpful in finding availability of the articles, or supplying photostats of them, given fair notice.

Appendix III is an aid, I hope a spur, for regional research, consisting of the grouping of makers with marks of known provincial localities, extracted from *OP, MPM* and *Addenda*. Thus London has been omitted completely, and also the rare early Edinburgh castle marks. All are of post 1650 approximately—the dates referring to the striking of marks. There are many more known makers whose localities are suspected. Many entries in the two latter books amplify *OP* entries. A glance will show huge tracts of the country as unrepresented; and absence during any period in the 200 years is less easy to descry. It does indicate what a wealth there is yet to discover in this one field.

There has been a slight murmur off stage that I have been precipitate or autocratic in devising names for types. Modern communication is emphatically visual, and I have purposely tried to produce names which are visually descriptive and recognisable (for example, 'bucket and ridge'), in place of seeking unintelligible archaic terms which would convey nothing but confusion. I follow the lead of the past when I use terms like 'beefeater' or 'baluster'.

2. The Pewterers Company
by C. J. M. Hull

The formation of craft guilds can be traced from the Middle Ages. The guilds, centred in the cities and large towns, were instituted by craftsmen to control and protect their local industry through ordinances granted by their municipal authorities.

Although pewter manufacture was active throughout the country, there is no doubt that by the fourteenth century the London pewterers held a pre-eminent position, due to the scale of their industry and the ability to distribute throughout the country from the capital.

It is evident at this time with the rapid expansion of their trade that the London pewterers wanted to extend their control of the craft, and in 1348 submitted a petition to the mayor and aldermen of the City for the regulation of their trade. These and a number of subsequent ordinances were designed to establish a high standard of quality and workmanship and to standardise the working conditions and practices of the 'fellowship' in London.

A milestone in the Company's history was achieved in 1474 with the conferring of the charter of Edward IV, providing the London pewterers with wide powers of control of the industry 'in the City and throughout the Kingdom of England', giving authority to search for and to confiscate sub-standard ware, and to fine offenders.

The granting of the charter was obviously of immense importance to the Company, although the implementation of this greatly-extended control over the whole industry proved extremely difficult in practice. Leading manufacturing centres—Bristol, York, Norwich, Exeter and a number of other towns—were represented by pewterers in their local craft guilds with ordinances based on those of the London pewterers, so the maintenance of standards throughout England cannot have been left solely to the efforts of the Company in London. The right to search however was vigorously taken up and continued up to the end of the seventeenth century, latterly relying less on assistance from the local guilds. Records detail a number of such searches, journeying as far north as Durham and westwards into Cornwall. The strain on the Company's manpower resources must have been considerable, but they indicate the difficulty of countrywide control and the gradual waning of local guild influence. An interesting side note in their searches is that they proved 'self-financing'—the value of the goods confiscated covering the costs of the expeditions.

12

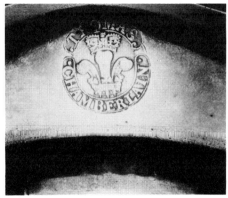

5. *Wavy-edge plate by Thomas Chamberlain–c.1750. OP* 873.

The Company has a fine dinner service comprising thirty-four pieces in all, both oval and round, representing the finest quality of flatware that can be found and is almost certainly in 'hard metal'. The hammer work on the bouges is immaculate and all the touch marks are struck—probably pressed—precisely and clearly, with the finish on the back of the plates almost as good as on the front. The twin beading round the edge of the plates was probably rolled in strip form and fashioned round and soldered on separately after the plates had been hammered and turned.

The Company is fortunate to have very detailed records of these times and note is made through the years of numbers of its members being reprimanded, fined and having sub-standard ware confiscated. In cases of gross misconduct a member could be expelled but, perhaps a little surprisingly, despite the many breaches of its regulations that are recorded, this ultimate penalty was only exercised extremely rarely, with—as often as not—reinstatement after a short space of time.

It is perhaps wrong to say the charter was granted to the Company, as it had to be 'purchased' from Parliament—an effective method of the times to raise revenue—and was valid only during the reign of the sovereign, a new charter having to be procured on the accession of his successor. Although no accurate figures of the cost of the various charters obtained by the Company exist, the costs must have been considerable and the Company appears to have been in fairly stringent circumstances through a good deal of its history. That the costs were met demonstrates the paramount importance to the Company in gaining these near-monopolistic conditions for the craft. In all, the Company was granted ten charters, the last being in the reign of Queen Anne (1702) under which the Company acts today.

As early as 1450 there is evidence of the craft in London being governed by a master and two wardens as assistants, an arrangement given perpetual status in the charter of 1474 and from that date a further ten senior pewterers were installed to form the governing body of the Company. The Company at this time comprised the ruling body of thirteen, the livery drawn from the leading and more wealthy master pewterers and the yeomanry, being the small independent masters, and the journeymen (that is, craftsmen employees of the masters). Whilst the governing body carried on the day-to-day business of the Company it would be wrong to conclude it was completely autocratic, as major decisions were regularly referred to committees which frequently contained liverymen and yeomen. In fact the journeymen, who would never have

13

matched the number of master members, can be seen to have enjoyed considerable influence in the drawing up of a number of the Company's regulations.

With its incorporation, it was necessary for the Company to have its own hall and in 1475 land and buildings were procured in Lime Street. By the turn of the century a 'great hall for feasts and general assemblies' had been added. The hall was used by the Company for its business and functions until the Great Fire of 1666, when it was destroyed completely, as was the great majority of its other property in the City and of

6 *Stuart candlestick.*
Base dia. 8¾in height 10in. Some earlier Stuart candlesticks tended to be of plain design but of handsome proportion. The date is probably mid-seventeenth century. Considering the amount of handling candlesticks received, the thinness of the section used on virtually all pewter candlesticks of this period is surprising.

course the premises of many of its members. With no fire insurance at that time, this proved a grievous blow to the Company's resources, but nevertheless a new hall was soon built on the same site, although to assist the Company's finances it was now also let for social and other functions. The hall was badly damaged by fire in 1840, losing many of its best features, but it was not until 1932, due to its poor state of repair, that it was finally demolished.

The industry reached its peak of prosperity in the third quarter of the seventeenth century—in the event very soon to go into decline—and it is interesting to note the composition of the trade at that time in London. The figures recorded in Guildhall give the average number of shopkeepers and master pewterers as 363 (this figure probably

14

included about fifty journeymen at the most) with the annual number of apprentices at forty seven for the period 1681–90. The average number gaining the freedom of the Company is given as approximately twenty, which indicates a large proportion of apprentices either failed to complete their term or did not follow in the craft. The figures also clearly show that even in this prosperous period for the industry, many master pewterers ran one-man businesses with the majority perhaps having only a single apprentice, with occasionally a journeyman. It is also interesting to see the

7 *Queen Anne lidless tavern pot. c.1702.*
Height 6⅝in with markedly tapering drum. Cast decoration on tankards is rare, although in the queen Anne period gadrooning is found occasionally on some pewter items, notably porringers. The handle has a 'boot heel' terminal. Note the 'A R' verification stamp.

methods of business followed in London, which were no doubt similar elsewhere in this country. The businesses fell into three main groups. First, the merchant pewterers who supplied large numbers of customers, both throughout England and overseas, and who produced only a portion of what they marketed; secondly, the master pewterer with his own shop, who sold retail and who put out and took in sub-contract work depending on the state of current business and, thirdly, the master whose business was predominantly that of manufacturing, most probably a limited range of pieces, and subcontract work, mainly relying on the merchant and retailer for the sale of his products. The individual wealth of pewterers therefore varied greatly, although by the setting up of a number of partnerships—incidentally disapproved of by the Company—it was possible for the less-wealthy pewterers to share the relatively expensive capital equipment—lathes, melting pots, hand and turning tools, soldering irons, and so on, and a range of bronze moulds—necessary to set up in business. (Some authorities have stated the figure to be as much as £500, although this does seem inconceivably high.)

The records show the Company to have had a stormy history, certainly over its first 350 years, both from internal and external influences. This is probably not surprising when one considers that over this period it was trying to control and adjudicate between fifty and 400, no doubt 'free thinking' master pewterers at any one time. Arguments between pewterers were frequent; from enticing away another's journeyman, unfair trading practices, employing foreign or unskilled labour, unruly apprentices and even to a complaint of aggressive language from the wife of a brother

8 *Cromwellian flagon. c. 1650.*
The sides of Cromwellian flagons are almost parallel, the cover only rarely having a knop. The thumbpieces are usually of the twin cusp type, but this flagon bears the 'twin kidney'. The exaggerated broad base on this flagon suggests it was for a specific usage.

9 *Cromwellian covered pewter tankard. c. 1650.*
A very early drinking tankard, very squat shape— 4in to lip—with slightly raised cover with cast rosette centre piece. Twin cusp thumbpiece. Mark 'C G' beneath a mounted horse. (Unrecorded.)

liveryman! Nevertheless, the 'fraternity' in London did have its social activities, which appear to have been robust to say the least. Feasts held at the hall allowed wives into the gallery who, by account, lowered ropes to haul up joints and other delicacies for their own consumption. Judging by the surprising disarray of some of the touches of the earlier Company touch plates, it is interesting to speculate if new freemen were admitted on such occasions, striking their marks at the end of the festivities.

The Company, for its part, enforced on the craft very specific standards of quality. All sadware—plates and other flatware that generally did not require cored moulding

—had to be made in 'fine metal'. This, according to the records, comprised 'pure tin with as much copper as its own nature will take', which would amount to no more than approximately two percent. 'Lay metal' was used in the manufacture of hollow-ware comprising tin mixed with lead of no less a ratio than four to one. 'Trifle', a third grade of pewter, was specified for tavern pots, candle moulds, toys and buttons. In later years some changes were made to these specifications as new hardening agents, such as bismuth and antimony, were introduced. It is interesting to note that at the end of the seventeenth century a variation of 'fine metal' denoted as 'hard metal' came into use for the highest quality flatware, which had very similar constituents to the Britannia metal of a hundred years later.

The regulations laid down by the Company over the years were extremely comprehensive, encompassing all aspects of the trade's activities. An ordinance of 1522 required all pewterware to be marked with the maker's touch, the touch marks being recorded on pewter sheets retained by the Company; that the premises and wares of members should be searched and tested at least five times a year; and that the number

10 *Porringers*.
Porringers developed from very simple utilitarian designs in early times, to much more decorative pieces with intricate fretwork ears and some with cast relief designs on the body and covers in the early eighteenth century. The near flamboyance of design in some late porringers is perhaps surprising, showing similarity to European types and one wonders if the porringers held some special significance in household chattels of the period.

17

of apprentices each master might have was subject to Company control—this move being designed to protect the journeymen's jobs and to match the numbers to those that could readily be absorbed by the London masters, and to discourage movement into the provinces. The minimum weight of certain standard products was fixed, as was the price of the various grades of pewter and scrap purchased for reprocessing. Any form of advertising was prohibited; a pewterer could be brought before the court of the Company for claiming his ware to be of higher quality than that of a fellow member. A freeman of the Company was prohibited from providing assistance to an unfree craftsman or in working in other materials, as a spoonmaker (John God) found to his cost when, improving the product, he made a few latten—a type of brass—spoons. Controls were also applied to certain techniques of manufacture. It forbade spinning or pressing; discouraged the repair of pewter; required that the bouges of plates be hammered.

The effect of these and many other controls introduced by the Company is hard to gauge today when one considers the number of practising pewterers throughout the land. Certainly in a number of metallurgical tests carried out on pieces from the Company's collection, virtually all have been within the specifications laid down, but it is probably not realistic to regard these pieces as a true cross section of the pewter actually made.

The Company tried vigorously to protect the industry from legislation that might damage its activities, and it expended much effort to ensure adequate supplies of tin from Cornwall when export markets were proving more profitable to producers and dealers. It tried to restrict the export of raw tin or have it taxed, and on occasion purchased tin itself as a buffer stock which was then allocated to members. Efforts were also made to restrict the importation of finished pewter articles.

By today's standards the Company's activities must appear totally autocratic and restrictive to competition, but when considering their approach, account must be taken of the prevailing trading conditions and general lack of government control of the times: you had to protect your own.

The decline of the Company's influence and that of the trade first became evident at the beginning of the eighteenth century, although the Company's loss of control was somewhat faster, due to the ever-increasing trading difficulties forcing individual pewterers to try to find their own salvation. The reasons for the dramatic decline are complex, although the technical improvements in the production of pottery and glassware and the wider use of brass obviously played an important part. The trade, which had adapted so well to changing conditions over previous centuries, failed to be able to take account of the fundamental social changes being brought about by the onset of the industrial revolution, and the epicentre of the pewter industry gradually moved from London to the new industrial midlands and Sheffield. It may have been that these areas were more receptive to new techniques of manufacture and style than the London craftsmen, who had so long been regulated by the Company, which for its part over the years cannot be claimed to have encouraged technical innovation.

Sad to say that to all intents and purposes the Company's influence on the trade had virtually ceased by the middle of the eighteenth century, while the scale of London-manufactured pewterware had become only a shadow of its former glory by the early years of the nineteenth century.

Today, in line with general Livery Company policy, the Pewterers Company is closely involved with a number of City institutions and charitable trusts and in conjunction with the City and Guilds Institute is hoping to set up standards for the

11 *Pair of marriage plates, 1661*

It seems to have been a fairly common custom for married couples to commemorate their wedding in this very attractive manner. The wrigglework decoration is particularly well executed. The plates are 9½in dia. and the maker is thought to be Nicholas Hunton, London. *OP* 2474.

19

training of young people in the pewter industry. To mark its 500th anniversary celebrations the Company has founded, with the Institute of Technology, a fellowship to carry out research into the effect of heavy metals on the brain and nervous system.

After approximately 200 years out of touch with the pewter industry, the Company and the trade again came together with the formation of the Association of British Pewter Craftsmen in 1970. The Association has been formed jointly to raise and maintain the quality of pewterware, to aid research into pewter, to provide benevolence for old pewterers and to encourage the training of young pewterers. In short, the aims of the ABPC are not so very far removed from those of the original 'fraternity' of the fifteenth century.

The Company's Collection

The Company's present hall in Oat Lane was completed in 1961. The formation of the collection stems from this time, being based on a number of fine pieces bequeathed by the late Dr Rex Godfrey Blake Marsh, a warden of the Company and past president of the Pewter Society.

The development of the collection to cover British pewter from its early guild beginnings was undertaken by the late Cyril Jossé Johnson who, with advice from Richard Mundey and the late Ronald Michaelis, for many years librarian of the Pewter Society, built up what is probably the most comprehensive collection of its kind in existence.

All pieces that are of good quality and known types of their period are felt to justify inclusion, and the Company's aim has been to provide a balanced range of pewterware through its long history so that as complete a record as possible can be permanently available for reference for those interested in the craft.

The collection currently comprises over 500 items and it is impossible here to give an adequate description of the pieces displayed. Early pewter is, sadly, extremely rare and there are in fact only a handful of items in the collection that can with certainty be dated prior to the seventeenth century. This is perhaps a little surprising and particularly tantalises the collector when one considers the vast quantity of pewterware in circulation at that time. The period of the seventeenth and eighteenth centuries—the golden era for British pewter—covers the bulk of the collection comprising flagons, tankards, pots, porringers, chargers and plates—many with wrigglework engraving—measures, salts, spoons and one or two items which appear specifically connected with the Company, such as the two-handled posset cup, commemorating the accession of Queen Anne, engraved with the Company's arms.

The pieces illustrated, some previously unpublished, have been chosen almost at random, but to some extent demonstrate the techniques of manufacture and show the considerable skill of the craftsmen of that period. The collection is in fact fully detailed in two catalogues published by the Company which illustrate the great majority of the pieces with, where possible, their touch marks.

The Company has originals of the five touch plates—flat cast sheets of pewter about $\frac{1}{8}$ in thick—upon which the marks of almost 1,100 master pewterers are struck. It is clear from the records that marks had been 'registered' in this way at the Company hall at least as early as 1550, but these early marks were destroyed in the Great Fire of London in 1666. The first of the existing touch plates was brought into use in 1667-8, but includes the restruck marks of some forty 'pre-fire' pewterers.

The touch plates have shown some deterioration with age and, because they are of

12   *Charles II restoration charger. c.1661–2.*
Broad-rim charger 16¹¹/₁₆in dia. Wrigglework engraved with royal arms surrounded by garter with lion and unicorn supporters between royal monogram C2R. The rim engraved with acorns, tulips, and thistles. Touch IF with harp between—possibly John French. *OP* 1775.

13   Postscript: Several dozen or so of Mr Charles Hull (author of this chapter) were liverymen (six were master) of the Company, going back to 1450. Here is the mark of John Hull, admitted 1685. *OP* 2452.

21

such immense historical importance, plastic replicas which are stable in normal atmosphere were produced by a member of the Pewter Society to provide permanent copies available for study.

Although not the subject for this book, modern pewter is also forming an increasing part of the collection, including Britannia metalware, Art Nouveau pieces of the early twentieth century and a comprehensive range of good-quality contemporary pewter.

(The collection can be viewed at the hall by arrangement with the Company Clerk. Telephone: 01 606 9363.)

3. Collecting

Perhaps you like the touch and feel of pewter—to absorb its sturdy subtle lines, to see its soft glinting reflections. Probably you like the intimacy of cleaning it, removing the unsightly dark scale which so often obscures the bright metal. By handling and restoring pewter you discover more about its manufacture, and learn to discern fake, foreign or made-up pieces. Hand in hand with such participant handling come knowledge and experience. If your knowledge leads, you will take deeper pleasure in finding worthwhile items for your collection and revel in the one-upmanship of having greater knowledge than the vendor.

We are all acquisitive—so go and browse in antique shops in hope. Take the opportunity to *handle* pieces. There is a rare leap of joy when you see that you are in luck. With your growing knowledge you can spot things of an age or rarity—or fake—hitherto unsuspected. One of the delights of pewter is that there is so much more to learn—paradoxically, particularly in the nineteenth century—and there are more pieces of that period to be found than of previous centuries. Its wares were too commonplace in the 1930s, '40s, '50s, and '60s—but now they are thinner. Hurry, and record and note everything so far unwritten.

When *BP & BM* was written, the position about finding pewter was changing. A result of this change is that tactics for collecting have also altered. Literature and the wider demand have bred much more general knowledge and awareness. Major dealers issue catalogues from time to time, some with most interesting text content. Unless you have limitless time and patience it is very unlikely that you will find many, or any, major bargains. If you do not seek specific items, though, you still have a chance of coming across interesting pieces, albeit of a later period than was the ideal of, say, 20 years ago. The trade is well organised in the sense that all strata know more or less what is what, and the values, so it is much more difficult to beat the market. I suspect that there has never been so much pewter available but such a large proportion goes through major or large salerooms that prices get pretty stabilised. Specialised dealers always have old, rare pieces—but at a price. With the major salerooms adding ten percent, plus VAT, the price even before the retail outlet has added his very justifiable profit is up, up. The dealer also has to think of his replacement. It is no profit to him if he sells a piece at an apparent profit if he tries to buy the piece's fellow next day at a higher figure than he took for it.

I would suggest that any piece has two prices—buying and selling: what you buy at and what the trade buys at. Do not grudge the trader his turn. He has driven many miles, advertised, paid his rent and rates, displayed his wares, and given you his knowledge and advice, all at your behest. Furthermore, this is his livelihood with a very justified profit, so with current predictions of future prices you must expect to wait 2 or 3 years before you can sell back at purchase price. Get to know shops which carry pewter and, if you know your subject well and have handled as much as possible, you will be aware of nineteenth and eighteenth-century pieces at not-out-of-the-way prices. One might wonder how anyone young can afford to collect at all. But it seems to me that there are more young people around who have £25 spare in their pocket now than there were with 2/6d in the early 1930s.

In towns' weekly sales, items do come up occasionally, and it is worth keeping an eye open, but you will probably be up against several freelance runners, and pieces sold may not stay in your town's antique shops. You should certainly go to a top specialised shop and be fairly certain of seeing something good, rare and old. You might be lucky in a provincial or small sale, you might be happy to keep on visiting countless smaller general shops. But in any case your chance of the hundred-to-one find or of significantly beating the market price is not great.

Auction frenzy is infectious and dangerous to your pocket. Embryo collectors often go out and pay high prices, but backed by no critical faculty; in almost every case they buy something they did not know about—a new thumbpiece may have been applied . . . or worse! There will be other collectors, shops buying for their own stock, professionals, perhaps, adding to their own private collections. Wherever you go, you must be your own judge. It is dangerous to let it be known what you seek, specifically. I do not know if fakes are being made today. I hope not, but expect so. In the 1930s the unsuspecting collectors let it be known that they wanted, say, a half-gill hammerhead, to make up a range. Surprisingly, within very few weeks one would be purveyed, with glamorous house marks, very 'old', battered, and repaired; technically made with complete knowledge of experts. Fake! It may happen today, tomorrow.

Collectors in all fields appear to be very hidebound and timid, and are inclined to buy only examples of what is 'in the book' and has been illustrated. Thus 'new' types can occasionally be discovered at a fraction of the price of pieces nearly comparable.

Occasionally enquiries are received from would-be collectors, seeking a society to teach them from scratch. No national society could exist with this purpose. What are books for? By all means make contact with other perhaps more experienced kindred souls. Members of the Pewter Society are delighted to meet learners and will give assistance. The Pewter Society (formerly the Society of Pewter Collectors) wishes to remain confined to forty members for wieldiness and for intimacy in advanced discussion. It is therefore esoteric. You do not join the MCC to learn to play cricket. In fact, you probably have a playing-in standard at your local tennis club. But those who have been through the mill, and will probably be able to fertilise other future collectors in the future, may be invited to join the Society. It is purely amateur. It will try to give assistance to individuals, as well as museums and the Church, and will also try to arrange for talks to antique societies and similar groups. There is also a large club in America—the Pewter Collectors Club of America—and a small group in Holland.

With any antiques it always pays to acquire pieces in the best condition, and beware of made-up items. There is a temptation in the early days to add numerically, and to accept perhaps a new lid on an otherwise entire piece; you will never be satisfied with it. Be critical in your mind of the piece in the shop. Do not purchase until you are completely satisfied with every replaceable part, or its authenticity. The dealer will not be very pleased if you complain later. You must particularly beware of confidence in high-price labels. Sometimes, I think, a shop may try to get rid of a piece it has discovered belatedly to be repro, by bluffing a very high price on it. I have seen what appears to be evidence of such a practice. Again, you must be your own expert.

As collections grow, conversely space diminishes. Good display requires room to see pieces individually, with plenty of air around. Successful collectors lose spaciousness and, dare I say, acquire a degree of clutter. One solution is to sell several to buy fewer, more expensive pieces. (But I regret having sold almost every piece that I have passed on.) Ringing the changes is the best answer, and to display only a part of the collection at a time. Putting it in the bedroom is unpopular, and in the boys' room unwise!

Where space is limited, you will find that the patience of the house-proud wife is also limited. Reference to photographs of any collection illustrates the point, and one can only say that some collections are more overcrowded than others. Do try, however, to be selective and show as few as you need. Try to weed out the unnecessary. A shelf is an excellent display stand, or ideally a dresser for plates, measures and small pieces. Spoons (which are rare) can best be displayed on a spoon rack and, while original racks are scarce and expensive, reproduction racks are quite acceptable: or make your own display shelf, preferably to show the knops standing up (contrary to antique racks).

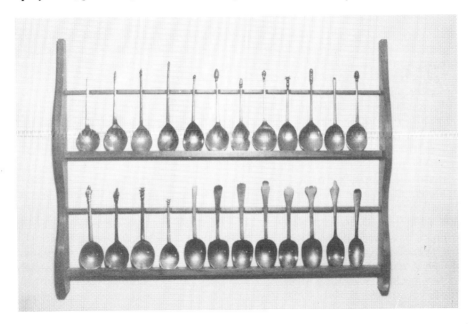

14   Genuine spoon racks hung the spoons downwards, to the detriment of admiring the knops. These excellent home-made racks honour the knops. (J. Douglas)

Although many collectors describe a piece as 'magnificent' because it is huge, does attraction really lie in vastness? Are not the smaller pieces more attractive? I would rather have a gill-sized hammerhead than a gallon. There are only two or three conventions in display which, in any case, follow normal artistic layout. Where possible have your larger pieces lower down; handles should be to the right for a right-handed person (although it is acceptable to balance a range of, say, bud baluster measures on the right by double volutes on the left, with the handles of the latter to the left). Pieces with handles are best displayed with the handle about 45° rearwards, to show off the thumbpiece and a little handle.

It seems quite hopeless to try to keep pieces of a close period together—it is far better to display aesthetically. On the other hand, there seems to be a psychological inhibition against mixing church pieces with other hollow-ware.

It is very satisfying to concentrate and specialise in some off-beat section like casters, or snuff boxes or funnels. Just consider how and what you would like displayed. Casters make an excellent showing, but I'm not so sure about funnels.

For safety, ease of identification, exchange of information by post and other reasons, it is highly advisable to photograph all your pieces. Also it is enormously useful and interesting to build up a loose-leaf catalogue of your collection. Allot each piece a number and record all details of acquisition, source, price, technical and recognition notes, and attach its photograph(s).

Good luck to your collecting. I envy with vivid memory the flirtation and romance of acquisition and experience going hand in hand. So often we are up against the universal difficulty in assessing dates of pieces caused by makers' working spans being seldom known. Worse, so many items never bore any maker's mark. In the not-very-distant past nineteenth-century ware was so ubiquitous that it was virtually 'infra dig' to be interested in it. It abounded, research was minimal. During the last war prices were low, scrap metal was needed, and most people had other things on their minds. As I have remarked before, the Americans and Canadians took almost as much fancy to our pub pots as they did to our girls, and swept both back home. Since then pewter has been universally and internationally popular and in demand—like girls.

Before that there had been many reasons for scarcity of old, really old, pewter. Styles changed rapidly in the seventeenth century, and trade-in value was about three-quarters of the cost of new. It is a soft alloy, easily damaged, and the Pewterers Company (which was a joint masters' federation and trade union under one hat, and a monopoly) forbade repair, even to the replacing of a lid. So into the melting pot went the trade-ins. Outmoded pieces, if not soon part-exchanged, would soon start to acquire the dark oxide and that would have reminded a proud housewife that it was, after all, time to update her decor. Another reason is that in contrast to silver, pewter is not a precious metal and therefore would not have been preserved automatically. Although of value, a spoon down the well was not a catastrophe, which explains why pewter spoons are so very much more rare than their silver counterparts. (Fortunately considerable numbers have been recovered during dredging, excavating for building, archaeological investigating of wells and so on.)

In the eighteenth century other media competed more and more and, whereas the power of the Pewterers Company had fought, and fought off, such competition in the fifteenth and sixteenth centuries, it could fight no longer, and the Company was relatively too weak to prevent the erosion of the popularity of pewter. With the coming of the Industrial Revolution, the harnessing and application of power developed a tremendous demand for metal and pewter was required in great quantity as scrap metal in the Napoleonic War period. So, too, in the wars of 1918 and 1939. In the latter, Britannia was of more value as scrap than as a perfect antique. Heigh-ho!

The history of collecting pewter, which started at the very beginning of this century, explains its popularity. In brief, in the very early years Massé put on an exhibition in Clifford's Inn. Just prior to that a small book on Sheffield plate and pewter by Redman had appeared. The only really significant point for our interest in it is that reference was made to the very great quantity of French reproduction pewter which was made in the last half of the nineteenth century. We see some of these items still, decorative, often repoussé, frequently with old makers' marks, dated, which had been handed down generation after generation. So you might find, say, a wavy-edge plate, of style 70 years after the mark was struck, but actually made 100 years later still! Massé followed up with another exhibition and, although written matter is scarce, I do have some interesting letters written by the new collectors of the period full of long, heavy, rolling phraseology. There was sufficient keenness for items to be brought out into the open, surprisingly widespread. It is still a puzzle to me that these early collectors were able to acquire so much superb pewter.

15   It is better to cast around and see what comes your way rather than decide prematurely what your specialisation, if any, is to be. A range of early nineteenth century pieces, and not a pot or measure amongst them.

In 1918 there was a landmark—the formation of the Society of Pewter Collectors (now the Pewter Society, in order to imply that possession was not a prerequisite—but that an amateur who *does* collect pewter is a potential member). This Society, and the few very keen enthusiasts, really laid the foundations. Howard Herschel Cotterell, an architect, was the greatest collector of all. He loved pewter and consorted closely with all the collectors, making his mark with his knowledgeable articles in magazines and in his books. He was the prime authority and a delightful personality. His books are worth seeking for the illustrations, as well as for the text—get any that you can. But here let us air a warning. As soon as one goes into print one is out of date, and old books are best read *after* the newer ones, because first impressions are those which stick.

In 1928 Cotterell organised a very fine exhibition of British pewter for *The Daily Telegraph*, held at Olympia, and opened by Her Majesty Queen Mary.

In 1929 Cotterell produced his magnum opus, and a colossal effort it was, his *Old Pewter, Its Makers and Marks*. He had a big subscription list. He had forsaken his profession, and it him, in the most difficult times (our dire financial crisis). The market could not take *OP*, and it was remaindered. It killed him. (It has, of course, been republished since the Second World War.)

OP is the one nearest reference book, with pleasant, wide-ranging text, but very little

27

about types, apart from the illustrations. The major part consists of the colossal recording of innumerable makers' marks. It is a tremendous work of research and analysis, and the author drew each mark himself. As I write I have Cotterell's own private master copy open beside me. Although Cotterell died his spirit thrived and pewter collecting has gone forward, no longer solely in the hands of professional men but in those of all occupations, here and overseas; latterly British pewter has won many ardent admirers in the USA, Australia, Holland—oh, all over.

16   A showcase of porringers at the Lincoln exhibition in 1962 organised by Mr White, Curator, and K. W. Bradshaw. A wonderful show.

1962 saw a very fine exhibition at Lincoln mounted jointly by the Lincoln Museum authorities and K. W. Bradshaw, with many of the quintessences from members of the Pewter Society on show.

In 1969 the Pewter Society ran a wonderful exhibition of the best pieces of all styles at Reading Museum, organised largely by R. F. Michaelis.

In 1974 was the quincentenary of the Worshipful Company of Pewterers, who arranged at Pewterers Hall a delightfully-presented exhibition, 'Pewterware with Royal Associations', all eighty-four pieces depicting royalty, or with obvious royal connections.

Some members, too, have put on public exhibitions; Norwich and Worthing come to mind. Since the Reading exhibition a little spare cash has been available in pockets across the board, pushing prices ever upwards.

Throughout the 30 years in which I have been in the Society there is a constant echo: with so much competition, how can one ever afford to collect? Perhaps we can't, but we do, and no-one has regretted his collection. As far back as 1920, only 2 years after the formation of the Society, they recorded that collecting was 'rapidly passing beyond the consideration of those of modest means'.

All are agreed that the last thing you want to hold is cash, and pewter, having moved from being an off-beat subject, is now a major consideration and in great demand, not

17   One bay at the Reading Exhibition, 1969, organised by Mr Gwatkin, Curator, and R. F. Michaelis.

only here but on the continent, where very high prices indeed rule, and in America. In that great country pewter collectors are even thicker on the ground than in this country; and in America there is a considerably larger percentage of lady collectors. There they pay greater attention to the products of individual makers, whereas in Great Britain the form and rarity are, I should say, the greater attributes of a piece. But this is a generalisation. Certainly in America, with fewer native pieces per capita of collectors, there has naturally been more intensive research of makers and their marks. The Pewter Collectors Club of America is a model of a large collecting society, while in England the Pewter Society, apparently the oldest collecting society, is hard put to remain in its intention small, esoteric and intimate.

We have exported an enormous tonnage of old pewter across the Atlantic and to Holland, Scandinavia and other European countries, Canada, and Australia. It amazes me that people can collect in some of these areas.

If you ask, 'OK, where do I start?' I would unhesitatingly say 'Read, and go out and see, but not to buy'. First read all you can of recent writings, handle all that you can in shops, or with a friendly collector. Get to know the difference between a repro and a genuine piece. Don't be in such a tearing hurry that you buy the repro before you buy the right ones. What you are likely to see first are the pleasant bellied measures which held sway all through the nineteenth century, a variety of pub pots and some plain-rim plates. We will simplify this a little later. Many other items will occur but what a pretty little start the three categories mentioned will give you, and with different sizes in the offing.

Many more seventeenth to nineteenth-century marks and makers have been published recently in *More Pewter Marks (MPM)* and in *Addenda to More Pewter Marks (Addenda)*. Finally, a full-colour booklet has been published recently, confined to nineteenth-century ware: *Let's Collect British Pewter (LCP)*. So your immediate needs for starting to collect are gathered all ready for you.

The two areas where you are most likely to see pewter are, I suppose, London and the Cotswolds—but I am not risking hints of backhanders by mentioning any specific shops. Of course you may see pewter in other areas, but those two always have several shops where you can be happy and, I think, satisfied. By the way, wherever you go it is useful to take a camera capable of fairly close-up shots, because you never know when you may see something you cannot buy, and it is well to photograph all the items which you would like to record. Likewise, do take pencil and paper and/or self-adhesive labels to record rubbings of any marks you think worthwhile.

There is a wide range of nineteenth-century items you will probably soon see—plain-rim plates, hot-water plates, pub pots, bellied measures, casters, salts, beakers, footed cups, snuffboxes, sports trophies, inkstands, spoons and candlesticks. I think that today I could go out and in one day get one of each of this collection for £250—£300.

You will also be able to see plain-rim and single-reed plates and dishes of the eighteenth century; and quite possibly a triple or multiple-reed dish of 15in or 16½in dating back to around 1700. In this group I have not included any Britannia ware, for the range is so wide, but probably you will want to be rather selective.

Britannia metalware you will see—mostly late, gross and over-decorated pieces—but however much we dislike their design, these are tomorrow's collectors' pieces. Other examples will range over a bigger field—teapots, coffee pots, church plate (flagons, cups), tobacco jars and a host of domestic items. Use your knowledge and taste. Britannia metal was also used as a base for plating—either beware or belove, according to your taste, pocket, and will for self-expression. But do try to select for style and date, rather than mere existence. Also Art Nouveau should be mentioned, although it is almost all post 1900. This has been eagerly sought more by collectors of that medium than by pewter lovers.

It may not be quite so generally realised that the lesser sales are possibly the 'best' places in which to unload the piece of repro, or of made-up pewter someone unfortunately had bought. You mustn't blame the auctioneer—he cannot be expert in all the many facets of sales. In shops—wherever you may buy, the principle of *caveat emptor* (let the buyer beware) is paramount. No matter how well meaning, and in the best of good faith, but perhaps not backed by the hundred percent knowledge you seek, there may be 'misunderstandings'. You alone must be the judge of the piece within your collecting parameters. Listen, and weigh up, then it is up to you. You are the guv'nor.

18 Another pleasant varied range of nineteenth century items, with a dish of *c.*1700. (15in dia.)

You do not necessarily need to be an owner to be a connoisseur. Massé wrote that he never owned a single piece, yet he was an early connoisseur, and he did some very fine repairing (all of which he 'signed' with a minute punch). To repair well you need to know your subject; repairing will sometimes take you into casting new parts, a lid for instance, a thumbpiece, or the terminal of a handle. You must get it right. So often one sees a new replaced part—and it shouts at you because it is not quite correct in design.

If you have a good camera, you could put together a marvellous collection of specimen photographs, and never own a piece. With the close-up lens you could spotlight marks, detail of manufacture, texture of oxide, all helping to build up a very comprehensive collection of records. But I fancy that somewhere along the line a piece (or more) will come home with you. If you are a very practical metal worker you could even *make* your own collection, provided that you have a workshop, and do not need the kitchen for your casting.

It is important to build your own confidence, although based on others' experiences. It has been mentioned that Cotterell was less than kind, less than tolerant, as regards Britannia metal. He told you how to differentiate, and how to 'lose' it. This tenet became such a shibboleth that it has hitherto been accepted practice, except to the wiser more catholic collectors in America, where Britannia forms a greater proportion of their shorter span of internally-made products. Do not be bound by what anyone

31

tells you to collect or abhor. Use your own taste and discretion, and develop your own confidence. To me the later (*c*.1870) Britannia-base electroplated teapots are abominations, and I have not held my tongue about it, but I hope that somewhere someone is saying 'silly old fuddy-dud'. I do think it rather appalling that many collectors feel a necessity to stock up with the same things as all the others. But collections are highly personal, and we all like to have the best range feasible—which often does mean travelling on the same rails.

It is unfortunate that most pieces in collections are without their history or provenance. Extensive travels of previous owners, runners, trade buying from far afield, major auctions—all contribute to fogging the traces of origin, which would be of great value. Marks are often initials only with no clue as to locality. Although we are learning much more of regional types, we are still sadly short of information. So, do keep your collection catalogued, note all useful details and see that your catalogue has a future home for perusal by others. But beware of repeating untenable but entertaining and fascinating lore from a well-meaning vendor or, as has happened, author.

There is much fine pewter in churches but . . . be careful! Churches may not sell their items, however damaged, without a faculty from the bishop of the diocese. Such pieces are not the property of the vicar, rector or churchwardens to sell, nor are these people without responsibility if any item is lost or stolen. I have had experience in recovering pieces, stolen and then sold by the thief, with plausible stories of sales in distant parts.

The phoenix says, both in its erstwhile and in its new life, collect from strength of knowledge, not strength of pocket. Read, see, handle and observe all that you can. The thrill of collecting lies in experience—knowledge and acquisitions going ahead in parallel.

4. Cleaning and Repairing

A great many people reading this book will own a few pieces of pewter and, to judge by the questions asked by individuals, how to clean pewter, or whether to clean it, rank as their biggest problem, greater even than knowledge on the various kinds of marks which are to be found on pewter. Therefore, to help those possessors in their logical sense of priorities, we are tackling the problems of cleaning early in this book.

Cleaning
The very title of this chapter will cause a minority of collectors to bristle. There has been an oversimplified rumour around for a great many years that pewter should not be cleaned. Let us look into the pros and cons. Pewter was made to look as similar to silver as possible. The finish was extremely bright and highly polished. It is possible that hygiene was tacitly taken as assured with cleanliness, but it is more likely that scouring was the order to make it shining and attractive. Is it now fair to try to make a tricentenarian ape youth? I think not—not to strip it bare of signs of age, then to buff it up to a very high polish. I know of no collectors who prefer this extreme: in this country such practice is thought to be garish and unseemly. Commercially one is told that demand has it so, and it is indeed the easiest way to treat pewter.

The pieces are immersed in strong attacking chemicals—either hydrochloric acid or caustic soda. The heavy unattractive dark scale is violently expelled off the face of the metal, leaving a very rough surface. This is reduced and smoothed on abrasive wheels, followed by buffing and polishing, so your marks have been removed too. Apart from bumps and dents all evidence of age has gone. It would seem to be reasonable to want each detachable part (lid, knop, thumbpiece, handle, body) to bear some trace of authenticity. At the same time, leaving traces of the black scale in all mouldings, interstices, spaces between rings and reedings, gives a very pleasing contrast of black and reflection. By leaving some scale on each part, one has almost incontrovertible evidence of age. I say 'almost' because it is possible to fake scale with the aid of chemicals or to use some other means of accelerating the formation of oxide. Furthermore, one must consider to what extent true oxide is a 'guarantee'. It forms quickly on some alloy mixtures, slowly on others, quickly under some conditions, slowly under others.

To return—we are dealing with cleaning pewter. If it comes to you in fairly bright condition it is easy to maintain. Any good metal polish (I find 'Glow' excellent) used twice a year is adequate, even in the smoke-filled, centrally-heated, double-glazed confinement of the modern home. You may wish to use it more often, but remember

33

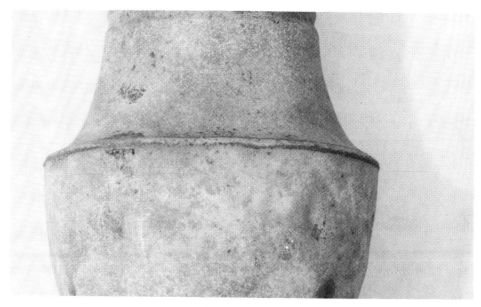

19 The surface after caustic soda or hydrochloric acid has removed the scale (or oxide). This is very rough, and requires judicious treatment to bring up a fine surface (which I have done on the other side of the caster). *c.* 1820.

that every polish is a little abrasive, so you must be losing something each time. To sum up—it is not difficult to have a bright, lively attractive room display, easily kept in condition.

It is more difficult to put it into the condition most collectors like, in which your pieces will show honest signs of age but will also be bright. We will come to that later in this chapter. First we must look into the very understandable objections to cleaning.

A minority of collectors prefer to keep every vestige of evidence of the passage of years carefully preserved on pieces. If they have acquired a heavy oxide scale, it is felt that you compromise their antiquity if you interfere. To the purist, a facelift is not *comme il faut*. Some want to keep the heavy scale as proof of age. Others prefer the glamour and mystery of only half-seen beauties. And others, of whom I am one, leave pieces of great 'archaeology' or pre-pewter history uncleaned, so that they remain untouched for future research. Furthermore conservation methods have not yet been officially determined. I fancy that there will be no one simple edict, for reasons that we shall see later.

The oxides on tin and silver can be converted back to pure metal by modern methods, and it is faintly possible, but most unlikely, that in the future research will enable the same with lead, and even tin and lead alloy, with the help of new techniques. Where there are pocks and breaks in the surface one cannot expect miracles—neither can one expect to reverse the conditions as neatly as playing a film or video recording backwards.

Furthermore, consider the following cases, both of which call for difficult decisions: first, where there is delicate decoration, such as wriggling, or a weakly-struck mark, will you lose it altogether if the scale is removed? Secondly, is the surface

34

so unstable with pocks and eruption that removal of the scale will allow these conditions to become worse? Until you have considerable experience in either of these cases, don't be impatient. You will be well advised to leave descaling for a year or two. Removal is irreversible.

20   Gadrooned salt (c.1705) cleaned bright, with the contrasting oxide in the interstices, TL, *MPM* 5767d. On the flask the oxide is too thick to be sure of a good surface beneath. It is probably very pitted. Furniture polish gives it a little vitality.

Finally, there is a very practical and human reason why you should not remove this really rather deadly, unsightly mask—it is a tedious, beastly, messy and laborious job, if the results I seek are to be achieved. More simply you can always bring a pleasing vivacity to heavily-scaled pieces with a couple of applications of furniture polish.

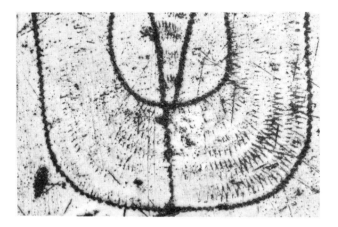

21   Very fine decorative 'wriggling' carefully preserved after the removal of an appreciable depth of oxide, through which I could barely detect the wriggling. Impatience would be dangerous to preservation.

35

Just what is this dark oxide, and what are the risks of losing marks underneath it? If pewter is left untended and exposed to alternating conditions of high humidity and dry air, plus other oxidising conditions such as natural deposits of dust (see how surfaces facing upwards such as lids are worst affected), then first a 'hume' forms, then a grey film and tarnish appear. This is caused by oxygen attacking the baser of the two metals in the alloy, and causing a skin of oxide. Low temperatures, too, are a contributory factor in the formation of scale, but this is nothing whatever to do with the glib, ignorantly-used term 'tin pest'. For now, 'tin pest' is not oxide or pewter corrosion, and is not applicable to pewter at all, under any circumstances whatever. We stick with 'oxide', 'scale', 'corrosion', 'eruptions' and 'pocks'. It is very important to appreciate that (with the exception of pocks and eruptions) the surface of the scale appears to be formed very accurately over the original surface, incorporating the finest detail of weakly-struck marks, or the faint lines of decoration. But underneath the surface of the metal is broken up more and more irregularly as the scale thickens, for the scale does not work upwards—it bites further and further into the metal, underneath.

Thus, in a nutshell, if you remove a thick scale completely a very rough, crystalline surface of the alloy awaits you, comparable with the appearance of snapped cast iron. This very irregular surface has bitten into and detracted from perhaps every trace of your weak touch mark—so note the detail *before* you attack your piece aggressively. I have seen a photograph of a sixteenth-century plate, later 'conserved' by a technician. A fine unrecorded maker's mark appears on the photograph, apparently very clear. On the plate, which was absolutely stripped, and which I have handled, there is now no trace whatever of this mark, for the surface is just a lunar landscape; it looks like something dug up out of a grave: literally revolting, with its great deep pits, even holes. But who is to say whether such treatment may or may not preserve the piece the better for more centuries than if the active oxide were left in position? No-one has yet said that oxide can be arrested by storage in such-and-such conditions; nor has anyone said that the plate will be the better preserved for being skinned alive. I do not think there is any certainty about the long-term effect of oxide—on, or stripped.

This oxide is more apparent in lower-grade alloys—and it is far heavier on some nineteenth-century pub tankards than on some seventeenth-century and earlier ware. So you can see that there are problems which you must appreciate before you begin to tackle them.

The fine-copper-content pewter of the early Middle Ages is very free from dark oxide (but does sometimes bear oxide-like gilding). To take an example from further back, a beautiful Romano–British pewter plate which I cleaned for Norwich Castle Museum needed only a minimum of treatment with very fine-grade emery. Its mint condition was probably because the river bank in which it had lain buried for hundreds of years was chemically neutral.

As well as the all-over formation of scale, I have mentioned pocks and eruptions. For some reason, probably impurities in the alloy, the oxide sometimes forms in pocks at a greater speed and more deeply, than on the surface and, as a result, is softer. These pocks are very unsightly and it is easy to see that chemical means of removing the flat scale will attack the softer oxide more strongly than the rest, leaving deep pits, even holes. Some years ago I acquired a flat-lid flagon whose previous owner, with the best of intentions but the minimum of experience, had dissolved off all the scale. It looked as if it had been hit with pellets from a sawn-off shotgun. If only he had left it for more experienced hands!

An even more insidious condition is eruption. Sometimes you can see bubbles of

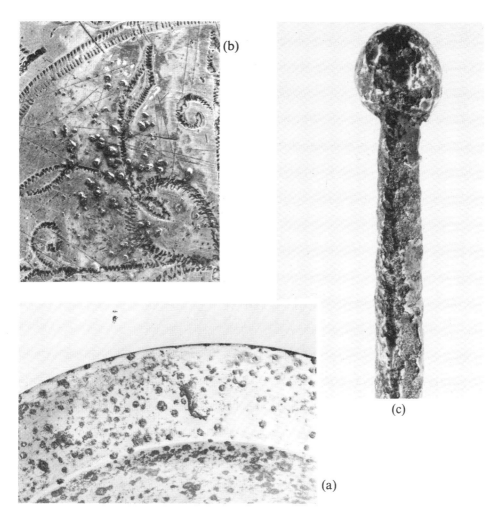

22   As well as corrosion in patches, (a) you may meet pocks (in this case on a piece recovered from an Armada vessel), and also (b) eruption. The latter consists of harmful 'boils' which damage the piece. (c) The ball-knop spoon (early fifteenth century) shows the disastrous result of stripping an ancient, or a heavily-scaled piece. Probably the surface of the oxide had perpetuated the true metal surface perfectly. (Fools rush in . . .)

pewter appearing, although there was perhaps no sign of them before you started to attack the scale. A few months after descaling, the surface may slowly quake up little domes of pewter about $\frac{1}{16}$in across, very reminiscent of horrible bubblegum. In this case it would seem that removal of the scale has unsealed an under-the-surface cause of oxidation. We do not yet know a method of neutralising it. The remedy, if you are patient, is to drill out each 'volcano' and replace it with matching metal.

These conditions of bad scaling, pocks and eruption have been confused with the term 'tin pest'. It was surprising to see Michaelis perpetuating this term, for surely

Cotterell in his *OP* had killed it, as far as pewter is concerned, and the leading authorities on tin confirm that this term 'tin pest' applies only to pure tin, *never* to pewter. We must not become so loose in terminology; let us hope that never again do we hear 'tin pest' applied to pewter. 'Tin pest' is a very rare condition, where occasionally pure tin which has been subjected to lower-than-normal temperature 'perishes'—loses its crystalline structure and cohesion. If it is in this condition and is disturbed it is liable to fall into a heap of dust. Furthermore, it is said to be contagious (which I doubt very much) and that contact with a sound piece at subnormal temperature can pass on the infection. I understand that if a piece is undisturbed or undamaged such affected tin can be restored to full structural strength by heating. I may add that I have kept some pure tin in my deep freeze for a long time, hoping to witness the phenomenon, but my tin is very conservative and unco-operative!

Alloying stabilises tin against tin pest occurring. As regards Britannia metal, the tarnishing and oxide are very much harder, and more difficult to remove. The lead constituent of pewter is replaced by antimony, and the oxide formed by antimony is very 'tight'. Also, since Britannia metal is hard, one is reluctant to do much work with abrasives, which could cause long-lasting scratches.

By this time our possessor of a few pieces, blinded with much non-applicable science, is no doubt getting worried and he probably decides to use only furniture polish. But he may be anxious about how best to take further steps. The short answer is, the less the better. Use the least aggressive methods possible. I do not mean that you should rely on Cotterell's extraordinary support for 'boiling in hay'. By all means try it. I think the only outcome is that you will need to boil it for so long to get any result that all the water will boil away, leaving in the bottom of the saucepan a little pool of bright molten pewter which was once your flat-lid tankard. Perhaps my hay, or my imagination, is not sufficiently strong. A great thought has struck me, I wonder if 'hay' was a misreading, or faulty typesetting for 'boiling in lye'. That would be less airy-fairy, and certainly would have more effect—probably horrible—but you still read of experienced people (the strippers) advocating it. Not this child!

If your pewter is already clean, then good metal polish is adequate. I think Cotterell's suggestion of using oil is bad, despite its sealing effect. Dust will adhere to the sticky oil and dust is notoriously corrosive.

If there is only a very little scale, and if you are sure you can cope with it, then use the very finest grade of wet-or-dry emery paper (600 or 800) used wet, with the initial cut of the abrasive taken down by rubbing it on, say, a screwdriver handle. Rub the piece in different directions. It is as well to stop before you have gone too far—you can always return to do more. I advise against using wire wool (often recommended) in any form, because some of the wisps of wire will lie along the direction of rubbing, and will cut deeply. It is a good idea, when the surface is dry, to smooth it by rubbing it hard with leather 'split'. I use 'split' leather mounted on a flat stick 18in long. This is my most important cleaning tool but it can only be used on outside curves. I have also made an asymmetric beech 'boat', some 7in long, also covered in coarse leather. The shape allows the rubbing of a remarkable range of concave (inside) curves, which will deal with a bowl, a bouge or a porringer very well indeed. Rubbing down is strenuous work, for you need to bear hard to bring up a fine texture. Britannia metal, being harder, is less amenable to one's efforts with emery, and you will have to work carefully to avoid scratching it. After rubbing down use metal polish, of course. The advantage of a metal polish with 'body' is its tendency to fill in scratches.

May I suggest that you read the whole of the chapter before rushing into any action

38

(b)

(a)

23 ℶ ⊃ (a) A fine piece most unwisely stripped naked of oxide. It looks a lot better now, after (b) handle repair and smoothing the metal surface. Height to lip 8⅛in. WW. *OP* 6028, 6031, *MPM* and *Addenda* 6032.

other than the use of metal polish. You may be tempted to employ some kind of mechanical means—a hand power tool or a static polisher—to get rid of film or oxide. My advice is, *don't*.

Although I have a slow-speed unit (980 rpm) and occasionally use it, I do not advocate the use of a power drill with various attachments. It generally revs much too fast; in mounting emery it is difficult to get just what is required; you are bearing weight in a direction for which the drill is not designed; it is one-hand working; it can 'chuck': there is always a risk of a metal mounting or some other part touching the pewter; and the desirability of using the wet of wet-or-dry involves a very real danger of electrical shorting—both of current and life; and being softer than the scale, pewter is in grave danger of being ground away while the oxide just laughs at your tickling. But there *may* be slow-revving (say 300 to 400 rpm) units into which you can mount your fine emery and apply pressure as you and tool wish, and with water remain compatible with electrical safety. Remember that if you overcome other difficulties, speed and pressure could 'burn', even melt the metal. It is far, far better to do it the long way, all by hand.

If you are faced with a piece with more scale than you judge removable by emery paper, you will need to use chemicals—either hydrochloric acid (spirits of salts) diluted, or caustic soda. I have used both. They are equally effective, but hydrochloric acid is more difficult to rinse off, and therefore harmful salts can be left in cracks and crevices in the metal, storing up trouble for the future. I only use them with the utmost caution, wiped on repeatedly—not immersed. I prefer, as so do most of my friends, to use caustic soda. Both are highly corrosive: murderous on clothes and carpets and satanic on the flesh. Wearing rubber gloves, first clean off any wax or polish then fill an egg cup with water, and drop in the caustic soda, stirring to dissolve. Soak a rag in the solution, sponge over the surface to be treated two or three times, then stand it on newspaper to dry.

By not attempting too-swift results you tend to prevent the chemical from boring down into the deeper holes—the deeper the swifter formed, therefore the softer and more soluble. So, oversimplified, the holes appear first! Having applied a smear or two of chemical you can start work with the wet-or-dry *(not* sandpaper), and alternate the use of chemical and hand work repeatedly.

Earlier we discussed the advisability of leaving some scale on every detachable part of a piece, and of leaving black scale in the moulding, and so on, to throw up a light and shade. If you strip a piece bare it is not only garish but you have removed vital evidence of its age. So it is well, and attractive in appearance, to leave some scale in all mouldings, fillets, reedings, angles and under the lee of other parts, for example, on the drum next to the handle. You can smear Vaseline on any part you want to protect but inevitably the emery will touch and pick up some, transferring it where you wish it not. A protective grease coat is really of more use to the strippers where they want to leave a patch protected during immersion. Better still, for more delicate work (in the lettering of engraving, or wriggling) I use black shoe polish. If you want to leave a mark unattacked just smear the protective coat over it. Little and often is the key word for application, each time using some 400 wet-or-dry emery, with water, to help ease off the scale. It is not as easy as it may sound: the scale is thicker in some parts; dents are more difficult to cope with; some patches come off easily. I can only leave it to you to be patient and persistent and gain experience. It is a very long job if you want to do it well—but most satisfying.

As regards the emery, start with 400 but be careful not to touch the metal with it. The metal is softer than the oxide. It is not easy, because you will not remove the scale evenly—you will come through it where it is thinner or softer, and it will be obstinate elsewhere. Use your rubbed-down 600 on the metal, and then rub it very well with the leather. You need to concentrate on this humdrum job because not infrequently flecks of emery will have parted company from the backer to be picked up by the leather and embedded in it, so encouraging comparatively deep scratches. Then use the metal polish, and inspect critically when polished. You will certainly need to repeat the work somewhere, to some degree.

We have talked of the evil of pocks. It is particularly dangerous to attack the scale too viciously in case there are deep soft spots. It is immeasurably better to keep some patches of scale than to have deeply-corroded bare patches. The only sightly and long-term remedy is to drill them out and replace the metal as a repair with matching alloy. So, wherever feasible, always use emery paper rather than complete removal. If a piece is one, two, three hundred years old it can wait a week or two while it is treated with loving kindness rather than with brash hastiness.

A week or two? Obviously, people who make a business out of buying and selling pewter cannot afford to spend so much time on one piece. It would make the cost of a nineteenth-century pot too high. So the trade strip and buff. You should be able to buy pieces uncleaned, which you can treat properly yourself.

It should be mentioned that some pieces can be treated not only with caustic soda, but by sprinkling granulated zinc on the surface of the piece which is still damp with caustic soda. This causes a chemical electrolytic action, but it is rather fierce, so it should be used with great care on *stubborn* patches. And that there will be some is certain. Cleaning your pewter, and handling it will teach you a great deal about the metal and make you wonder how the piece was made. You will soon become aware of the seams running round most pewter and Britannia hollow-ware, but down straight-sided Britannia coffee pots. You will start to wonder how handles were attached and how pewter was assembled.

On acquiring pieces of pewter one may find many dents; the rim of a plate may resemble the brim of a wet felt hat! Two forms of very elementary restoration present themselves—to tap out the dents, and to bend the waves straight. Tapping must not be done with a metal hammer as this will damage the pewter and even a brass pestle with a rounded end makes very sharp dents. Use a hard rubber hammer. Always tap from the inside against a surface, not forgetting to turn the body of a curved piece so that the small area tapped has a firm anvil. Take great care not to distort by over tapping. With a metal as soft as pewter it is only commonsense to hammer lightly and very frequently—in bottom gear. Tapping may fracture the very brittle scale and cause it to flake off, so you will have to decide whether or not it is worth removing the dent at the risk of damaging the scale. Many tankards, plates and suchlike will be misshapen, but can, with patience and care, be worked back into shape by hand—forefingers, thumbs and the ball of the thumb. It is far safer to do a little at a time and allow the metal to settle and readjust. As with tapping, only a small alteration to the shape may cause the very brittle scale to flake off extensively.

Sometimes in reshaping battered wells of pewter plates and dishes I find it a great help to take off my shoes and work the flat of the well into shape with my heel and ball of the foot on a smooth floor. But first one needs to be certain that the well is flat—not all types were! I find it a great help to immerse a piece for a few minutes in a saucepan of hot water. You will find that raising the temperature to boiling point makes the metal more malleable. Then, wearing gardening gloves, one can work the slightly-softened metal more easily while it is still hot. This is particularly useful, even important, in

41

24   Before and after. A fine little tankard used as a flagon in a small church, restored to a degree of respectability. Maker Henry Seegood, *OP* and *MPM* 4169 and 5922a *c.* 1690.

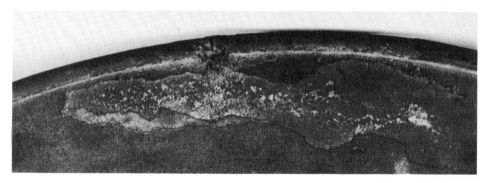

25 Oxide is very brittle, and flexing the metal causes the oxide to flake off.

working solid parts such as thumbpieces which have been crushed. It is fatal to try to reshape them too quickly.

Repairing
Repairing is a most satisfactory craft to master—but most frustrating to attempt and not master. It is a skill for which one either has or has not the gift; no halfway. If, like me, you, are bumblefisted at delicate, precise jobs probably with an inherent optimism and impatience that bypasses adequate preparation, then I can only recommend innumerable practice joins and dummy runs on scrap pieces. They should show one hundred percent success before you risk tackling a favoured piece. Don't forget, too, that it is not easy to mock up the repairs to simulate the varied difficulties you will face when you come to the real thing—the rim separated from the lower part of a plate, a leak in the mouldings at the base of a tankard, or the replacement of a handle. Furthermore, each repairer develops his own quirks of technique.

Perhaps one should mention that some minor repairs can be tackled while you are still not an expert, but nevertheless in a practical manner, by using epoxy resin and polyester adhesives. No heat is required. One adhesive which is metal filled and quick curing—as little as 5–10 minutes—gives adequate results on pewter of no great value. It dries to a powdery grey colour which does not match (so repairs should be out of sight) and if not perfectly mixed is suspect when immersed in hot water. I have used it with complete success to replace handles and fill minor holes. I have even backed up small holes in wafer-thin sections of pewter with very small patches of a fine linen handkerchief soaked in the resin. It is, however, difficult to judge the amounts required in a mixture of two ingredients of differing proportions—ten to one. You must get the proportions right. These adhesives result in a repair that you want to stay hidden, not to advertise your technique!

It is a good idea to save all the flake and coarse powdered oxide from your cleanings, and reduce this to a fine powder. Work this into the surface of the adhesive which is showing just before it sets. Later, of course, smooth it down.

Prestige does follow skilful metal running, using either a bit or blowpipe. Your bit should be large enough to hold the heat from dispersing too quickly, the temperature as low as you can keep the solder running. For solder, it is best to use pewter or Britannia metal, as this will give a closer colour match. Where it will be visible it is important to get the colour of the metal you are using right, not only for the appearance when clean, but because you will probably find that solder will tarnish more than your piece under repair, soon to show a darker blue–grey. So you may need to add more tin to your solder. If the repair is out of sight (the re-attaching of a handle for instance) you can get away with low-grade metal. Meticulous cleanliness of the bit and the surface to be joined is absolutely essential. Conversely, you can limit the area of adhesion by leaving oxide on the surrounding area. The running metal will not adhere to oxide.

26 Marvellous result of skilful repair of a wrecked flagon, lid missing. Would you have spotted that this is a new lid? Body *c*. 1625. Lid *c*. 1970. (S. Shemmell)

It is a good starting point to get some pewterers' solder (which has a low melting point) and to start with easy repairs, where there is a really good substance. Never mind if you add too much—you *must* add too much to allow for taking down exactly to the surface, by power tool, dental-mechanic's accessories, or by file, scraper and emery cloth. It is essential to maintain the contours of the piece to be repaired. You can always take more off later. Naturally, one needs plenty of substance of metal (not including oxide!) to absorb and disperse the applied solder. If you add a mass of molten metal to a wafer-thin part, the latter will disintegrate.

At all stages ingenuity, patience and deftness are essential. Practice on scrap or worthless pieces. Do not be too ashamed of not completely trimming away all the surplus fringe—experience of old pieces shows that very seldom was the job mechanically perfect. Herein lies the charm of hand work—the irregular minute imperfections.

Although one can give an idea of how to set about the job, repairing is a very personal craft, and anyone undertaking it will adopt and adapt within their own capabilities and equipment. Do remember that it is not like planting out a flowering annual—many people are going to own your piece after your period of guardianship is over.

5. Marks

We have seen how the control of the pewterers was completely in the hands of the Pewterers Company, occasionally reinforced by Parliament, and that their control and checking were jealously guarded—certainly up to 1550. From then on there were increasing creaks and groans, developing into dissension. One would have thought that what was established as a craft by the mid-fourteenth century, and received its charter in the fifteenth century, would by that time have instituted a method of checking back—of identifying the makers by some means of marks.

No one single piece of Romano-British pewter (except possibly one, from Cirencester) bears any form of maker's mark. But it is more surprising to find that none of the earliest-known medieval pieces is marked—the sepulchral chalices buried with monks in the twelfth, thirteenth and fourteenth centuries. Nor are the few reasonably-dated medieval flagons or plates. This throws new light on the Act of Parliament of 1503, whereby the marking of pewter was made compulsory—perhaps for the first time. Scotland followed in 1567. Presumably the Company's searchers had had to catch the quality evaders redhanded. Perhaps they had long been enjoying trouble-free trips out into the country. They should have been seizing faulty wares, imposing fines and, in the later fifteenth century, marking faulty pieces with a broad arrow. No genuine such pieces are known due chiefly not to normal wastage but to the fact that these pieces would have been melted down to be recast. I have seen one spoon with the broad arrow, but it was a fake. With no means of identifying wares, the searchers must have had an uneasy sinecure.

The Act of 1503 changed all that. Henceforth every piece had to be marked. (There had just been a reference to the Company buying marking irons for the hollow-ware men.) The evidence is most easily seen on spoons, the most numerous kind of ware of the period still existing. In the fourteenth and fifteenth centuries they were seldom, if ever, marked, whereas nearly all sixteenth-century spoons bear delightful, excellently-made touches. But it is not until 1550 that we read of a tablet on which every (?) man's touch was struck. It seems highly unlikely that all or many provincial pewterers came to London to 'touch' the tablet (or touch plate). We know that very many later provincial pewterers for one reason or another did not strike their touch mark. But despite the implied guarantee of quality given by signing pieces, the troubles with debased alloy, trickery, poaching and so on increased. We cannot hope to see this touch plate, for it was lost in the Fire of London in 1666. A new touch plate was immediately put into use, and every pewterer was required to restrike his touch. Cotterell in his *OP* unravelled the seemingly-anomalous sequence, pointing out that, after the master and wardens, they struck in seniority, to be followed by the new

27 Beautiful work in the die for maker's mark in a sixteenth century spoon bowl. The earlier fifteenth century mark has no border.

brethren as they were given leave and before they could set up in business. However, there are very many marks which are missing from the touch plates, but which are recorded in *OP*; many, many more have come to light, published in *MPM* and *Addenda*. Perhaps significantly, the large proportion of the 'new' marks comes from pewter of pre 1650, (which, thank goodness, continues to emerge from ground, mud and sea) and post 1800.

Seventeenth-century pieces of beautiful technique, metal and design are often found unmarked—for instance it is most unusual to find one of the magnificent and numerous, always excellently made, 1605 type of church flagon with a touch. Why the makers were so shy of putting their touch on their wares is not known. Were they in trouble? Were they not fully qualified, making pewter pieces as a moonlighting sideline? Were they too poor to buy an iron? There are several records between 1520 and 1670 of fines for not marking pewterware (including one for $2\frac{1}{4}$ cwt of tavern pots in 1595—I wish we could see just *one*!). So, as with present-day shopping, judge the piece not the label.

The only other two centres known to have had touch plates are York, whose plate has long since disappeared, and Edinburgh, whose two plates still exist. The Edinburgh marks range from *c.*1600—*c.*1760. All the early Scottish marks are very similar, consisting of the three-towered castle with maker's initials and sometimes the date of striking.

Welch delved most thoroughly into not only the Company history, but the history of marking pewter, which is admirably laid out both by Cotterell and by Michaelis in his *Antique Pewter of the British Isles*. They trace the growing unrest within the Company, and show how beset by surges from below, intensified by competition from other media, and vacillation by the Company, all control was lost by the middle of the eighteenth century.

We have seen that irons were provided in the last quarter of the fifteenth century, and that marking of pieces was made compulsory in 1503. Constant friction developed throughout the century, including makers encroaching on one of the few marks placed on pieces by the hall—the rose and crown (in that century), which, although records are confusing, appears to have been a mark struck on goods for export—an emblem for 'made in England'. Those who offended had their goods seized, were fined or were required to strike a new touch. Presumably this was intended to let them turn over a new leaf, and not be dogged by their past faulty wares. Competition arose from stone pots, and the Company tried all kinds of devices to suppress this new threat, even to petitioning that all measures should be made of material which would take the impression of a seal. Perhaps that was the origin of the pewter lids on stoneware pots known to have been made here as well as in the Germanic countries. (Their descendants are made to this day in Austria and Germany.) In the seventeenth century the old complaints reappeared, and after the Fire there is much evidence of emancipation of thought and deed. The spoonmakers, a group on their own, seem to have been up to some trickery, for in 1666 they were all ordered to have new touches. There were also more complaints of anonymity. (Come to think of it, with London ravaged by fire, and the effects of the Plague, competition, economics, and the expansion of design consequent upon the Restoration, is it not obvious that the whole scene was set for enterprise and emancipation—for branching out? This concept goes far to explain the enormous explosion in this freedom of thought and deed immediately after the Fire.)

We will deal later with the form of the marks, but will now discuss their content. Early marks had appeared to be simple and direct—just two initials—but from the early years of the seventeenth century symbols begin to appear. They indicate the name or address of the maker. You do not have to guess long at the name of the maker whose touch is TB and a bell. Others are more punning and less obvious; Lucas shows a shaft of light (Latin *lux*). This was the fashion of the period, and continued in the next century. The copper token 'coinage' of 1649–72 abounds with this same pictorial representation of name and address, which was read so easily by the illiterate. Our company symbols today are similar, but much more abstract: a visual recognition and identification.

Perhaps the pewterers took a lead in self-advertisement from the token issuers. In the past this was just 'not done'. To help to maintain their business, makers now put their names in full in their touches, added 'London' and their addresses and finally a sales message such as 'Superfine Hard Mettle'. The provincial pewterers, to the annoyance of their citizen brothers, also put 'London' on their wares, and, as it turned out, there was nothing to stop them, the get-out being the implication of '*tin* from London'. In the meantime some London makers again encroached on the use of the rose and crown, and adopted it for their touches.

There are several other types of mark which each individual pewterer used, broadly classed as secondary marks, including 'hallmarks', cartouches, rose and crown, and X crowned, none of which was struck on the touch plates. There are very helpful drawings and text relating to these in *OP* pp. 50 and 51. These are dealt with later in this chapter. There are also capacity-checking marks. But the touch is the basic vital factor of interest. In the chapter on the Pewterers Company, we have seen how the company was organised. Understanding the organisation, particularly of the point at which our pewterer was allowed to strike his touch, helps one to understand why so many yeomen are shown in *OP*, *MPM* and *Addenda* with no marks. They may never have opened up on their own, and therefore had no need of an iron. As already suggested, perhaps they were provincial and did not travel up to strike their touch; perhaps they died before making many pieces, none of which has survived.

If a maker struck his mark on the London or Edinburgh touch plate he has earned a number, for example LTP 1021. There are five London touch plates, with a total of nearly 1,100 touches. If he is recorded in *OP*, then his identity is Cotterell's alphabetical sequence number—for example *OP* 2440, which also goes for *MPM*, and for *Addenda*, where further information on a man is found under the *OP* number perpetuated therein. The latter books are complementary to *OP*—and they include very many visual entries for makers unknown to Cotterell. There are almost as many marks again—new, and amplifications, corrections, and so on. This has involved the use of suffices to slot in makers between existing successive *OP* numbers. How else? Cotterell had drawn each mark beautifully, and it is now proved and accepted that very occasionally a little imagination and artistic licence were involved, corrected where there is evidence, in *MPM* and *Addenda*.

The latter two are compiled by reproducing marks exactly as received over the last 50 years (since *OP*). So you find rubbings (reproduced same size where possible), good drawings, rough sketches and photographs—especially, where possible, including rubbings reproduced same size to key accompanying photographs, sketches and drawings (and several in *OP*) to their correct size. The compiler/publisher kept as tight an editorial eye as possible on marks received, date ascriptions and validity as to whether they were British, (sometimes overriding submitted opinions) and interpretations of lettering, refusing many which fairly obviously included creativity and enterprise. Facts only, even though as rough sketches, are published. There was so much important feedback, particularly from America and Britain, that unexpectedly soon 'Addenda' was merited and required, to disseminate the information for the common weal—collectors, dealers, libraries and museums. There is also a section in both books for marks recorded as fake marks. Fake marks can have been applied to fake pieces and also to true pieces, presumably mistakenly to give extra appeal. There is no disadvantage in owning a fine seventeenth-century unmarked salt, flagon, candlestick, baluster or what you may. Anyway, these two books do make a most useful complement to *OP* for the serious collector, and for others who may have practical use for them.

Cotterell decided wisely to compile his list of known pewterers alphabetically, for easier cataloguing and reference. Alphabetical sequence keeps together members of the same family who sometimes used very similar marks, and identification is easy if the beginning of the surname is legible. Uncertain or blind allocation necessitates a separate section, and unallocated marks with no initials a further section. Not for the first time may I say that Cotterell should be read! I am grateful to Batsfords for permission to reproduce a few typical entries from *OP*, these having been struck from *c*.1750 onwards. A few entries from *MPM* and *Addenda* are shown. You will see that these contrast radically against *OP* as being essentially collectors' tools. The small selection of later marks from *OP* have been simplified to give just what is known of the span of that mark to help in dating pieces.

The book you are now reading does *not* set out to be a makers' reference, but rather an overall guide to turn to frequently not only for the text, but particularly for the illustrations. Most of the latter are previously unpublished.

Touch marks
The development of the shape of touches is a valuable clue to dating, even if the maker is not identified, and so it is well worthwhile to inspect and analyse the shapes, types and designs in fashion from 1600 to 1850. Better still to look at photographs of the touch plates in the back of *OP*. It must be clearly understood that observations are in broad generalities, particularly after *c*.1660, and that it is trends and tendencies which are mentioned. The older styles continued to be struck concurrently with the new, and a piece was not likely to have been made in the year of striking. The maker probably continued to use his original iron, or a replica, all his working life—say from the age of

49

25 to 65. I have pieces widely varied in date style, bearing the same touch. Once again, develop your judgment of style, not relying solely on mark identification; and do not ascribe the date of striking, *ipso facto*, to all pieces with that touch.

Cotterell's 'Old Pewter . . .' Mark Numbers

38. Alderson, Sir George, London: July 1817, Y.; 21 Aug. 1817, L.; 1817, f.S.; 1817, f.R.W.; 1821, U.W.; 1823, M. Sheriff of London 1817. Died 1826. Touch, 1084 L.T.P.

40. Alderson, Thomas, London: *c.*1790–1825. He made the pewter-ware for the Coronation Banquet of George IV.

118. Ash & Hutton, Bristol: *c.*1760. Partners, Gregory Ash and William Hutton.

158. Austen, Joseph & Son, Cork: Were at 54 North Main Street, 1828–33.

1 Anne spoon rack, with much earlier spoons. Knops: diamond, *c.*1400. Two small latten-knopped, fifteenth century. Stump end, *c.*1450. Horned headdress, *c.*1475. Writhen ball, early fifteenth century. Peach ball, early fifteenth century. Mitre, early fifteenth century. Golf ball, late fifteenth century. Globe ball, mid fifteenth century. Lion guardant, fifteenth century. Crown, fifteenth century.

2 Thirdendale', or 'hooped quart'. Gorgeous early seventeenth century measure. Only one other is recorded. Mark is SC and a daisy, (*MPM* 5527b) and HR on lid. Capacity is 45 fl oz. Dr E. Roberts has elicited that in 1671 information from Statutes from *c*.1600 onwards was repeated that the yeast and froth of ale and beer effervescing and working on being poured, was allowed for in these 'quart' measures. No proportion or capacity was mentioned specifically, other than 'being a small quantity somewhat bigger ... in respect of the working and ascending of the yeast and froth.' Not a very sophisticated method of measuring such erratic and ephemeral froth — and guaranteeing it with the HR stamp! (Dr E. Roberts).

740. Bush & Perkins, Bristol and Bitton, Glocs.: Partners, Robert Bush, above, and Richard Perkins, q.v. *c.*1775.

873. Chamberlain, Thomas, London: In the lists of Openings and Touches, leave was given to Thomas Chamberlain to strike on 20 Mar. 1734. 3 Aug. 1732, Y.; 24 June 1739, L.; 1751, f.S.; 1754, R.W.; 1764, U.W.; 1765, M. His Trade-card, q.v., gives his address as King Street, corner of Greek Street, St. Ann's, Soho. He is mentioned until 1806. He was later a partner in Chamberlain & Hopkins.

962. Cleeve, Bou(r)chier, London: 16 Dec. 1736, Y. and L.; 1744, f.S. and f.R.W.; 1755, f.U.W.; 1757, f.M. Was given leave to strike his Touch on 22 June 1738. Was in partnership with Richard Cleeve, vide Welch, ii. 194. Lived at Foots-Cray Place, Kent.

1547. Ellis, Samuel, London: 28 Sept. 1721, Y.; 1725, L.; 1730, S.; 1737, R.W.; 1747, U.W.; 1748, M. 1773, died. Touch, 746 L.T.P., which he had leave to strike on 10 Nov. 1721. He was succeeded by Thomas Swanson.

1576. Englefield, William James, London: Was an apprentice in 1867 (with John Jarvis Mullens). 21 Mar. 1875, Y. and L.; 1890, f.S.; 1907, R.W.; 1908, U.W.; 1909, M. Touch, 1091 L.T.P. Englefield's business is of very ancient foundation and traces its descent as follows:
Thomas Scattergood, 1700, Y. Succeeded by
Edward Meriefield, 1716, Y. Succeeded by
John Townsend, 1748, Y.–1766, then
Townsend & Reynolds, 1766–1777, then
Townsend & Giffin, 1777–1801, then
Townsend & Compton, 1801–1811, then
Thomas & Townsend Compton, 1811–1817, then
Townsend Compton, 1817–1834, then
Townsend & Henry Compton, 1834–c.1869, then
Elmslie & Simpson, c.1869–1885, then
Brown & Englefield, 1885–present day.
(The above notes were corroborated by Mr. W. J. Englefield in the years immediately preceding his death.—H.H.C.)

《SUPERFINE 》
《 HARD METAL 《

3317. Moyes, J———, Edinburgh: in 1872 his shop was in West Bow. He was the last pewterer to practise the trade in Edinburgh.

3334. Munster, Iron Co., Cork: c.1858–c.1905. (Cf. Austen & Son.) c.1833 onwards.

3694. Pitt(s), & Dadley, London: Touch, 1043 L.T.P., struck c.1781. Partners probably R. Pitt, 1780, W.; and E. Dadley, 1799, W.

3732. Porteous, Robert & Thomas, London: Touch, 999 L.T.P., struck c.1762. Of Gracechurch Street. Successors to Richard King, hence the ostrich.

3817. Ramage, Adam, Edinburgh: In 1805 he was apprenticed to James Wright.

4379. Smith(e), Samuel, London: 17 Oct. 1728, Y. Son of Jno. Smith. Touch, 796 L.T.P., which he had leave to strike on 21 Mar. 1727/8.

4442. Spackman, Joseph & James, London: Touch, 1045 L.T.P., struck *c.*1782.

4795. Town(s)end, John, London: 16 June 1748, Y.; 21 Jan. 1754, L.; 1762, S.; 1769, R.W.; 1782, U.W.; 1784, M. Died in 1801. Touch, 928 L.T.P., which he was given leave to strike on 16 June 1748. He was apprenticed to Samuel Jefferys in Middle Row, Holborn. Commenced his business at 47 Prescott Street, Goodman's Fields.

4876. Villers & Wilkes, Birmingham: In 1805 Directory they are given as wholesale braziers, pewterers and dealers in metal at Moor Street.

4959. Wardrop, J. & H., Glasgow: c.1800–1840.

4968. Warne, John, London: Founded in 1796. Of Blackfriars Road. Now incorporated in Gaskell & Chambers.

2824. Langford, John. On a plain rim plate, *c*.1750. (A.S.G.)

2828. Langley, Adam. 'H.ms'. d. before 1693. (A.S.G.)

2839. Langworthy, Lawrence. Touch dated 1719. Emigrated to U.S.A. d.1739, Newport, Rhode Island.

2843. Lanyon, Thomas. Fresh touch and ? alternative or amended 'h.ms'. (A.S.A.)

2861. Lawrence, Edward. 'H.ms'. (H.H.C., & A.S.G.)

28a Showing the presentation of *MPM*.

2704. Kelk, N. Note 'h.m' 4 – "S.I." See 5929b.

2714. Kent, John. 'H.ms' on a p.r. plate, *c*.1750. (R. Touzalin)

2720. Kenton, John. Also appears on fakes; see page 112.

2738b.b King, George. Liverpool, 1823–1835. Transfer from 6049a. (succeeded by Thomas Holdgate).(I. D. Robinson). See 5687. See also 5757c and 6049a.

2741. Probable connection with 1973.

2748, -9, or -50. King, Richard. On a 6" bowl. (Mrs. Paul Young).

2749 or -50. King, Richard. On a 26" dish. (W. F. Kayhoe).

2751a. King, R. Transfer from 6243. (Mrs. Paul Young)

28b Showing the presentation of *Addenda* to *MPM*. Note how *MPM* and *Addenda* to *MPM* are complementary and additional to *OP*.

29   A typical ³⁄₈in touch on a flagon handle of *c.*1630, CB, *MPM*
5417e, and one of ⁵⁄₈in of *c.*1685, John Emes, *OP* and *MPM* 1567.

The early marks—pre 1620—are so rare that we need not pursue them. If you come across a piece of this date it will speak for itself. We can deal briefly with spoon marks which, of course, must be small to fit snugly in the lee of the bowl. A few early marks have no border, and may depict a fleur-de-lys, or a pewterer's hammer, for example, but in the sixteenth century and up to *c.*1660 they are nearly all small (⁷⁄₃₂—¹⁄₄in), very well made beaded circles, with two initials and perhaps a key, sword or pellet. In the early half of the seventeenth century the many marks to be found on the handles of flagons are all small, neatly-beaded circles of ³⁄₈–¹⁄₂in, having two bold initials with a star, pellet or other simple decoration. They rarely bear a date. I have seen one with 1616, but that is exceptional. Towards 1650 emblems join the initials increasingly, and the diameters are enlarged up to ⁵⁄₈in. This question of size is important—beware the piece whose mark is out of step in size! Ninety-five percent of the marks struck from 1650 to 1660 are circular, but an entirely new fashion in touches now appears—a large oval 1in high, with soft palm leaves within the sides emanating from the lower banner, and supporting the top banner, which bear Christian name and surname respectively.

In 1666 a spate of small marks suddenly appears on the touch plate, but this is no new fashion; it is the troubled spoonmakers mentioned earlier who were all ordered to strike new, dated touches.

One still finds occasional small circle touches, with dwindling frequency. For instance LTP 911, struck as late as *c.*1745, could have been struck 90 years previously to judge by style; but touch plate no.4, on which it was struck, was not in existence in 1655.

By 1670 the circular touches are larger, and there are a few more 'ovals and palm leaves', to be followed immediately by a flood of the latter. Also, a very large number of pewterers struck their touches—200 in 10 years—despite the danger signals of the economy in our 'golden age'.

By 1673 inclusion of the names was the rule rather than the exception. Pewterers had realised that here was quite good advertising space and, as far as the regulations went, they got away with it. Only 'quite good' advertising space, because the touch marks were shyly tucked away on the backs of plates and dishes, on the rim. You would have been unpopular with your friends if you had declared 'By Charles, this is a fine pewter dish—who made it?' and simultaneously turned it and its contents over, in order to scan the touch. From the earliest examples we have, until the arrival of the early eighteenth-century 'single-reed' type of plate and dish, the touch had been almost invariably on the back of the rim. From *c.*1700 the touch, for no apparent reason, is always on the back of the well. Perhaps it is because touches are bigger, and need a flat area for even striking. From 1670 to 1694 most of the freshly-struck marks are upright oval, ⁷⁄₈–1in, with palm leaves at the sides very often supporting the design. Addresses,

30 Fashions of touch mark shapes. Large oval, *c.*1660/70. Upright oval, *c.*1670/94. Three-sided dome top, *c.*1720+. Banners, *c.*1735+.

31 Without this touch dated 1685 depicting a dome-lid tankard we would have dated the tankard *c.*1695, probably. IS. *OP* 5930.

too, were occasionally added. (Remember that so far we are speaking only of touch marks, not subsidiary marks.) One very interesting mark, LTP 420, dated 1685, includes a dome-lid tankard in the design. This appears not to be the earliest type even, to judge by the rather heavy base. Without the evidence of the date in the touch, one would have dated such a tankard as 10–15 years later.

By 1692 the palms tend to dwindle, and the outline often becomes waisted. There are still a few beaded-circle touches usually ½in diameter. The designs sometimes show the maker's wares—a baluster, a still and so on. For the greater part, however, the emblems are punning (sometimes extravagantly so) on the surname or addresses, or else are well-executed 'important-looking' designs. By 1705 nearly all new touches were large and more elaborate.

Touches remained similar in appearance until by 1720 a new outline had appeared. This was three sides of a square, the top being curved into a shallow dome. The sides of this design are no longer filled with delicate palms, but with strong-fluted pillars. It must again be emphasised that new touches of the various types were being struck each year so that types overlapped.

By 1735 the touches had an air of grim starkness, and were less well designed. While the pillared touch was popular, a more-or-less circular touch of 1in diameter was even more favoured. There were now prominent banners top and bottom for the name of the maker. 1760 saw the start of other shapes, and in 1780 two or three shields were used. By 1790 some simple ovals appeared, some upwards, some across, and smaller than previously. Only twenty new touches were struck between 1820 and 1825, nearly all flat ovals. Pewterers were no longer members of the Company and/or did not bother to strike their touches.

An interesting fact is that very, very few baluster measure makers' marks are recorded on the touch plates, and Cotterell, too, recorded a lower-than-average proportion.

If you wish to record marks there are two or three ways. Everyone knows how to make a pencil rubbing. They are best stroked diagonally, and it is a good idea to do one north-east/south-west, and then try north-west/south-east, to get the best result. It is normally impossible to get a mark from the bottom of a pot. Put a self-adhesive label over the mark, and rub that; you have got rid of the left hand for better use elsewhere. An excellent method of getting a rubbing is to play the smoke of a candle flame over the mark, then place stickytape over it, and rub suitably: peel it off and put it down on white card. The result is a very good black and white mark, not the graduation of tone of a pencil rubbing, and it is protected. If you wish to photograph a mark make certain that the light emanates from *above* the mark. Somehow many people contrive to light from below it. That results in the optical illusion of relief appearing to be incuse, and vice versa (just as an aerial photograph of a feature on the ground, such as a barrow, with the light or sun coming from the bottom of the picture, makes the barrow appear to be a depression).

32 Cover the illustration on the right before looking at the left. This gives the impression of depressions in the design, due to the light coming (unacceptably) from below (our mind knows it cannot issue from the stomach, and so reverses relief into incuse). Now see the photograph on right, correctly lit—from above.

Secondary marks
In addition to the maker's mark, starting from the sixteenth century, pieces are found bearing other marks, some of which are easy to accept (initials, for instance) as being those of an owner. Later there are other types of mark which will either help or confuse you. By name these are:

    Class A 'Hallmarks'
        Rose and Crown
        Crowned X
        Labels or cartouches
        hR, WR, AR, GIV and some WIV
    Class B 'House marks'
        Verification, or Board of Trade stamps

    Class A marks were applied at source, by the pewterer. In Class B house marks and verifications were probably nearly always applied after distribution.

'Hallmarks'

'Hallmarks' first appeared about 1635, and the goldsmiths very soon protested. They are *not* hallmarks, since they were not applied by, nor related to, the hall—they are simply extra marks of each pewterer, to foster the illusion that pieces might be silver. They infer neither date, town nor quality mark nor a 'registered' maker's mark. They are the choice of the individual pewterers, and each cartouche is his own design. That is why they are always written in inverted commas. The goldsmiths were worried and complained repeatedly, without getting any satisfaction. The 'hallmarks' of each pewterer are sufficiently distinctive to enable a piece to be identified often by only one mark, if it is clear, and it has been clearly and accurately recorded. But only very occasionally can you do this.

33 The small 'hallmarks' of *c*.1635–1660, ND *MPM* 5551a and the larger, longer lived, *c*.1660+. JF (Black letter), *OP* 1791.

The general fashion of styling varied a little—perhaps by so little that one cannot describe the difference—yet a little experience gives the 'feel' of the period of striking, so if you see a set of 'hallmarks' you can judge the earliest possible date of striking. There are usually four, until the nineteenth century, when occasionally three or five appear. They are nearly always struck in a line. At first very small and dainty, they were larger by about 1680, and often an old set of small irons was discarded for a set of bigger cartouches and shields which now had serrations round the border. By 1675 they were in very common use—still on the front of the rims of plates and dishes, and on flat-lid flagons and tankards, but on no other wares. Occasionally flat-lid tankards and flagons around 1700 bear 'hallmarks' apparently struck at random, both on the lid and drum. After about 1700 all 'hallmarks' took shame and hid on the back of the well of both plates and dishes, but are to be seen on the top of the drum of flagons and tankards both lidded and lidless, after c.1720.

Occasionally the 'hallmarks' of one pewterer appear on a piece touched by another. There had probably been a change of ownership of the firm and the 'hallmark' irons handed on, either within the family or by purchase of the business. Very occasionally two different makers 'hallmarks' appear on one piece: in these cases it was probably sub-contracted out, and both showed their credits.

34 'Hallmarks' struck individually at random. Far less common than in a line. I think this is a Midlands and North Midlands peculiarity. WW, *MPM* 6032.

'Hallmarks' of all periods consist of heraldic and non-heraldic devices, black letters, and maker's initial or initials. True silver hallmarks are sometimes closely copied. 'Hallmarks' are little more than a means of identification, and much less informative than the touches. In the mid-nineteenth century they are very often two devices repeated; occasionally earlier than the nineteenth century.

By the way 'hallmarks' do *not* appear on genuine salts, flagons pre 1640, scarcely ever on candlesticks of the seventeenth century, baluster measures (although on these, occasionally, the one initialled 'hallmark' may be used for the mark), lidless tankards or dome-lids before 1700, and very seldom on porringers. That is an almost inflexible rule, and any pieces mentioned so adorned should be greeted with the greatest discourtesy and suspicion. There *may* be some; the fact that I have seen or heard of so few does not mean that they could not exist elsewhere. Experience has taught me the danger of making positive and exclusive statements!

'Hallmarks' arrived in Scotland a little later and in Ireland very much later—well into the eighteenth century. In Scotland the thistle was usually incorporated, and in Ireland the harp.

It may help to know where to look for faint marks, or to be assisted in dating.

Positions of touches and 'hallmarks'—approximate generalisation.

Period	Spoons	Plates & Dishes		Flagons		Balusters	Tankards		Pots		'Sticks	Salts
	Touch ('h.ms' NEVER to c. 1700)	Touch	'h.ms'	Touch	'h.ms'	Touch ('h.ms' NEVER)	Touch	'h.ms'	Touch	'h.ms'	Touch ('h.ms' NEVER)*	Touch ('h.ms' NEVER)
pre-1500	Seldom	Front or back of rim	nil	?	nil	On lid	?		?	nil	?	?
1500–1620	On bowl	Front or back of rim	?	Very seldom	nil	On right of rim	?		?	nil	?	?
1620–1660	On bowl	?	Front of rim	Lower handle, then under base	nil	On right of rim	In base	On lid	?	nil	?	?
1660–1700	On bowl, then on back	Back of rim, or of well	Front of rim	In base	On lid	On right of rim	In base	On lid	In base	nil	On lip	Some under bowl
1700–1730	On back of stem or handle and 'h.ms' ditto	Back of well	Front of rim	In base	On top of drum	On rim or none	In base	On top of drum	In base	On top of drum	Only Tyne area (base)	nil
1730–1790	Ditto	Ditto	Back of well	Ditto	Ditto	None, or on lip or rim	Ditto	Ditto or none	Ditto	Ditto	Ditto or none	Ditto	nil
1790+	Ditto	Ditto	Ditto	Ditto	None	None	Ditto or none	Ditto	Ditto or none	Ditto	None	Very scarce

*Never? A huge pair with wide flared bases bears 'hallmarks' on the flange, also on the sconces. The only instance I know of.

Rose and crown

How far back goes the use of the rose and crown by the Company is not recorded, but it was in use in 1566, and in fact pewterers were warned then not to add their initials to it in making their touch. It is obvious that it was, for some reason, a mark of quality. (Tin ingots were similarly stamped.) It may imply that, where warranted, the pewterer applied the rose and crown. I am fortunate to own a plate of at latest 1570—probably earlier—which bears this rose and crown struck on the face of the rim. The fact that there is no touch mark could incline one to believe it to be of fifteenth-century manufacture but the rose and crown may place it as probably first half of the sixteenth century. It was still regarded as a symbol of quality, and by c.1680 pewterers struck a rose and crown as an additional mark on their plates and dishes, alongside their touches, of the same size and principles of design. Each pewterer used his own design of rose and crown, and so with diligence and adequate recording, theoretically, one can trace a maker by his rose and crown alone. Before long several were defying the Company and incorporating a rose and crown in the design of their touches. This persisted well into the nineteenth century.

Before leaving the rose and crown, bear in mind the difference from the Low Countries' use of it as a touch. There the petals of the rose are filled with fine radial lines, and/or the crown bears, or contains within its outline, the makers' initials.

35 Rose and crown amongst other marks and continental-type rose crowned.

The crowned X

Although this mark appears in the base or on the lip of so many Victorian pieces, its history goes back to the end of the seventeenth century, but its use earlier still can be inferred by the injunction to stamp the X only on 'extraordinary ware called hard mettle'. Certainly, pieces of this period that bear it *are* hard, and may have a higher tin content than normal or are of antimony alloy. Only extensive analyses can prove the points from an adequate sample, Cotterell points out that basically it may be a use of Roman numerals to denote a ten-to-one proportion of tin, which is known to have been laid down on the continent as the standard for best-quality use. This would reduce the lead content to less than half the old standard for hollow-ware. The relative proportions of lead: tin in 'extraordinary' and 'standard' are thus 1 to 10 and 2.3 to 10.

Of course, it may be much simpler—X may be short for 'extraordinary ware called hard mettle'—antimony alloy. This is not so whimsy as it may appear. Analyses are expensive, and much could be undertaken; but it is hard to persuade institutions of research who have the necessary equipment to have the necessary time, free. It is quite likely, I think, that the X is for 'extraordinary . . . ' and that it is the strength and resilience resulting from antimony as the prime alloying metal which is 'extraordinary'. The comparatively few analyses have shown many divergences from what has been written as laid down. We find in pre-1700 instances:

Tin/copper approx. 81:19, 96:3, 98:2

Tin/lead approx. 81:19, 80:20 (there are other traces in most of the above).

64

Antimony was used, probably significantly, after 1660, often in conjunction with copper:

	Tin	Copper	Lead	Antimony
c.1660	98	0.65	0.3	0.45
c.1750	97.2	0.2	0.4	1.7
c.1750	95	0.65	0.1	3.9

Various wares, various parts of wares, used different alloys. Plates and dishes (flatware) needed finer grade than pots and flagons (cylindrical). In the nineteenth century it is very noticeable that the lower section of a body made in two sections is of a quite different (harder) alloy from the remainder—in order to resist being misshapen. Don't do as I did in my inexperienced days—I discarded a magnificent two-handled gadrooned cup, thinking it could not be right since the handles and body were composed of obviously very different alloys. Ah, me!

Antimony had already been used with tin on the continent in the sixteenth century, and was already in use for printing type, for which it gave a crisp edge, amongst other attributes. There are many, many pieces existing from the whole eighteenth century of extraordinarily hard, lovely alloy. I do not think it fair to try to disprove this suggestion on the evidence of some poorish-quality nineteenth-century pots bearing the X—they may well have been made by a backslider. On the positive side, just see how hard and firm are the great majority of pots and plates which bear the X, and also 'superfine', 'sonnant' and so on.

Labels or cartouches

We have seen the pewterers' sudden desire for self-advertising, and some of the opportunities taken in the latter seventeenth century. There was no holding those publicity-minded boys. In addition to touch mark, 'hallmarks', rose and crown, questionable use of X, the enterprising pewterer further attacked the market with cartouches bearing at first 'London', then 'Made in London', for prestige purposes. Provincial pewterers followed their example and did the same—'London' included!— and it transpired that nothing short of an act of Parliament could stop them. The London makers stepped up the campaign by adding their address, perhaps in even another cartouche, and several added others containing more-or-less meaningless jargon. Presumably their 'commercials' paid off, for such labels persisted throughout the eighteenth century.

House marks

This is the title given to marks very similar in appearance to touch marks, but which denote the ownership of the piece—an inn, abbey, corporation or institution. They are struck with an iron just as a touch was, on baluster measures and occasionally on plates and dishes. (Engraved ownership does not come into this category.) It is fair to include corporation ownership such as the Great Yarmouth coat of arms to be seen on eighteenth-century plates and balusters. In Peterborough Museum there is a much earlier example, a sixteenth-century plate bearing a ram on the rim. This is a rebus for the abbey at Ramsey, near which the plate was excavated. Usually these rather rare marks appear on baluster measures. Note that true house marks are struck from irons as well made as touch marks. Beware any that are crudely made! These will be fakes, and there were many on the market before the Second World War. They are still in existence, of course, prized and changing hands, both at home and abroad (see chapter on fakes).

65

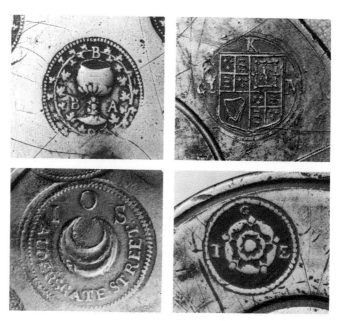

36 Some house marks on baluster lids. The craftsmanship of the die
makers is superb. (Museum of London)

The house mark almost invariably contains the two or three initials of the innkeeper, and the emblem of the house. It is usually struck three or five times on the lid of the baluster. Earlier it was also struck once inside the neck. Besides this mark, the measure will very often carry the same initials of the landlord stamped on the lid and on the handle for thorough security. A very rare form, so rare as to be almost negligible, is the house mark branded on the inside of the base. But after, say, 1650, where used, they are always prominently placed.

Owners' initials

Owners' initials are easily accepted, bearing in mind that 'I' often stood for 'J' to the end of the eighteenth century ('J' starts to appear c. 1720). Whereas previously only two punched initials had designated the (male) owner, from c. 1670, very loosely, gradually the triad took over, bringing in the wife's Christian initial—a slow overlapping changeover. Given the triangle of initials, for example, I $\overset{I}{}$ M, the top initial is that of the surname, the others are the initials of husband and wife. In this case it could have Jones, James and Mary. Occasionally initials may be found surmounted by crowns. Think nothing of it, for it has no known significance.

In Scotland it was more usual to use, not the triad but the two pairs of initials. This is not exclusive to Scotland, for certainly it was used abroad as well, but in this country whether it is a north country feature, or whether erratic I am not certain. I am inclined to the latter.

Note that the triad of initials can refer to a parish—S $\overset{N}{}$ P = Norton St Peter. Pairs of initials on handles of flagons and on pairs of dishes can refer to officials in parishes, institutions and so forth. On a pair of dishes you may have one pair of initials on one, and two pairs on the other—rector and churchwardens or similar hierarchy.

hR, WR, AR, GIV, WIV (each usually with a crown)

The first of these caused much misdating at first. It was assumed by Massé that this stood for Henricus Rex—Henry VIII. Very reasonable, seeing that it occurred on battered, early-looking buds and hammerheads, and that some other balusters and tankards bore AR and WR. It looked as if these marks, struck on the lip or lid of balusters, referred to the reigning monarch. Thus some buds we now know to be of *c.*1700 were dated as mid-sixteenth century. Then it was suggested, after a logical redating of styles of measure, that they referred to the standards of measure enacted in those periods. They need inspecting separately.

The small hR is not solved to everyone's satisfaction. Michaelis, in *Antique Pewter of the British Isles*, suggests that in view of the interest in correct measure of 'muggs' by

37 Applied by the maker, hR, HR, WR and AR refer to capacity measures enacted in those reigns. GIV and WIV refer to being made in those reigns (and are Imperial standard).

the clerk of the market of the queen's household in 1708, it stands for 'household Royal' (or more likely 'Reginae'). It seems far fetched to think that the many different makers whose measures bear this mark all belonged to the royal household, but this official's position included jurisdiction over an area where at least stone pots were made, so there may have been pewterers too under his control, or even markets where the 'muggs' were sold.

First we need to reconcile the many balusters made long, long before 1708. 'Rex' would still stand, excepting the commonwealth period (for which, anyway, we cannot prove a baluster's date). The late Stanley Woolmer, who was also a keen coin collector, pointed out that in the style of lettering on coins of the sixteenth and seventeenth centuries, the apparently lower case 'h' is, in fact, a capital. In the face of this very strong pointer we can probably accept that hR does stand for Henricus Rex, or rather the wine standard of Henry VII. I am still not convinced, because balusters bearing it are by no means of the same or proportionate capacity. At present it just means that you have something of an enigma which looks very well on balusters. WR was used on balusters and tankards, and is undoubtedly the seal of a verification check of capacity, conforming with the act of 1688, standardising the ale and wine measures, which explains why WR appears on some of either capacity range through the eighteenth century, right through to 1826 presumably, when Imperial measure came into force. (I have a 1-gallon Society flagon of 1819 bearing this WR—eleven years before William IV.)

Carving a gap, AR was applied, where used, for Anne's acts of 1704 and 1707. How long after her death this was continued we cannot say. We *can* say that AR on a piece guarantees that it is not pre 1704, but does *not* guarantee that it was not made after her death. AR on pieces is not very common, and my impression is that they fade out fairly soon—say within 10 years, loosely. So these three—hR, WR, and AR refer to standards enacted in those reigns, not to those reigns; and for hR and WR they are predominantly posthumous; for AR, mostly in the latter part of her reign.

38   GIV and WIV in relief—the maker's guarantee. Incuse—verified 'outside' by inspectors.

On the other hand, GIV, which appears first — perhaps pre-Imperial — with a very large magnificent crown, next, much smaller, and finally incuse, and WIV (relief and incuse) were stamped as a guarantee of Imperial measure, and are often accompanied by a stamp of Imperial. I am not completely satisfied by the apparent tautology.

Verification marks
Here is a very brief summary of the standards we are most likely to meet. But I do warn that you will find measurements are far more in the breach than honoured.
I calculate the following fluid ounces (Imperial) per pint:

Ale	Henry VII	Wm III	Anne	Imperial
	1497	1688	1704	1826
	? 'HR'	WR	AR	
	19.36	20.33	19.63	20.00

Wine	Henry VII 1497 ? 'HR' 17.72	Wm III 1688 WR 16.15	Anne 1707 AR 16.65	Imperial 1826 20.00

We will only touch on capacity standards by referring you to the summary chart and by noting that in 1826 Imperial standard was implemented.

About this time the capacities began to be verified by stamps using 'GIV' (whose reign was 1820–30) and in turn by 'WIV' (1830–7). We have assumed that workshop-produced goods which were denominated and stamped with these 'royal' stamps were verified at source, but subsequently measures sometimes bear a sequence and multiplicity of verification marks. One wonders if certain innkeepers were regarded with grave suspicion, and the authorities chivvied and hounded them constantly: or perhaps the publican was an easy touch for a beer. I have seen about fifteen verification stamps on a single tankard. Note that it is not only measures which are verified, but also tankards in general use. After the omnibus GIV and WIV stamps,

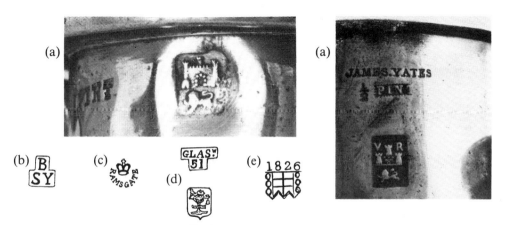

39 A few county and borough verification marks, 1835–1878. (a) Norwich. (b) Surrey. (c) Ramsgate. (d) Glasgow. (e) City of Westminster. Note that Westminster, apparently alone, verified measures as far back as the 1750s, using a portcullis without a date.

county and borough stamps were used, usually being a simplified reproduction of their heraldic arms or crest. To date, nowhere have these been published for general perusal but we now have hopes of their being made available in the not-too-distant future.

In 1879 central control and standardisation was more or less imposed, and the stamps were the monarch's initials crowned, with a number and, in some districts, a letter, for example, $\frac{VR}{159}$. The number was allocated to a county or borough, the letter denoted a district. The numbers were issued one by one, as applied for—*not* usually as a group. Thus two consecutive numbers could possibly be from widely-different localities. A few districts did not take up the new functional stamps, but kept to their own ideas, mostly pictorial ones. A two-digit number, notably 82, on a few non-uniform stamps indicates 1882, at which time about sixty-five districts in Britain had opted not to take

40 Standardised 1878 stamp (Norfolk).

(a)   (b)

41 (a) Rather curious verification marks—CS with P beneath: County of Southampton (i.e. Hampshire), Portsmouth District. (b) Opposite side of cup. Portsmouth crest, and initials of inspector Hugh Moncrieff.

up a 'uniform' stamp. Often you will find two-digit numbers on the rim as well; sometimes many pairs: 97, 00, 11. These are year stamps of verifying in 1897, 1900 and 1911.

In Ireland there is a slight difference in the 1878 stamps. A harp is the central motif, in lieu of VR, with a number, say 33, even as high as 555, comparable with the British numbers. But in Ireland these are constables' numbers, amongst whose duties was verifying.

There are one or two oddities amongst verification marks. One is the portcullis, which serves double duty as the emblem of both the City of Westminster, and the Department of Weights and Measures. It is very frequently found on pots and measures dating anywhere from 1826 to 1878, all the while bearing the date 1826. However, in 1758 (no later) the City of Westminster had laid down that all their measures and pots should henceforth be stamped with their emblem.

42 Several counties and boroughs opted out of the new formalised 1878-type stamps, and continued using their existing, or modified or designed afresh. Northumberland, Bristol and Higham Ferrers for a very few widespread examples.

One of my own pots is marked with a 'Turkish-looking' verification, a crescent with star between points and HM, and elsewhere on the same pot is C + S. The latter is County of Southampton, P (Portsmouth) District, and the former is for Henry Moncrieff, inspector. Occasionally elsewhere other inspectors' initials are included; sometimes a letter, like a single digit, denotes sub-district.

6. Romano-British, Early Medieval —to end Sixteenth Century

The Romans came to England, not primarily to make pewter, as you and I might think, but for other economic and prestige purposes. They knew of our tin, and as well as using it for consumer and military products they copied silver in it. Tin, however, is very harsh, and liable to decompose. Somehow—perhaps just to make up substance—some lead was added, and the alloy no doubt proved easier to work, and certainly better in use. The well-known hoard found at Appleshaw in the middle of the last century included items containing varying proportions of lead to tin. The 'Fish' dish was ninety-nine point two percent tin, other pieces varied down to ninety percent; other pieces of Romano-British in the country go down to only forty-seven percent tin! Soon they appear to have settled at sixty-two to eighty percent—which latter was the medieval standard. The hoards have been discovered principally in East Anglia, and the pewter was virtually confined to the civil zone south-east of the Fosse Way. East Anglia was subject to fierce, violent raids in the fifth century AD. Warning was short— a hole rapidly dug and the pewter hidden—the raid successful; the owners were left in no fit state to recover their fine dishes. There the dishes remained until they reappeared during deep ploughing, and building of many airfields. So East Anglia has provided perhaps disproportionate evidence of distribution due to fifth-century raids, the Second World War and deep ploughing.

Manufacture has been proved at sites in the Bath area, notably at Camerton (see *Excavations at Camerton* by W. J. Wedlake). Tin was brought from Cornwall, and lead, stone (for moulds) and coal were available close by in the Mendips. The products are invariably well made, some of superb craftmanship. For design, technique, decoration and enigma, the octagonal flanged bowl with Chi Rho and other presumably Christian decoration, now at the Museum of Archaeology and Ethnology, Cambridge, is perhaps the finest piece of pewter in the country of any period. This is probably true judged on any two of these points, excepting the decoration. This consists of Chi Rho, the Greek symbol of Christianity, and other emblems of the faith not yet elucidated. It is very clear, and obviously of great potential interest. Items made in the period range from chargers of 32in diameter down to saucers of 5in diameter; little cups for sweets, sauce or spices; bowls, plain or with circular or octagonal flanges; ewers; jugs; caskets (perhaps for cremation remains); even to a candlestick.

Some of the dishes bear a decorated panel in the centre, based on geometric and what can best be described as squirl designs. The rim types vary considerably in detail, and some are very similar indeed to the single-reed plates of the eighteenth century. They were cast in stone moulds and trimmed on a lathe, but they were not hammered for strength. One certain method of identification is that *all* plates and dishes carry a

71

43 Perhaps the finest piece of pewter of all, considering all factors. Fourth century AD. Ht 4in. (Dept of Archaeology and Ethnology, Cambridge).

44 Three remarkably sophisticated and well-made Romano-British ewers from the Fens of Cambridge-shire. (Dept. of Archaeology and Ethnology, Cambridge)

support ring underneath, of approximately half the diameter of the well. Therefore they were used to carry weight—probably a jug or ewer, for knife marks are never to be seen on them. Also the great majority have three or four concentric grooves on the top of the plate, from a quarter to a third of the diameter of the well. No piece has been found with a maker's mark. ('Romano-British Plates and Dishes', Christopher A. Peal. *Proceedings of the Cambridge Antiquarian Society*, Vol.LX, 1967.)

Indeed the Romans evolved pewter in Britain, and several museums have pieces on display (see Appendix I), but there is evidence of its use elsewhere much earlier: 'The earliest known example of pewterware was found in a grave at Abydos in Egypt . . . confidently ascribed to 1580–1350 B.C.'—(Hatcher and Barker, *A History of British Pewter*, Longman). Just where China stands is not known. The Romans very soon achieved a high standard of workmanship and established desirable alloy standards. I wonder if the early medieval pewterers were aware of their predecessors' skill. When the Romans left Britain, trade and communications collapsed, so pewter manufacture lapsed as a trade.

A few Anglo-Saxon brooches of base alloys are the sole existing representatives of a millennium ago. We have no evidence of domestic ware until 10 years after the Norman invasion. Perhaps the Normans are a significant link, for it is not known how or where or whence pewter was resurrected.

1076 is an oft-quoted date, for it is the first historical record of pewter, in which it is referred to as 'tin'. This confusion of term persists in German and French, for their nouns are 'Zinn' and 'étain'. 'Étain' mutated to English would be 'stin' and the common derivation (Latin 'stannum') is obvious. 'Pewter' is a corruption of Old French 'peutre'.

The record of 1076 refers to 'tin' being allowed for church vessels, and Michaelis comments that there are other written evidences of church pewter in the eleventh century. We now meet the first examples of early medieval pewter—the sepulchral chalices, and occasionally patens, which were buried with priests in their coffins in the twelfth and thirteenth centuries. This was specifically requested by the Bishop of Winchester in 1229.

There are one or two spoons of very early date, probably of the thirteenth century. There are four very fine and well-preserved ecclesiastical cruets which are most probably of that century, or the next, at Ludlow, Weoley, Victoria and Albert Museum and Tong, Shrewsbury c.1350. Remarkably they form two pairs. In 1348, another memorable date, the first recorded representations were made which culminated in the charter being granted for the founding of the Pewterers Company in 1474. Obviously for much more than this hundred years the makers had been getting together for their self-protection, and determining standards of workmanship and alloy (see chapter 2).

In the fifteenth century there were founded not only the Pewterers Companies of London, but also of York, Bristol and Edinburgh. At the same time guilds of freemen of associated crafts were established at many other centres. Records refer to very many types of ware which are not defined, and of which we have no knowledge. In fact in many cases it is not clear whether the reference is to type or size. Michaelis, *Antique Pewter of the British Isles*, quotes many instances and gives his references such as 'Voyer', 'Dobeler', 'Tanggard potts', 'Stope potts', 'Bow potts', 'Ephram pots', 'Guiny potts'. There are so few pieces of hollow-ware belonging even possibly to this period, that we are left as frustrated as we are intrigued. Two domestic flagons come to mind, at Norwich and Hitchin museums respectively.

45 A very early spoon of unknown use or significance. There appears to be a strong Norman influence in the design. (P. Hornsby)

46 This cruet is in sharp mint condition, and its condition implies that it was dropped new, down the fourteenth century well from which it was excavated at Tong Castle. The archaeological evidence (Mr Alan Wharton leading the Tong Arch. Group) is very clear as to date of deposit, as mid-fourteenth century. It is marvellously preserved, and speaks volumes for the standard of workmanship existing at the time that the London pewterers started to petition for a charter. With this cruet was a very fine little paten. *c.*1350. (Photograph, Graham Lawley)

It is possible that some of the very early slim balusters (Mr R. Mundey's, for example) are of the fifteenth century, but it is more likely that they are a little later. The greatest numerical evidence of the period is in spoons, and this is in the time when the pewterers' lobbying and pressure appears to have virtually stamped out competition. The spoons are with fig- or pear-shaped bowls, and the thin diamond-shaped stem has now been tapped on top and underneath to form a hexagonal stem, which by the end of this period became rather heavier. (Homer, *Five Centuries of Base Metal Spoons*). The types which run in the fifteenth century include writhen ball, diamond ball, acorn, stump end (which is very different from slip top), horned headdress, melon, some maidenheads and some earlier latten-knopped spoons. Do not forget that some types ran well into the next century—the diamond knop had a life of some 200 years, and while *some* acorns are early, most are sixteenth century. Latten was used occasionally to simulate the gilt knops on silver spoons. The horned headdress is the most commanding of all types of knopped spoon, and has been aped by the fakers, and so has the acorn, and probably others as well, including the maidenhead. Be very wary!

47 Sixteenth-century flagon. Examples are very
rare indeed. Probably *c.*1550. Hitchin Museum
(North Hertfordshire Museum Service).

Whereas all items in silver were carefully preserved, old pewter was only good for
scrap. So all presently existing pewter spoons had been lost and have been recovered
from drains, wells, the ground, river, mud and so on—which helps to explain why
pewter is so very much more rare than silver. There are a few spoons on show in the
Victoria and Albert and Salisbury museums, and many examples of very early pewter
spoons are in some museums' stores. It is not fair to say which, for risk of too much
enquiry. To a lesser degree many museums have single or a few examples of fifteenth
and sixteenth-century spoons—and plates—on display.

Some of the bumpy-bottom plates almost certainly belong to this period. A hoard of
some twenty was discovered in 1899 during extensions to Guy's Hospital. They are of
copper–tin alloy, exceptionally fine, and each bears an ostrich feather in a long
rectangular mark on the front of the rim. This was the emblem of Arthur, Prince of
Wales (1486–1502). Specimens of early bumpy-bottom plates probably of that century
may be seen at the Department of Archaeology and Ethnology, Cambridge; Weoley
Castle; Museum of London; and Victoria and Albert Museum. Most, however, belong
to the sixteenth or early seventeenth century.

75

48 Fifteenth-century spoons (photograph printed upside down, to show the knops the better). In this illustration, l. to r., mitre, diamond, melon, gridded ball, golf ball, peach ball, writhen ball, horned headdress, stump end, two early latten-knopped, diamond. (Approximate date sequence is the reverse order.)

Sixteenth century

These charming bumpy-bottom plates continued, and reflected light throws up their design most attractively. The rim is rather wide and plain. A pity that they are so rare. Specimens may be seen at Hampton Court and the Museum of London. Two similar in type are known, both dated 1585, but with punched decoration forming a series of scallops.

Although there are many records of the doings and misdoings of pewterers, which we have already touched on, only a few types are described, and our examples of hollow-ware of the period are woefully inadequate. We know that tankards and pots were made. We have none. Stone pots with pewter lids threatened the Company, and were probably similar to foreign examples as in, for instance, Fitzwilliam Museum, Cambridge.

Undoubtedly some of the early baluster measures are of this period (Museum of London, Victoria and Albert), and cannot be later than sixteenth century. Although we have no archaeological evidence, few pictures or descriptive evidence to define styles, and we cannot *with certainty* date earlier than the end of the sixteenth century either, it is very likely that these were made continuously over a longer period. The thumbpieces were either a large hammerhead, or a ball, both mounted on a slightly-curved flattish triangular attachment. One of my own, unfortunately without lid or thumbpiece, shows exceptionally early lines—with a pure curve and narrow base. Who is to say that any of these is the first of the type to be made? I feel that balusters, in some form, certainly existed in the fifteenth century, perhaps earlier, and that some existing examples may date to then. Some writers have suggested that these balusters were sired by the leather black jack, but a glance at medieval pottery jugs surely gives a stronger line on their conception.

49 A very early baluster indeed, perhaps fifteenth century. I regret not knowing the provenance or any owner at any period, but it is too interesting to omit. (The Pewter Society)

Candlesticks were made with a bell base (and probably other styles as well). One is to be seen at the Victoria and Albert Museum, but the base of this has been mis-reshaped. This type is recorded recognisably, as of two sizes.

Salts, both bell and trencher, were made. None of the latter has been identified, but I found the base of one of the former acting as door stopper in an antique shop. Identical styles were made in Holland. The goods of the Heemskerk expedition of 1596 were recovered early in this century, and there are several identical examples from it in the Rijksmuseum, Amsterdam. (Note, any remaining diehards of the 'tin pest' phrase—the intense cold of 300 years in Novaya Zemlya did not cause 'tin pest' in the pewter. Nor, to be fair, is there much evidence of corrosion.)

Probably very little pewter, if any, was used in the churches in this century, but a

50 Very fine elizabethan dish. Dated 1585. (Dr R. F. Homer)

most interesting example which is more likely to be domestic and is probably of this
period, is at the Pewterers Hall. This is bulbous, on a thin stem over the foot. The
weakness at this point may account for this being the sole survivor of the style. It is
similar to silver examples, but one should add that it appears to be somewhat similar in
style to a flagon depicted in the well-known touch of EG of about 1630, and so it is
possibly very early seventeenth century. A fine flagon of the mid-sixteenth century has
been recovered from the wreck of the battleship *Mary Rose*.

The porringers of the day were akin to the plates and dishes, but are much more rare.
At first they had very gently-sloping walls, (or bouges), with three-lobed, trefoil or
fleur-de-lys-like twin handles. The walls became more vertical through the century,
and the handles more ornate. The bases were either flat or bumpy-bottomed. (See
Apollo 1949, July, August, September, October, R. F. Michaelis. It is masterly.)

The sixteenth century saw the heyday of pewter spoons. Many types of knop are
known of this period, including gauntlet seal, lion sejant, 'peachstone' ball, maidenhead, 'chrysalis', apostle, melon, hexagon, seal, baluster, diamond, horsehoof, and slip
top (the top of the stem cut off). You can hope to acquire an example of this type,

possibly acorn, and hexagonal knop, too, maybe others, with patience and cash—but beware . . .

The spoons at this time were bigger and more heavily made. The now heavier hexagonal stem was hammered flatter, no doubt to give strength to the rather unsuitable medium. It is as well to study spoons carefully, for they are the one category of pewter that one can confidently expect to see of the sixteenth or even fifteenth century—but this will probably be in a specialised dealer's shop, or major saleroom, or museums. (The big heavy-handled round-bowl spoons one occasionally sees are Dutch, easily distinguished, and of much later date.) Hilton Price pioneered the subject of pewter spoons (and latten) in his *Old Base Metal Spoons*. In *The Connoisseur* issues of April and July 1970, 'Latten Spoons', I have traced the development of the spoon, and drawings help in dating at a glance, for the types are almost equally applicable to pewter, and the two media are considered together. Here I must again recommend Homer's *Five Centuries of Base Metal Spoons*.

Spoonmakers' marks are delightfully struck from beautifully-made irons, being beaded circles with initials and emblems. But trouble and competition suddenly sprang up, and were tackled by some pewterers joining the new faction in the second half of the

51 Sixteenth-century spoons, on their rack, printed upside down. L. to r., decorated slip-top, crown, seal, maidenhead, baluster, hexagon, latten-knopped baluster; lion gardant, maidenhead, apostle, chrysalis baluster, acorn, gauntlet seal, lion sejant. The lion gardant and the crown are probably fifteenth century.
(Approximate date sequence is the reverse order.)

79

century. Latten (brass) was now allowed to be made in this country, and it must have been realised that it was a far more satisfactory medium for the leverage imposed on the stems. Some pewter spoonmakers took to making latten spoons—and ructions followed (see *The Connoisseur* articles mentioned above). This appeared to take place at a critical time for the Company. There had been many reports of misdemeanours; the Company had difficulty in maintaining control (makers were always finding fresh ways to kick over the traces) and it was a bitter struggle which, in effect, the Company lost, for latten spoons became the larger proportion of the examples which have survived from this period.

Wills often provide our best sources for the names of items—but alas, wills were not illustrated. Here are relevant extracts from one in Norwich, dated 1589. Only three rooms are mentioned, 'Parler', 'Chamber', and 'Chetchin'. I am sure that you would prefer me to preserve the original spelling—it is comprehensible. The total estate was £23 13s, of which pewter was exactly five percent. The most valuable effects were 'One English gowne' at xxxvis viiid, and 'vii payer of Shetes', at xxxs. Of the pewter, 'viii Dishes' at iiis iiiid, and 'vii candlesticks' at vs were the most valuable 'lots'. Three porringers for 10d (not 'p', mark you) seems a good buy, and I would make an effort to raise 1s for the quart pot. On a serious note, compare the price for a quart 200 years later, listed on the trade card illustrated later in the book—new quarts were by then approximately 1s 6d to 1s 9d. While 1s looks a lot for the tudor pot, we are not accustomed to only fifty percent increase in inflation cost over 200 years.

In the Chetchyn

i charyer		xxid
iiii platters	iis	
i basen of pewter		vid
i basen of pewter		vid
viii Dishes	iiis	iiiid
iiii plates of pewter		xiid
vi Saceres		viiid
iii porrengers		xd
iii Salt Selers		xiid
i Botell of pewter		iiiid
i lamp of pewter		xid
i chamber pote of pewter		viiid
i quart pot of pewter		xiid
i Jug covered with pewter and acrustonered with pewter		viiid
vii candellstickes	vs	

('Certen other things in the chitin' are mentioned which may include some pewter, such as a 'poudring tube'.)

7. 1600–1660

Now a new series has appeared, around 1605—church flagons—and very numerous the specimens are in churches and collections. There are very few other items from this period still existing apart from occasional plates, dishes, balusters, porringers and spoons. A few special museums have examples—for instance the Victoria and Albert, and the Museum of London.

52 Dignified, simple church flagons of the first quarter of the seventeenth century. (a) Curiously, the superbly-made first type, of 1605+ only very seldom bear makers' marks. This is 8⅜in to lip. (b) RI, *MPM* 5730a. (c) EG, *MPM* 5614a. (d) CB, *MPM* 5417e.

We cannot be sure that uninscribed flagons not now in churches were not domestic. Almost all other domestic hollow-ware is now missing—worn out—while flagons were preserved in church keeping. But they may have been also domestic. One I know bears a wriggled (zig-zag) pictorial domestic scene, so that is one precedent. However, I do feel that it is unlikely that many people would choose ecclesiastical styles for home use. Conversely, there are many instances of domestic pieces, in domestic styles, subsequently taken into church use. Where inscribed they bear evidence of being gifts, probably when the churches were hard up. Offhand I recollect a plain flat-lid tankard, (later, several inscribed dome-lids) and even baluster measures.

The Church had been despoiled—particularly of the silver plate—and thus impoverished it was allowed in 1603 to use pewter for flagons for bringing the wine to the table. So starts a really fine series of the most dignified ware in pewter—the rather rapidly-changing styles of church flagons. The first ('1605' type) ran till about 1625, and is very solidly made, of simple and most effective design, slightly-tapering drum with a little entasis. The base spreads a little, and the lid is faintly like a skull cap, with knop surmounting. The thumbpiece is the most remarkable item, being an adaptation of a German design—solid, towering. The bottom of the container drum is curved, and does not touch the table. It was made in various sizes, and very seldom carried a mark. Those marks I have seen are on the back of the thumbpiece. This type is supplanted quite suddenly and universally, as though the Company ordained it, by the 'muffin lid', in which the lid is waisted. There is almost always a touch mark on the lower part of the handle.

It is not clear whether the knopped version preceded the plain lid, or vice versa. I am inclined to think that the knop is earlier, because of the natural follow-up from the last type; another reason, because of one maker's idiosyncrasy of a detail which appears in both the 1605 type, and the 1625 with knop; another reason being that there is a rare early type of thumbpiece like a tall flat 'chair back' which occurs only with the smaller knopped ones. In fact the knopped are often dubbed 'the 1625 type', and the same style without knop, 'the 1640 type'. Perhaps it is safer to regard them as coeval, over a span of some 35 years. A probable dating pointer is in those whose drum bottom is rounded like the 1605 type, as against those whose whole flared base is open to the contents (flush with the table, for better stability, and more capacity). The maker's mark now starts to appear under the base. The thumbpiece is now a strong bar across the top, a heart-shaped piercing beneath, and two side projections, the whole tapering somewhat, which has allowed some to have been broken off in the thirty-four decades of wear and tear. Have a good look at this point in examples.

One cannot pass beyond this type without commenting on one maker—EG, whose identity is not known at all surely. He must have had many apprentices and journeymen because his flagons appear all over the country. I do not think any distribution map has been attempted, if only because so much church pewter has not been examined by knowledgeable people (and so much has left the churches). I have often wondered how such heavy and rather vulnerable items as large church flagons were carried to the numerous and remote parishes of, say, Norfolk. I pity the poor packhorses, *and* the flagons because of the joggling. None of the several scores I must have seen bears obvious signs of travel wear and tear. EG's mark is one of the few touches incorporating a 'style illustration', his bearing two flagons—one bulbous, footed on a stem, the other (surprise, surprise!) of a typical EG flagon. So perhaps the footed one was also a popular product. Or was he reminding the public that he was a successful maker of the tall type, and now how about one of the bulbous? I guess that this was a type which he made, but the weakness of the stem design means that all have perished. To reinforce this idea, the bulbous illustration is lidless, and is an ewer, and so is domestic; the wear and tear would have sent it to be recycled after only a short working life. True, there are very few not dissimilar ewers such as those at Shrewsbury Museum. I wonder if there *is* somewhere, an example of EG's 'other type', which appears to be lidless?

In the 55 years up to the Restoration it appears that only the three types ran—the

3 (a) Three vessels recovered from the *Mary Rose* which was sunk in Portsmouth Harbour in 1545. Obviously a pottie — of any period. The flagon — our best example of a first-half sixteenth century flagon, or in fact of all pre-1600 examples. See and compare with the illustration of the Hitchin Museum flagon. On the right are two fragments of another flagon. (Copyright, Mary Rose Trust).

(b) Porringer — the most perfect example, for design, condition, workmanship and age. *c.*1695. W.B., *MPM* 5487a.

4 Very fine wriggled flat-lid with twin love bird thumbpiece. By Samuel Billing, *OP* 425, whose mark includes
the castle and elephant of the Arms of Coventry. *c.* 1685.

53   A marvellous flagon of *c.*1635 of the Weavers Guild of Exeter. 15½in overall.

1605, and the knopped and knopless muffin. A great many flagons exist in churches and in collections. A vast quantity of domestic pewter was made at this time, most of which has perished, but church flagons have been preserved by inactivity and security in the Church; only a few in collections can be matched by a faculty to prove that such permission for sale was ever given. It is unfortunate that there seems to be so little opportunity for the Church to display such treasures with safety, and they command more interest in collections where they can be seen and used in research and study. Presumably each flagon had a plate on which it stood. These, when specially made, have a very shallow bouge, and a shallow groove round the well into which the rim of the flagon base nestled. They are now very rare, perhaps because they are really rather insignificant to the uninitiated. They are about 7in in diameter, plain rimmed. Communion cups are very rare in this century.

Plates proved to be of the early seventeenth century appear to be almost non-existent but, as mentioned in the previous chapter, it is probable that many bumpy-bottom plates considered to be sixteenth century are, in fact, of the first quarter of

54 The first tankards (Cromwellian) that we know of—in the seventeenth century. Most insignificant in detail. This one has been used (and preserved) as a church flagon, and made by Francis Seegood of Norwich and King's Lynn. *c.*1658. Approx. 5½in to lip. *MPM* 4168.

this century, particularly those with slightly wider rims, for this was probably a style in fashion from 1600 to 1650, with the rim diminishing in size latterly. Cotterell has illustrated the rim with a single incision 'reed' on a fairly broad rim, with dated touch of 1621. These are very rare. The bumpy-bottoms continue, and two I have bear 'hallmarks', and so would not be earlier than *c.* 1630. Two plates which I take to be of this period have 1in wide rims, and gentle bouge, with the bottom of the plate not so much bumpy as crowned. One is a gentle dome, the other a very flat cone. Both have 'hallmarks' on the rim and are therefore about 1630-50. The

55 The famous and prolific maker "EG", so far not identified. On the right of his mark he depicts very faithfully one of his well-known style. But where is an example of that on the left?

deductions of dating are simple overlap of features—the bumpy bottom tailed off when striking 'hallmarks' started *c.*1630: the gentle bouge and plain 1in rim together usually occur with late bumpy-bottom plates before very broad-rim plates and the more intricate reedings appear. Of the two plates the 'hallmarks' of one are larger, square. This tends to be *c.*1650 onwards. Dishes and plates with rather deep wells followed, and have a fairly narrow rim—of about 1in—and a gently sloping bouge. One in my possession bears a touch dated 1646, and is probably pre 1660.

While the bumpy bottom was waning, the broad-rim dish and, to a lesser degree, plate, waxed in popularity. It was well established by *c.* 1640, and rose to its peak at the time of the Restoration, after which the rim dwindled. The greater proportion of the heyday broad-rimmers were plain, but no doubt the light line bred the idea for the rare dishes with two deep grooves, so soon to yield to the shallow mouldings of the young multi-reed dishes, so soon again to be heavily emphasised.

I think it fair to suggest that knife marks did not appear to the same extent on plates actually in use pre *c.* 1650 as subsequently, due to the more genteel dining table

56   A bumpy-bottom dish-plate of late Tudor to *c.* 1620.

manners after then, in the small private dining room. But, of course, older plates which survive to this day could easily have been used for decades after manufacture. Conversely, later ware might have been in servants' quarters, to be treated to more basic table manners.

Porringers henceforth in England were always one-handled. They are just as rare in this period. At the start of the century they continued with a very deep bowl with vertical walls, with a shell handle or 'ear'. The body suddenly melts, and goes 'splodge'—to become shallow and wide, but with straight sloping sides curved at the bottom; and the handles are very simple, symmetrical fretted. The bottoms were usually crowned. Again, see *Apollo* magazines in 1949.

We know nothing of salts, barring a probable early seventeenth-century specimen in the Victoria and Albert, of a 'spool' design.

Of candlesticks we know a little; they are rare and seemingly trumpet shaped at first; then, or perhaps concurrently, with heavily-knopped stem, a drip tray, and rather low bell base. Magnificent.

There are a few very rare cups and goblets bearing fine-cast decoration, perhaps derived from Germany. The vogue was very short lived, *c.* 1616.

85

57 Three styles and proportions of broad rims. On the left, one of the Mount Edgcumbe service, with bad corrosion adequately smoothed. (The backs of these plates have a most unusual tin-like appearance). A good conventional b.r. dish, of *c.*1660, 18¼in dia. On the right is a very rare reeded broad rimmer of *c.*1645. Left, ND, *MPM* 5551a; centre, SI, *OP* and *MPM* 5741; right, WS, *OP* and *MPM* 5961.

The series of baluster measures is uninterrupted. In the sixteenth century they had borne a ball, or a hammerhead as thumbpiece. Nowadays most collectors do not accept that a 'wedge' type was made with no thumbpiece—maintaining that it is the strut leading to a missing thumbpiece. Surely it needs a firm leverhold? How would stubby thumbs have coped? Every single other type of lidded vessel is set up with a very imposing thumbpiece. No, a 'wedge' is an emasculated 'ball', or a hammerless hammerhead. The earlier balusters were thin and slim, and are likely to have been inspired by medieval pottery. So they followed the lines—slim, simple and gently curved, not flaring out at the base in very early specimens.

The bottom handle attachment fitted very flush with the body, and the mark was usually on the lip. But now they swelled, and grew a wider base giving more stability. Up to, say, 1640 (very roughly) the lids were trimmed thinner round the 'edge', with a distinct 'step' to nestle into the rim of the body, tending to obviate lateral wear on the hinge.

Like other items, pre-Restoration balusters are very scarce, and there are some very attractive fake hammerhead, ball and 'wedge' balusters around. I do wonder how many have been destroyed after recognition! The Pewter Society would be very grateful for donation of any fakes for its 'chamber of horrors'—its 'awful warning' collection of fakes. Beware these early-looking balusters, probably overloaded with glamour house marks, hR, and pocked surface. By the way, the measures were for wine and spirits, and were in Old English Wine Measure which is five-sixths Imperial (still the standard fluid measure in the USA).

The ball dropped out of use except in a very rare type, but the hammerhead continued into Queen Anne's reign. In the meantime, in the middle of the century, the body had become squatter and more curvaceous. It is not enough to judge the date, as one writer has said, by thumbpiece type and for these two types at least it is far better to judge by body type.

58 Two porringers of the period, found by a holidaymaker in the river bank at St Benet's Abbey, Norfolk. As found and after restoration by R. F. Michaelis. (The late Charles V. de la Mare)

The spoonmakers were in obvious trouble, to judge by the comparatively few specimens left to us. Whereas the church flagons particularly show us superb design, craftsmanship and finish, the spoons had become weak and crude in design and execution by comparison with those of the previous century. They were assailed by the far more practical latten spoons. The latten spoonmakers—some of them known to have been pewterers—now piled on a mortal blow: they tinned their yellowy-gold brass spoons, and turned out ostensibly pewter (or silver?) spoons of great hardness and

59   A fine quart so-called 'wedge' baluster, which in fact has lost its ball
or hammerhead thumbpiece. Note the slim lines. This is the baluster
bearing a bull house mark in the base, c. 1635. 7¼ in to lip. DB *MPM*
5421. On the right is an earlier gill, the lid being stepped so that it nestles
in the neck of the body, so restricting lateral play. c.1625. 3¼ in to lip.

resilience. You may come across a latten spoon still completely covered with tinning,
but more usually showing only traces. The types of pewter spoon you may encounter
are baluster, seal, possibly late maidenheads, and of course pre-eminently slip top.
These bear no knop, the stem appearing to have been cut off on the slant, like a pruning
cut. Stems in this period are very much flatter and bowls very much more round. Odd
examples of extremely debased but recognisable styles belong to this period. Obviously
these pewter spoons are at the very bottom end of the trade. Moulds were possibly of
wood, or made of clay from a crude master spoon, and probably they were made by
itinerant tinkers.

8. 1660–1710

This is the narrow period when an enormous amount of the most attractive types of pewter was made and has been preserved. All pewter of this period is irresistibly attractive and forms the greater part of established collections, and the ideal of newer collectors. The most popular date ascription would seem to be *c*.1690!

It would certainly appear that the flamboyant enterprise with which the makers threw off the heavy control of the Company, and the stimulating effect of the country's release from the stern repression of decoration during the Protectorate, together with the attack with which competition was met, unleashed an unbridled freedom which was exercised with the utmost good taste. There is a remarkable number of survivors.

Emerging free enterprise was spurred on by keen competition, not only because of increased output of pewter, but also from the growing intrusions of pottery, and possibly silver, which was just within the reach of some of the pewter clientele.

So wide is the field, and it is so necessary to cover it adequately, that it is difficult to know where to begin and what to omit. Certainly a few inevitable omissions as to type, styles or details are bound to disappoint some readers.

60   Church flagons—(a) beefeater, 8⅜in to lip, *c*.1665. Thomas Lupton, *MPM* 3016a. (b) Rare two-band flat lid (with date 1588 stamped on the drum! Commemorative dates are frequent) *c*.1685. IF, *OP* 5591; (c) John Emes own design of lid in particular. The drums are most attractively hammered *OP* and *MPM* 1566, 1567, *c*.1680–90. (d) This type seems to be largely confined to an unidentified maker 'WW', (*OP*, *MPM*, and *Addenda* 6032). The centre of distribution appears to be approximately Nottinghamshire, *c*.1680–1700.

Church flagons continued to change in style, even more dramatically. The first type after the Restoration is perhaps the best known of all—the 'beefeater' (from the similarity of lid to cap). The base is widened considerably, giving a lower centre of gravity when filled, and therefore a greater stability. The thumbpiece is usually a pair of hemispheres, or 'twin cusp', although in the western part of the country, and/or perhaps a little later, a form of twin kidney with projection was popular. The mark was usually inside the base, and for the first time we find 'hallmarks' on the flat lid top. This type is very pleasing, and is probably the least rare. It was made by many different makers.

There is a most handsome type, most of the few I have seen being in private hands, while the others are in Sussex churches. This is not to say that there are not more in churches elsewhere, for one is in a Norfolk church, and another came from a Hertfordshire church. The sole maker was John Emes (*OP*, 1566–7) 1675–1700. Emes' touch is on the handle, the handles almost always being weak at the swelling (due to inadequate spread of metal in the 'slush' casting, in which the molten metal is swung about in the mould until it congeals). Perhaps future research would elicit whether he ever became aware of his inadequate slushing, and hence deduce dating of those concerned. His drums are always beautifully hammered—small and very regular impressions. And he used several different thumbpieces, one, at least, of an eagle.

Towards the end of the century flagons took on a new look. They have less base diameter, the body bears two hoops, and the tall flat lid of tankards is adopted (*c.*1685). It is noteworthy that the body of this rare type is similar to the hooped coeval tavern pots (but is almost cylindrical). Following this is a type which seems to be by one prolific midlands maker—WW (*MPM* 6032)—the distribution of his hollow-ware in churches radiating (very roughly) around Nottingham. This flagon appears to be his monopoly, and is of very handsome proportions with its tall tapering sides, and a shallower (earlier-looking) flat lid. Who is this WW? We do not know. He is one of the few makers who applied his 'hallmarks' scattered in a loose diamond area, instead of in a neat short line. One would have thought that others would have made this type, or

61 Three unusual tankards. (a) By 'WW' (see previous fig.) *c.*1680. (b) Note the thumbpiece more usually on beefeater flagons, and the solid handle, 6⅜in to lip, *c.*1680. (c) An early, probably provincial dome lid. Perhaps this most unusual shape was the dawn of the 'tulip' shape (see chapter 1710). TB, *MPM* 5466.

very similar, but I do not recall seeing examples. His other types include an earlier type of flat-lid tankard, and a later dome-lid.

Now to spoons. Somewhere, and why not here, I should say that for every knopped spoon, you will probably see twenty to forty slip tops. Spoons in pewter were now fading out, and are largely represented by very debased and poorly-made 'things'. Latten, usually tinned to simulate silver, possibly to isolate the brass, really held the stage. But there *are* pewter spoons either ahead of, or trailing behind latten, and they underwent a revolution in design in a very short while. Puritanism had kept styling in check, confined to the slip top (excepting the poor tinkers' jobs). By now, in place of a knop, someone had hammered the top of a slip top perhaps in rage, perhaps to flatten it slightly, to give a little lateral stability leverage.

Someone else went a step further and hammered it harder for greater flattening—and in so doing caused two splits at the top. Someone, whether in silver, pewter or latten, visualised the possibilities of developing design from this modest start. Spoon-makers too, were ready to burst out with enterprising design. The spoons developed more oval bowls, flat wide stems, a finger running down the back of the bowl for support, and the top of the stem became a wide flat with a progression of detail—all emanating from the two nicks. It is particularly interesting that decoration and mantling grew around the edge of the top of the handle and the bare centre was used to bear successively William and Mary, and Anne. It is strange that although spoons in both latten and silver bear the surrounding decoration, in those two media it is almost always left blank in the middle and only in pewter does the royal portrait occur. No doubt *they* were ready to back any horse. Trust pewter!

A moment's thought shows how logical it is to take porringers next. If you were well brought up you used your spoon in a porringer. But it puzzles me why the porringers of the earlier part of the century had been straight sided—and as a corollary, why spoons had become round bowled. Perhaps the porringer makers realised that there was something amiss in their liaison with the spoonmakers, for from 1650 the curve in the wall was reintroduced for the spoon to scrape the bowl efficiently. There may be a little confusion over the term 'porringer'. Its use was for eating any porridge-like substance such as a thick soup, or stew. However, what we call a 'two-handled cup' or a 'loving cup', the silver lovers call a 'porringer', and they refer to our porringer style as a 'wine taster' or a 'bleeding bowl'. I wonder how much wine tasting was undertaken, and how many receptacles for blood letting were of silver, not graduated?

We will not go into the minutiae of R. F. Michaelis' articles on porringers previously mentioned, but will summarise what you may see through glass, or faintly possibly without restriction of view. Many of the types are single or only very few, and several examples were culled from the stores of the Victoria and Albert, and from what is now the Museum of London. There had been a developing range of one-eared porringers from, at latest, the early sixteenth century. Although Michaelis identified some dozen types to the seventeenth century, they are mostly very rare, except those of William and Mary and of Anne. By now they have become very rectangular in section, with the bottom of the wall curved. The perforated fretted handles are more ornate, including some with relief figures—dolphin, crown and so on. Then starts the voluptuous arc-like curved walls. One type probably accounts for ninety-five percent of all those you will see outside museums. There are various permutations of the thicknesses of base and walls. Again the bottoms are mostly crowned, but some are flat. Various designs of the handle are their greatest attraction.

An unaccountably-rare class of domestic ware is salts. The pewterers drummed up business in many types of ware by rapid changes of style—probably none more so than in salts. Therefore presumably comparatively few were made of each style. Rare indeed they are . . . but you never know!

Salts, like spoons, are well worth studying in other media—for instance silver and pottery. Until mid-seventeenth century the ceremonial use of salt necessitated the great standing salts of silver, with smaller trencher salts round the tables. No doubt the base section of the three-tiered salt played its part in such a custom nearly 400 years ago. After puritanism had suppressed all ceremonial, the upper crust who had been 'above

62　Salts are unaccountably scarce. The collared salt is very rare (fakes are much more common), 1¾in high, *c.* 1660. At about 1700–1705 gadrooning swept in, and out so soon.

the salt' in the hall now dined in a separate room. Apart from the bell salt just mentioned and the spool of the early seventeenth century we have no salts until the very attractive wide octagonal collar salts of about 1660, of which very few genuine specimens still exist. They were soon outmoded by capstans which, plain, ran from about 1675 to, gadrooned, up to about 1700. A completely new conception of design now appeared, smaller than capstans and, instead of being waisted, bulbous; the smaller, simpler probably being the earlier. Note that the bowl of all these types is a

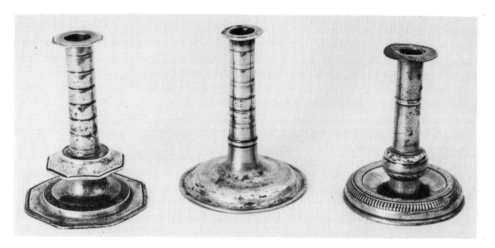

63　Candlesticks—(a) Skirted 'stick with cast floral decoration on the base, *c.* 1685, height 6½in. (b) Rare, similar style, no drip tray (because wax was improved and was almost completely consumed) *c.*1690. RB, *OP* 5452. (c) Gadrooned. The stem usually rises up out of the base, but this example shows no signs whatever of having been compacted.

separate well—the salt is not contained by the outside wall. Very broadly speaking, earlier salts have the smaller wells proportionate to the pieces.

Candlesticks follow salts if only because the moulds for casting the octagonal collar salts were used sometimes for casting the base of the very much sought-after driptray type. Some magnificent specimens still existing were notable for the balusters and knops in the stem, and their drip tray. These are rare, and their attraction and whole stature ensures very high prices. Then the balusters and knops are omitted and the stems are lightened by fine multireedings, or else wide, slightly-bowed 'sections' (for such they appear at first sight to be). The lip, drip tray and base are usually octagonal, and sometimes the base has a ring of grape and vine decoration cast into it. Not for the first time when describing fine pieces I warn you to beware of the several fakes. Candle wax improved in quality towards the end of the century, spluttering fat no longer scalded the hand, nor clogged the clothes, so drip trays fell out of use. Exactly where the large knop variety fits is not known for certain. Perhaps they were of the same period. Certainly some have gadrooned edges to the base, placing them at about 1700. Probably the knop followed the abandonment of the drip tray.

There is a further complication with this type—in some the stem stands up tapering out of the base; in others the stem grows out of a well in the base. These have not been compacted downwards—if that had been the case wrinkles and fractures of the metal would show. When marked the touch is usually on the top of the lip in all types, but very occasionally under the base—so far all the fakes are marked under the base!

Plates and dishes are an obvious essential to any display and this period sees the biggest range, changes, and prettiest styles of the whole history of pewter, some running concurrently. We left the early part of the century with bumpy-bottom plates and dishes, and rather bowl-like dishes. By the Restoration, broad-rim dishes had made their appearance in a range of widths.

Around 1660 or a little earlier, the ultra-broad-rim dishes and plates were made, *some* being used as patens, but mostly for domestic purposes. It is difficult to imagine these as everyday plates for meals, as the well is so small and shallow and the ratio of contents to strain on the seam and rim is poor. Nevertheless, they show many knife cuts. What was the day-by-day tableware from about 1660 to 1675? Perhaps they were the dishes with rather broad rims and either incised rings or deeply-grooved rings—but plates of either type are very rare. About 1675 the two types 'triple reed' and 'narrow rim' appear. These have from two to four rings or reeds *cast* near the edge.

In case you are despairing of ever coming across any 300-year-old pewter—the most likely seventeenth-century ware to be seen are the decorative triple (or multiple-) reed dishes, probably of 15in or 16in diameter. And a noble basis around which to show your pewter. Conversely, narrow-rim dishes are very rare indeed. It is very tempting to make out a case of type development to show that narrow-rim plates started with bold reeds, and gradually grew a plain band inside the reeding, on which 'hallmarks' and owner's initials were placed. It grew until this style is almost indistinguishable from triple-reed plates and some might regard the triple reed as the ultimate development. The difficulty is that narrow-rim plates are usually provincially made and, from what good evidence we have, tend to be slightly later on average than triple-reed plates. 'Hallmarks' were placed in the well of the very narrow-rim plates, otherwise being on the face of the rim. Touch marks on triple-reed dishes and earlier types are on the back of the rim: from *c.*1680 on dishes and plates they are on the back of the well.

64 Although narrow-rim plates are not desperately scarce, dishes certainly are, and this, at 16⅛in, seems to be the largest recorded, c.1690.

At the turn of the century the rim was greatly simplified—with only one ring—the 'single reed'—still with 'hallmarks' on the front in the early years of the 1700s. The triple reed and the single reed overlapped for a short while.

Before leaving plates and dishes there is a large subject which must be introduced—decoration. We have discussed the reedings on plates, dishes, candlesticks and salts; the cast decoration in vogue in 1616; the knops on spoons, in candlesticks and on flagons; the fretting of porringer handles. All these were an integral part of manufacture. We now need to look at art applied after the piece was made, although probably applied by the actual pewterer. We have touched on the punched decoration which appeared in about 1585—this scalloping reappeared, very rarely, in c.1685.

94

'Wriggling' swept the board in the whole of the latter half of the century. It probably existed in the previous century, for I have a plate of undoubted tudor period, which bears traces—but wriggling does not seem to have caught on until the Restoration. Then suddenly there appear the big wonderfully-decorated Carolus Rex dishes (Victoria and Albert, Museum of London, and Wisbech museums). There are many in existence, very prized, and possibly some are fakes. (I have never recognised one as such, but most have been much cleaned.) Wriggling is, I suppose one could say, a form

65 Triple (c.1690), narrow (c.1685), and single-reed (c.1705) plates showing different craftsmen's wriggling.

of engraving, but instead of cutting the lines deeply (and weakening the pewter) they are formed by 'waddling' a chisel along, pivoting on its corners at each step, zig-zag. The design was first traced, then different-sized screwdriver-like tools were used, and varying pressures applied. As well as on these magnificent Restoration and Marriage to Catherine of Braganza commemorative (1662) dishes, wriggling was used particularly on narrow-rim plates, flat-lid tankards, and occasionally on dome-lids showing the contemporary forms of flowers, birds and busts. There are some rare coronation souvenirs of William and Mary, and this was the period of its greatest popularity, waning by about 1720. In this connection it is amusing to note that coronation souvenirs were as trashy then as at the last few coronations—the pewter in one plate is little better than Dutch cheese. Engraving was the normal treatment for arms, crests and inscriptions, of course.

Wriggling on flat-lid tankards! Probably everyone who knows what pewter is would like above all to have a decorated flat-lid. It would not deter them to know that when plain they are more rare. Perhaps the latter were so little regarded that they were traded in, while the wriggled ones were kept carefully. There are fakes, reproductions—so, as usual, take care.

So to tankards. Two, of c.1645, are the earliest I have ever seen and when I say flat lid, at this time it really was a *flat* lid; the plainness of the whole makes them so featureless as to be almost unnoticeable. By 1655 the lid had a shallow crown with a single tongue projection, with insignificant base (flush to the table), over-curved handle, twin-cusp thumbpiece and squat drum; and is nearly non-existent. In the middle period (c.1675–85) they have a little depth in the lid, and the handle has a long tongue dropping from the top to give a good attachment to the body. The thumbpiece is possibly a 'ram's horn', twin crescents backing, twin love birds, a chrysalis-like

95

structure (very rare), or even a crown (on a possibly-unique example). There are probably five projections at the front of the edge of the lid; some, probably the earlier, being perforated, and very delicate they are. Some, possibly because of this, have been filed off in antiquity—or recently. The 'hallmarks' are on top of the lid, and the touch mark is in the base. A good look at the illustrations will convey more than wordy descriptions.

Subsequently, the base is heavier, the handle more solid looking and butting onto the body. No doubt the fragility of the perforated projections (or denticulations) had proved itself, for they now become unperforated. The shape also changes. The body becomes either more squat or taller and thinner. Whereas earlier drums had a marked entasis (outward bowing), which conveys parallelism to the eye, they are now straight and tapering—sometimes even convex. The development of handles from solid to hollow, the details of curvature, and of their terminals can also be seen in the illustrations. The type ran until the early eighteenth century.

66   A fine group of varied flat lids. Note the curious curve in the two left-hand handles, and all other detail of these two handles (c.1680–5). See also the fine decoration on the handle of second from right, c.1685. (Price Glover).

It is generally thought, erroneously, that dome-lid tankards followed after flat lids, but they were certainly made in 1685, for we have seen that touch no.420.LTP (*OP* 5930, identified as Thomas Smith, 4361a—*MPM*) depicts a dome-lid and '85'. The remarks as to body, handle and thumbpiece apply equally to dome-lids as to flat-lids, except that quite early dome-lids adopted an approximation to a clenched fist as thumbpiece—the scroll: Dome-lids are best dated by body and handle type. In the period under review, they had at first a high dome and small squat body, with small base—and *may* be earlier than 1685; then a little lower dome, overwide brim to the lid and body with marked entasis. The handle on both of these types runs down the body. The denticulations are bolder than on the flat lid. Both bodies are plain—free of encircling rings. In some cases these purely joyous-purpose items have been taken into use in small parishes as flagons.

It is puzzling that almost all containers of liquid appear to have been automatically provided with a lid. One needs to go back to Romano-British times to find lidless containers—the ewers and flagons. *All* subsequent examples—flagons, tankards and measures, except very rare ewers—have lids. Hygiene and safety of contents were probably not the reason. Perhaps the Company ordained that lids were to be made, to keep the price up. Perhaps it was further evidence of the rebellious enterprise of the 1680s, in the face of a trade slump, which led to the production of the lidless 'tavern

67 Two rare examples of flat-lid tankards—(a) the engraved ship, b/ R. Hand(s) *OP* 2117a. (D. Peatling): (b) Crown thumbpiece (C. C. Minchin).

97

68 Four variations of dome-lid design. They make a fascinating range and study (a) WP, *OP* 5866. (b) WW *OP* and *MPM* 6028, 6031, 6032. (c) TB *MPM*5466. (d) RB, *MPM* 5455a.

pots'. Their design differs from the lidded tankards, being tall, slightly-concave sides, with two bold bands or hoops round the body, and usually bearing an engraved inscription showing ownership. Those prior to 1700 are very scarce indeed, and those of the early years of the eighteenth century only slightly less scarce. Whereas some of the household flat-lid tankards had been *preserved*, the tavern pots, in use much more numerous but now much more scarce, have *survived*. The eighteenth-century tavern pots, smaller in capacity, have two narrow fillets. At first they have solid (thinner) strap handles, soon to adopt the heavier-looking hollow ones. These early ones had their bases flush with the table, soon to be raised clear—*c.* 1705. Perhaps starting before this type are some very rare larger capacity pots with one high fillet and strap handle, which appear to be English, but the only three I have seen or heard of have turned up in America, with evidence of original habitat. So they may have been exported, or they may have been American made.

Two very attractive types of pot with similar decoration appear early in the eighteenth century, with shallow close diagonal fluting (gadrooning) cast in the mould. One shape is like a neolithic beaker, but with a handle, the other with tall tapering sides. They really are glorious examples of pewterers' design and work. Occasionally rather squat two-handled cups with this fluting may be seen. A large proportion of these gadrooned items were made by one maker—William Hux (*OP* 2498).

The last category to be dealt with is measures—baluster measures—perhaps the most interesting group to understand fully. They are pre-eminently suitable in design and function for pewter, and do not appear in other media—certainly not silver, although I have seen one of gallon size of later date in brass. We have already met them in the earlier periods—as ball, and hammerhead. The latter continued to be made after 1660, apparently up to the end of our period, since one I have bears the AR verification stamp.

By now the hammer thumbpiece was usually very thin and emaciated and whereas formerly the lower handle attachment was flush to the body now it stands off, connected by a strut. Formerly tall, slim and of little curvature, by 1660 they are invariably more squat with fuller curves, including the base flaring out. The original three sizes recorded in 1480 as 'pottell' (half gallon), 'quarte' and 'peingte' had been

98

69 Tavern pots. (a) The very striking 'two band' of c. 1680–90, 6³⁄₈in to lip. J. Donne, *OP* 1415a. They are usually engraved with the innkeeper's name and address. (C. C. Minchin has one with the pithy 'If sold, stole'.) (b) A very rare type—only two others are reported, and are in the States. It is possible that they are American made. No maker's mark. The details look English, certainly. However, assignation of provenance is rather speculative. If English, c. 1690–1700. If American, perhaps c. 1780. 6¹⁄₂in to lip. (c) A slightly later North Country English pot, c. 1720. IH, *MPM* 5654a.

joined by 'halfe peingte' in 1556 records, and now by gill and possibly half gill. Again, be well warned to avoid a quarter gill, however twee and tempting.

The series of balusters must have run for 350 years or more—starting at latest c. 1480 and ending in c. 1820. By about 1670 the 'bud' thumbpiece makes its entry, so-called for want of a more descriptive name. Each end is a 'leafed' projection faintly like a bud, and comparable with car springs dressed together. These are most desirable and not unduly rare, and specialised dealers can usually show one or two. It is almost true to say that no two buds are alike, for even when two come from the same mould they will have different grooves cut round the body. Like humans, some are tall, some are solid, and they carry their curves in different ways. Grooving bands were very often used, but only on balusters with this style of thumbpiece, and some late hammerheads. Some

70   Most attractive example of a transitional ball baluster twixt the early ball type, and the slender. Baluster shapes are very varied indeed. RB, *OP* 5452. This may well date from earlier than our chapter. (New South Wales Art Gallery)

have plain bodies—and the nuances of different curves of the outline are limitless. The handles are heavier than in the slim earlier measures. The lids, too, bear rings of varying number and distance apart. The thumbpiece sometimes bears a little pip in front, which also occurs on some later hammerheads (and so can be taken as evidence of the late seventeenth century). The thumbpiece is attached to the lid by a three-tiered flat wedge. The touch marks in early specimens are small and may be either on lid or lip usually to the right of the handle or, particularly on later examples, there may be no mark. At first slim and plain-bodied, curves and rings developed. Occasionally they

100

were made without lids. It is surprising to find two touches on the London touch plate—nos 362 and 564—both of which depict a lidless baluster of bud form. These would have been struck *c.*1682 and *c.*1700 respectively.

With so much styling variation one would think them easy to date. Unfortunately, it is the very opposite. In the seventeenth century they nearly always bore a maker's mark, but few bear dated touches, which would give only earliest possible dates. Few are by known makers—and dates of deaths are scarce. With experience one can feel fairly confident of dating some to within 10 years. Sometimes luck may help; if a bud bears a touch with date (say, 1680) and bears AR crowned on the lid, the piece is not likely to be more than 40 years later than striking. Therefore the latest date would be *c.*1720. But AR would not have been used before 1702—so its dating is 1702–20. If you have a bud with a pip on the thumbpiece, and/or the handle very closely attached to the body, then it will be early—*c.*1680–1700. It would be more misleading than helpful to try to formulate any rules of dating by design. Of all types, these appear to be subject to the fewest rules in details of style (and capacity). For this reason it will be more convenient to take this class beyond our terminal date of 1710. The capacities had been laid down, but the variations within a given size are enormous—up to about plus or minus ten percent.

Dr Homer and I have at different times carried out wide surveys of buds to try to find reasons for the erratic departures from the standard, but we have had no real success. Provenance is invariably unknown, date difficult to define, and the result means nothing. It was not intentional short measure, for most are over standard. One interesting clue was three (quart, pint and half pint) by different makers, and of different styles; each bore the same owner's initials. They are exactly in proportion. There are three other types to note. The ball baluster continued now in bud-like body proportions, but only in the smaller size ranges. Most of those I have seen have been half gill, although I have come across a gill with touch dated 1662. The lid attachment

71   A harlequin (mixed makers and/or types) range of buds, from quart to half gill. The half gill is almost as rare as the half gallon and gallon, but the latter are rather large for small houses. I think that the variation in line and proportion make buds the most attractive type. The wings of the half gill thumbpiece are usually very weakly formed.

101

at first is a high ridged bar, which later becomes more flattened. One of mine is plain, early, with a 'pip' under the ball, exactly as in some hammerheads and buds. Dating is difficult since they are scarce. However, I have seen one with the touch of A. Hincham (*c.*1710–50) and I think the timespan for this type of measure must be *c.*1680–1730.

There are also those called 'slender ball balusters', from apparently the very north of England, since they conform to Scottish measure, not OEWS. The only sizes of the five or six I have seen are the three smallest. Delightful they are, but I can find no

72   These three probably belong to this period. Gill slender ball. The bull-neck is slightly reminiscent of the later Newcastle balusters. 3⁵⁄₁₆in to lip. IH ?*OP* 5666. Centre—the rare spray baluster (one example bears date 1704). The half gill is possibly later than the current chapter.

Scotsman bold or rash enough to claim their nationality. I reckon them to be *c.*1700–*c.*1740. Another type also from the north—Lancashire to Northumberland, is the very rare 'spray' type, again mostly conforming to Scottish standard, but not consistently. These I have only seen in 'quart' and 'pint' (approximately) sizes. John Douglas has shown me one engraved with date 1704. I have no reason to think it anachronistic. Like the slender balls, there are one or two other points common with Scottish design—the anti-wobble flange under the lid; and the long straight under the hinge. I have a strong ally in Dr P. Spencer Davies in rejecting Scottish provenance. They have all turned up in England, and apart from very rarely in London shops, all from the north Midlands to the Border. And none in Scotland.

Buds appear to be discontinued by about 1780–1800. With great reluctance and nostalgia we leave them, and the seventeenth century.

9. 1710–1825

We left trade in a bad state, and have seen the reasons for the spate of new ideas which were rife from 1660 to 1720. Anyone aged 80 in 1720 must have been subjected to changes of designs far more extreme and sudden than we complain of today. Trade continued to be bad; there were many insolvencies. The Company's weakness and vacillation came home to roost—it was disregarded. With the coming of the House of Hanover, designs became teutonically heavy, and largely gross and mundane. Inspiration and attempt to float new styles deserted the pewterers. Instead of meeting competition by upgrading design, they kept costs down by using the same plant for a long time, and their moulds had to pay for themselves over and over. Decline was general. There were some extremely successful pewterers but only a comparatively small proportion. Pewter faced competition from pottery, porcelain, silver, brass and, later, other base-metal alloys.

Up to 1750 most styles have been fairly comprehensively illustrated in books, but when we get past that date, while there are well-known standard types, for example, an Eddon dome lid, or a Chamberlain wavy-edge plate, there are many different types which are individually scarce, but collectively have had little attention, particularly from c. 1750–1820. This makes this period exciting for the enterprising collector—casters, salts, funnels, even pots. True that the three former types are reasonably common in the nineteenth century—but do you know which are nineteenth and which are eighteenth century? Nor, often, do I. So here is a field for both collecting and research. Once again, difficulties are that styles changed slowly, and that on several items, certainly three mentioned above, virtually never do you see a maker's mark. In salts there must be a better sequence and dating than we have so far been able to produce. Almost all that has been published about salts, for instance, apart from a modicum in *BP and BM* is Cotterell's dating of the grapefruit-cup-like salts as 'c.1740, c.1750' and some very optimistic dating of later types. But am I fair? To an extent I think so, for the base mouldings on one example illustrated, for instance, are of 50 years later, referred to later in this chapter. Later the same types have been given a longer span, to 'c.1800' and I am convinced that this large-cup-salt type is found late in pewter history, into the middle of the first half of the nineteenth century. Casters should be a tremendous area for seeking the truth. Maybe a wide, tolerant study of other media will show probable dating, but do bear in mind that pottery, silver, treen and Britannia metal ware will all have been made by different methods of manufacture from pewter, so varying emphases of style may show in one or another medium. Enigmatic as dating is, it is the pewter industry's own fault for not having given us makers' marks on them; not that this would have given us close dating, probably, since

103

73 (a) The wavy style of the dish and plate was adopted from the French for a short while, made and marketed most successfully by Thomas Chamberlain. *OP*873. Dish length, 18¼in. The strawberry dish is very rare, and is another more enterprising style than is usual in English pewter. Similar date. G. Beeston *OP* 353. (b) A most satisfactory George I dome-lid with typical fishtail terminal. (Holt Collection)

in general one mark was used in a lifetime. Possession alone is a poor qualification for a collector; we are only temporary guardians of a national heritage. It is only courteous to talk to one's pieces, and get them to talk back. Now that possession is more difficult, from scarcity and cost, inevitably those interested will veer more and more into researching multitudes of unknown or vague facts. I hope that this book will be grossly out of date in 30 years time, thanks to each of you, individually. There are many, many lone collectors who have something to contribute; so frequently I have found that some of those who appear on the scene, not being dyed-in-the-wool collectors of early pewter, are already well versed in their later, off-beat speciality and, thank goodness, contribute worthily to discussion and knowledge because they have dug out facts for themselves.

I have intentionally taken you for a ramble into unexpected products and dating, so that we can return to collecting in this period with an open mind but sharper eyes—eyes to spot the early piece of a type which appears to be much later. By contrast, here are some items which may be met, which were presumably too commonplace to advertise on the late eighteenth century trade cards: church flagons, bowls, plates, footed plates, communion cups, porringers, bleeding bowls, tankards with lids (of various types), early nineteenth-century pots, candlesticks, spoons, tea caddies, snuffboxes, chamber pots, tobacco stoppers, seals, whistles, medallions, mantel ornaments, to mention only some. There is plenty to go for; but the ability to recognise them is required.

Let us start with church pieces. We know that styles now seldom change. There are really only two basic types of English church flagon for the whole period. Initially a nearly-flat-lidded type was produced, apparently in England first, but it was adopted almost universally in Scotland for probably 100 years to about 1820, and by far the greater number of these were Scottish, for as English they are quite scarce—and many collectors have overlooked their English origin. This type soon had a successful competitor—the rather heavy first edition of the 'spire' flagons. The early type has a plain handle, and lowish dome lid. However, it was soon made more slender, with higher dome, with knop, wider base, and, most important, a very well-designed 'broken' handle. Note that the lower section of the broken handle is the lower part of the same handle mould. The total result is that this delicate, neat, always exceptionally-well-made and beautifully-proportioned piece stands out like a fairy amongst Hanoverian soldiers. To my mind it is one of the short-listed most attractive styles ever made—perhaps the winner.

Regionally there are two outstanding types of flagon—the 'straight-sided York' and the 'acorn York'. It may fan smoulderings of the Wars of the Roses, but I suggest that the straight sided is more truly Lancastrian, since it seems to be distributed in churches in that area.

One should remember the fairly frequent use of domestic dome-lid tankards as church flagons. Many exist in churches with such inscriptions as 'ex dono . . . '. Other tankards and balusters marked with only the name of the village are perhaps village measures, not church flagons.

There are one or two other general flagon designs which have been published. There are sometimes odd ones, too. Just recently I handled a really 'made-up' affair—but it had been made up originally. It was about 3 pints capacity, the lower section of the body being that of a typical pot with fillet, with the upper inch or so cut off; in lieu of this an extension had been added, all in the same tapering line. It had a nice late domed lid, with 'open' thumbpiece; the handle was an undersized 'broken' one, probably designed for a pint mug. This was made by John Curtis of Bristol whose partnership

74 Examples of the early dome-lid flagons developing on towards the beautiful
spire style. *c.*1710–35. (C. C. Minchin, and Holt Collection)

was bankrupt in 1793, so I guess that as he tried to pick up the pieces, when he had the opportunity of a job, he made do with what moulds he had, or could borrow. Normally the tapering drum would have been made in one piece. Made-up, but quite attractive.

From flagons we pass to communion cups. They are very rare in the previous century (when they had small cups) and were omitted from this text. In our present period they are of large capacity, with either a very flaring out lip, or remaining straight sided, with no beading at the lip; very unfinished these look. Usually the cup slightly tapers down towards the pillar of the stem. I think that they never bear a maker's mark. Why, I wonder do some of these good pieces seem to have missed out using their due place as good advertising space? Most of those engraved are nonconformist, and the English specimens are much less frequent than Scottish. Perhaps most churches had silver cups.

75   Three Yorkshire flagons (although I think the straight-sided one to be more truly Lancashire). (a) c.1720, 9$\frac{1}{8}$in to lip. IW *OP* 6002. (b) The open thumbpiece of the very small acorn indicates c.1760. (c) There is a twin to this very fine flagon with a similar inscription. (The church is demolished.) Date engraved is 1750. John Harrison. *OP* 2162.

To patens is the next step. Early in the century they were often narrow-rim plates mounted on a circular foot. Sometimes this was beaded, more often plain. After c.1730 a normal plate stood duty for a paten, and several are inscribed as proof. Plates and bowls were used for alms and collecting. Some churches stood a bowl in each porch. One church in Norwich has four such narrow-edged flat-bottom bowls, engraved on the rim 'St Andrews Church, North Porch', and one for each of the other three porches. (There were a few reeded bowls in the seventeenth century, sometimes engraved, but very few outside the churches.)

Plates are almost always plain rim of about 1in (the single-reed rim ran out by c.1730) and there are also soup plates with similar rims of the late eighteenth century. The only difference at first sight between these and those of c.1660 is in the bouge. The earlier type is much more gentle in curve and, correspondingly, the diameter of the bottom of the well of the later is much greater. For a short period c.1760 there was a

76 The small-bowl communion cup is obviously the earliest, say *c.* 1750, height 5¾in. The other two are *c.*1820.

vogue for copying the French style of cast wavy-reeded-edge plates and oval dishes. These are most attractive and break up a display of plain- or single-rim plates to great advantage. As we can see in the trade cards later on, octagonal plates were made, but are now very seldom in circulation. Another rare earlier class of dish of *c.*1728, 12–16ins, is of lobed decoration hammered out. Very few are known, including two pairs, but probably there are others in private hands, which may turn up very occasionally. They were probably made for decoration and ceremonial use, being like silver and gold rosewater dishes, and similar to the earlier brass Nuremburg dishes.

Identical in form with the church collecting bowls were those for domestic purposes. Obviously there were countless kitchen and household uses, and I think it interesting that a fine mahogany dressing table I possess has one drawer with circular cut-out containing a pewter bowl, exactly like the church bowls. This is by Aquila Dackombe, and reference to *OP* shows that he was insolvent in 1761, and struck out of the Company in 1773.

Plates, dishes, bowls . . . to porringers. Like nearly all other products, porringers were very similar throughout the period: one fretted ear, on which the perforations remain very similar. There is only one good reference, which is the very painstaking work by R. F. Michaelis in *Apollo*, previously referred to.

The most common type has bulging sides, and nine different ear types are found with this body, all of them multi fretted. These date from *c.*1675–1760, although Michaelis lists one Bristol made porringer as *c.*1775. Porringers do not display very happily; at best they can be hung on hooks on dressers, rather, I think to the detriment of pieces behind them.

Many like to think that porringers were bleeding bowls, but the latter are always graduated in 4, 8, 12, 16, even 20-oz rings. Oddly enough, these are the only British measures of any type giving 'read-off' markings. Whereas porringers are round walled, bleeding bowls are straight sided. Never willing to yield to the cant of antique dealers,

108

77 A typical porringer ear. This and similar styles ran on to about 1760. (Indeed, porringers were still on offer in *c.*1850.) (After R. F. Michaelis, courtesy of *Apollo*) (A. Bartram)

who seem to think bleeding bowls very desirable, I do not see why this type should not have served equally well and far more often as kitchen measures; and why should not many pieces such as bowls have had many uses. People ask me 'What was it used for?'. The answer is simple: 'What do *you* use a bowl for?'. I like a piece, *regardless* of its possible use. These 'bleeding bowls' do not bear marks, and I take them to be late eighteenth century, with probably a long run.

78 Bleeding bowl. Dr Gusterson has seen them in use in a hospital.

Salts, candlesticks and spoons followed very different courses. Salts had reached the stage of low-sitting bulbous trenchers. After 1710 these became rectangular, with the corners cut off, in the well-known silver style. About 1750 a radical change occurred—they were made like a grapefruit cup, always without a mark. The container was the cup—single-skinned for the first time. These continued into the nineteenth century.

A great variety of minor differentiating outlines of small cup and trencher salts

109

occurred around 1800, but in the absence of marks and other evidence we cannot get nearer in dating. It does not seem good enough to dismiss a range of household articles as '*c*.1800' when one cannot be certain whether it could be 1780 or 1840, but that is the situation.

79 The octagonal salt is well known in silver, and is therefore datable at *c*. 1728. The bowl for the salt is separate from the wall. The cup salt, dia. 4in, seems to be the next style, and henceforth in a different conception—usually footed, the cup being the container. In the absence of marks dating is problematical. The illustration puts forward a proposed progression.

Candlesticks had a broken career. We left them rare and expensive in 1710–15. Excepting a very rare Newcastle type they disappear until about 1790! (There are some Dutch specimens of the period.) One can only presume that pottery and brass ousted pewter candlesticks, but they came back in full force with several designs involving knops, teardrops and balusters. The overriding recognition mark is the iron pushrod for ejecting the candle stub. No marks are struck on these candlesticks.

Spoons. At last it seems that although they had been good enough for parents and grandparents, it was now realised that pewter spoons were not much good to anyone—except apparently the Dutch (Dutch spoons are very heavy and gross and the bowls almost hemispherical.) What English spoons there are follow the slim styles well known in silver—the forerunners of georgian and victorian shape; ladles, too, were made into victorian times. Spoons and ladles were one of the greatest beneficiaries of antimony alloy, whose use indeed was more and more widespread over almost all products. In the nineteenth century some are stamped 'Ashberry Metal'.

A very interesting historical link survives with society flagons. In the middle of the century the workers in a trade used to get together locally and pay into a fund for mutual insurance. In towns each major industry had its society. (From these, development was natural, but in two different directions—friendly societies, and trade unions.) Each society had one or more engraved flagons. Perhaps Norwich has more than other towns and cities—there are at least five guilds' flagons existing—and there were also the Mancroft Ringers—the bellringers at the famous church; not only the flagon but tankards too exist, similarly engraved. Often these flagons are not engraved with the society's function, but bear arms, and/or the supervisors' and headsmen's names. Their occupations (and thus the society's function) can be found in electoral rolls. The same style, but lidless, turns up in half-gallon size as pub jugs.

Two-handled cups on a stem can be taken as of the early part of the nineteenth century; those whose bowls sit at table level, as of the mid half century of the eighteenth.

Leaving tankards to the last, we will deal with measures—baluster measures. Since

80 Newcastle produced very attractive 'sticks, by G. Lowes (c.1710–1765) and his successor R. Sadler (c. 1730–1780) *MPM* 4088. These do not carry the push-rod ejector which was universally adopted after c. 1790. Height, 7in.

we have already investigated buds for their whole run (due to difficulty in dating), one might think that only the double-volute thumbpiece type is left. That is by no means so. For instance, there are the bud-type bodies which were made lidless. The earlier are taller in proportion, the late eighteenth century are very wide rimmed, and the end of the handle is fitted flush to the body, like a soldier's hand as he stands at 'Attention'. Buds were overlapped by the double volute (so called as the thumbpiece resembles the decoration on ionic columns) in sizes from the gallon to half gill.

In this type the thumbpiece is attached to the lid by a fleur-de-lys (in the smallest size the fleur-de-lys is cast on a flat flange). The handle, with a ball terminal, is attached to a diamond-shaped plate on the plain body for greater adhesion. Just occasionally a bud may bear one or two of these transitional features. Conversely, early double volutes sometimes bear rings round the body, and sometimes have a touch mark on the lip, and very occasionally house marks. One presumes their life ended in 1824 when the Act was passed establishing Imperial Measure, and abolishing Old English Wine Measure. I have never heard of one in Imperial capacity (remember they were measures for wines

111

and spirits), although in Suffolk the lid was stripped off and an extra piece added to the lip to bring the capacity up to Imperial. I have seen only the half pint and the pint so modified. Very occasionally lidded or lidless they have had a band added to the belly to make up the capacity to the new ale and wine measure.

The ball, slender ball and spray balusters were referred to in the last chapter and these overlap into our present period. However, they are all very scarce and it is difficult to place terminal dates. I suspect that they each extend into the first quarter of the century and perhaps a little later.

81   (a) A lidless bud-type body. Peculiar that the maker used a pot handle rather than a baluster handle. Certainly this removes the hinge boss. (b) A double volute thumbpiece baluster, with engraved inn sign.

Not truly measures, but containers, the pleasant rural-looking ale jugs are usually dated 1780–1810 and are found in five sizes, half gallon to half pint. I think they should date at least a decade later, at each end. They used to be very plentiful, and I don't suppose any have been melted down—so they are still about.

Under measures I have omitted pots which bear capacity check stamps, for as in the seventeenth century this guarantees only the contents, just as now some of our glass tankards are engraved with the capacity.

At first thoughts, the subject of eighteenth-century tankards and pots would seem simple. Tankards, just dome-lids; pots . . . well, almost nil. But already we have seen that there are many details of ancillary parts which are crucial to assessment. I have included a chart which attempts to give their date span, and their weight of survival (see pp. 114–15). We must be openminded as to some dating—some styles starting earlier than expected, and others later. Please realise that this chart shows only my impressions.

Let us climb up over some general facts to set the scene for a simple overall analysis. Lidless tankards continued to be rare for many decades. It is not until *c*.1770 that lidless and lidded exchanged popularity. Almost immediately the proportion of lidded became very small indeed. I wonder why: probably the soaring price of metal. In any case did we not wonder *why* lids in the first case? There were more pewterers at work in the very early years of the century than at any other time (although lack of trade soon reduced the number) and no doubt for the tavern pots, in their constant clattering service, mortality was high. Yet here we are with a great many bud balusters around, with their prominent thumbpieces and their lids with fragile hinges—just asking for damage—but these have survived somehow in much greater numbers than the eighteenth-century pots.

82   Cider or ale jugs. One of these is repro. Which? The double curved wrists grasping each other is the most usual handle. That on the right is the repro. (Miss Jane Russell)

Beer had become very expensive by the end of the seventeenth century, at 3d a quart, while gin was cheap and strong. It was much more popular than beer in London, if not the whole country. Then in 1763 heavy duties were imposed on gin, thus giving a fillip to beer.

Dome-lid tankards were very well established by 1710, and thrive they did up to the time that they tailed off rather suddenly, their final disappearance being around 1825 (to reappear on the sports trophies of *c*.1845–*c*.1885). Their dating features are primarily body and fillet; handle grip under the thumb; terminal; and thumbpiece. The bodies tended to be rather squat, and were adopting the fillet by 1710—at first lower than at any time thereafter, and the fillet remained on truncated cone dome-lids, although on the other main eighteenth-century dome-lid body type, the 'tulip' or 'pear', it was inclined to be absent from *c*.1790.

From 1730 the lidded tulip tankards had cut in parallel to the truncated cone dome-lids, but with no fillet. Then they adopted both the fillet and the pierced thumbpiece, to about 1790, once again to omit the fillet to remain plain and lidless through the nineteenth century. Note the earlier converse behaviour compared with the straight-

113

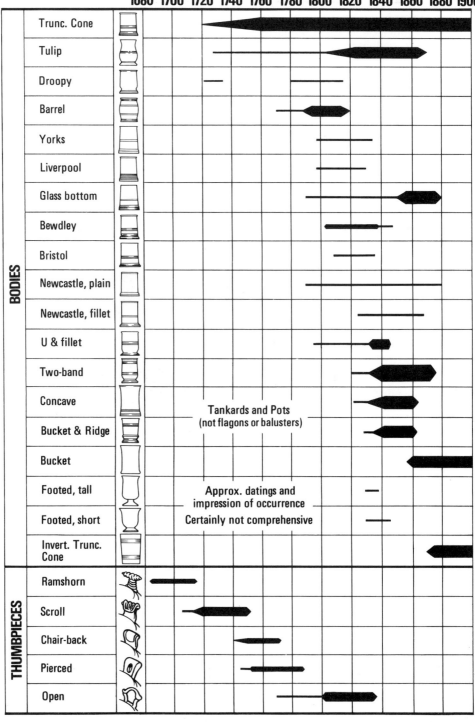

		1680	1700	1720	1740	1760	1780	1800	1820	1840	1860	1880	1900
BODIES	Trunc. Cone												
	Tulip												
	Droopy												
	Barrel												
	Yorks												
	Liverpool												
	Glass bottom												
	Bewdley												
	Bristol												
	Newcastle, plain												
	Newcastle, fillet												
	U & fillet												
	Two-band												
	Concave					Tankards and Pots (not flagons or balusters)							
	Bucket & Ridge												
	Bucket												
	Footed, tall					Approx. datings and impression of occurrence							
	Footed, short					Certainly not comprehensive							
	Invert. Trunc. Cone												
THUMBPIECES	Ramshorn												
	Scroll												
	Chair-back												
	Pierced												
	Open												

114

		1680	1700	1720	1740	1760	1780	1800	1820	1840	1860	1880	1900
FILLETS	Two-band												
	Two narrow												
	Very high												
	Very low												
	Low-mid												
HANDLES	Solid												
	Hollow												
	Standard												
	Broken												
	Tongued												
	Escutcheon												
	Frisky Horn												
	Crank												
	Oozy tongue & pip												
	Grasped wrist												
	Long invert. U												
TERMINALS	Shield												
	Heel												
	Spade												
	Fishtail												
	Ball, hooded												
	Ball, plain												
	Yorks												
	Attention												

115

83 A fine large 3½-pint Eddon flagon/tankard is shown with a very pristine plate also by him. Note the complete purity of shape, and the base is distinctly conical. Also it shows the occasional result of the cutting of the surface, for the monogram has allowed the oxide to form more quickly, precisely, and attractively.

sided 'cones'. The terminal of the handle was at first a sort of short spade shape, to c.1720; at the same time there might be three little transverse bars cast on the upper part of the curve of the handle, making a more stable thumbgrip. This feature was soon lost; and the terminal became a large and imposing 'fishtail', to c.1740. A modified form of ball terminal which included a 'hood' (rather like a lapping wave) took over from about 1725 until c.1760; this was followed by a plain ball terminal. Finally the 'broken' or double curved handle ousted all other handles on tankards, c.1780.

The thumbpiece too, changed very markedly. At the start of our present period it was like four clenched fingers; then it was a solid chairback, which in mid century was perforated by an oval hole, which seems to have been used more frequently with the tulip body. This gave way about 1760 to the 'open' thumbpiece which is of square-section casting, comparatively very thin, and correspondingly weak and fragile. This carried on through the remaining years of the dwindling lidded tankards.

The lids themselves throughout are not very noticeably different, until compared side by side. Very loosely, the normal tendency is for the dome to lose height with the decades, and towards the demise the crown of the lid is flattened a little, but this had started by mid century. By the way, if you find you have a brass hingepin, welcome it, as some makers used them around the middle of the century.

84   A range of mixed dates, styles and sizes of tulips, from quart to gill. That on the right rear is obviously the oldest, c.1740–50.

And now to the increasingly exciting pots—lidless pots—in the latter-day dark ages of pewter. Although some fall into fairly clear pre-Imperial (PIP) types, many more look to be one-offs. Since the moulds were big, cumbersome and very costly they had to be used to the utmost, so there must have been many thousands of every style (unless they really were extraordinarily short-run styles entailing clay, sand or wood moulds, or were made-up pieces). So the chances are that there are many more survivors, unappreciated that they are just that bit different and therefore probably earlier, and they may be ready to come out into the air. We do want to fill the gap with reasonable assurance. What a pity that such a vast quantity must have gone into 'liquidation', being melted down for industrial and munition purposes; and probably in the last 50 years a large proportion of eighteenth-century pewter has been discarded due to its similarity to nineteenth-century. It has not until recently been sought and recognised—but there is a lot of scope ahead yet. Let us temper the optimism by remembering that there was such a surge of contemporary demand attendant on the advent of Imperial measure, and the huge increase in the number of pubs in the 1830s; and contrast this with the economic pressure to gather in all scrap metal possible in the 1780–1810 period.

Pots! We have mentioned the one high-fillet type in the last chapter. It seems to have lived in the north, until *c*. 1725. One unusual feature is that most specimens have a very bold, wide base. The two-fillet also just ran over the start of this period, and the bases on the later (*c*.1710) ones were raised up, clear of the table, and must have finished, to all intents and purposes, although there are some with later styles of handle. I have not inspected these latter, and so cannot say if the handles are later replacements, or

85 A fine Bristol tulip, by A. Bright, *OP* 574, *c*. 1750. (H. W. Buckell). Another, maker indistinguishable (Holt Collection).

whether the type did run later than expected. But what now, *c*. 1725 onwards, take their place? So few specimens exist with any evidence of date. There are a very few pots with rather droopy bodies looking rather compressed (see *OP* p.142 (a)). There are some dome-lid bodies whose hinge lugs were filed off in infancy, there are a few tulips, both with and without fillet—but in all these there is no clear-cut dating; where there are marks often they are detrited and, as we know, a mark is seldom adequate evidence for narrow dating. You might think that silver should help—but probably the same reason obtains why there are no silver baluster measures—that they were pub ware, and much too liable to abscond. The lovely gadrooned pots—yes, they occurred in silver, but very obviously they were not pub ware. There are, more hopefully, a few straightsided tapering pots ('truncated cones') and these are a little clearer in date having some of the features mentioned under dome-lids, and shown in the chart. I must say that I think the 'droopy' and the 'tulip' bodies have been considerably pre-dated at '*c*.1720'—and I think it wise to err on the side of conservatism until evidence stretches dating. Otherwise many people will be grasping at a misunderstood detail, and grossly optimistically dating a piece. The tulip certainly had a very long run anyway. If we start it at 1740, and it was still going strong in 1880—even 1900, maybe later—it has had a life of 160 years. Probably by 1780 the fillet was being gradually dropped, inexorably. As with so many other designs, we do wonder from where they originated. No, there are no obvious fillers of our huge gap, to *c*.1750. After the mid-eighteenth century gradually shapes which are not quite the same as the usual victorian styles begin to emerge, but still their dating is very hypothetical.

Handle detail is of the greatest importance. A handle has four basic elements—

118

86 (a) Some pleasing PIPs, for comparisons. On extreme left a grand Bristol 'droopy'; then a London droopy; centre, closely dated at *c.*1822 by the ownership inscription; right, verified Worcester (illustrated again a little later), and a fine-ringing quart, probably from Wigan. (b) Another range of PIPs. You can pick out so many points of interest. Note the similarity of Wigan, fourth from left, with Liverpool, with the multi-rings around the base. That on the right is 15 fl oz, mentioned elsewhere. We have come to call all the tapering cylindrical pots (correctly) 'truncated cones', but the centre of (a) is the most typical example.

87 Thumb rests and terminals. Oozy tongue and pip, with rounded asymmetric terminal; oozy tongue, no pip, and asymmetric triangular terminal; tongued thumb rest; a few bars across the thumb rest (and note the one heavy fillet); on right, normal heavier bars as thumb rest. All these are common, but are details well worth spotting and seeking. All pre-1830. Four truncated cones and a two band.

119

handle shape; thumb rest; detail behind thumb rest; and the terminal with the sweep of curve bearing it. By now all handles are hollow, so their dimensions are greater than if they had been solid, and therefore they look heavier. With the economy of plant many handles ran for a very long time, with small variations. One universal economy which typifies the ingenuity is in the earlier flagon 'broken' handles, where the bottom section is a duplicate of the lower part of a complete handle, and very happy this liaison is, visually. Somewhere, probably about 1770, the 'attention' handle appears (so called as being like the flattened hand of a soldier on parade), and this must be a strong clue in dating. I guess that some apprentice in an excess of strength in a quiet moment just bashed the badly-cast end of a handle, and then bashed it again, when his master strode in, and instead of thrashing him, the master colloquised 'Eureka', and immediately adopted it. It made an easy terminal which adhered strongly. Unfortunately it is characterless and insignificant. This terminal runs for 100 years from c.1780, at first almost circular, then an asymmetrical 'oval', like a victorian tennis racquet, finally to be squared off making it into a flat triangle.

For a long time the thumb rest ended in a flat, lazy tongue pointing laxly backwards, which gave way gradually from perhaps as early as c.1780 (still lasting to c.1830), to a 'crank' handle—a hump under the thumb, below which are either a couple of ridges for the thumbnail to fidget with, or an oozy, drooping tongue barely in relief, which then started to adopt a 'pip' or 'pellet' below it. I am sure that comprehensive research on datable pieces, or makers, will elicit much clearer dating facts.

The 'cranked' handle was probably started around 1790, and continued to c.1830; usage, I rather think, to the whim of individual pewterers, and/or regions; but probably more prevalent from the Bristol, Bewdley and Wigan pewterers.

Before the crank handle appeared the broken handle was in evidence, scant it is true, from the first half of the century, and had settled down by c.1770. A plain curve round the top of the handle may well be in the earlier broken handles, to be followed by a frisky little horn standing up, followed by a reversion of the lazy tongue after c.1825—thenceforth the two latter running together. A few glances at illustrations will make this much clearer.

The attachment, too, has importance. M. Boorer was the first to spot, from trade cards, the true meaning and use of 'escutcheons'—the reinforcing 'U' and oval handle attachments on lower-grade alloy pots of around c.1790–1820. Probably concurrently a simpler method was in use, but which had probably entailed using new moulds—no very great hardship at this precise time of huge beer consumption—the lip of these pots was a very heavy bead. (From 1815 onwards, increasingly the stronger, harder antimony alloy was used for all products.) What a lot of minor points can tell one so much—and still have much more mileage in their conversation yet! Keep your eyes open for re-shuffling.

The broken handle had appeared in other media and on other pewter products c.1730, and became formalised about 1790 or a little earlier, and both this type and 'attention' ran away into the second half of the nineteenth century.

The 'barrel' body (at last a clearly recognisable descriptive name) appeared probably about 1785 and combined public relations with sales promotion by its point-of-sale inference. It has been dated by one authority back to 1753, only on the strength of an inscribed date—but we see innumerable examples of both pre- and post-dating inscriptions, of which one must be very wary. In view of the aching void of 1725 to 1790, we must be prepared to be accommodating trying to date a certain style. Illustrations in books are very scarce for this period, and some dating ascribed is probably more dogmatic than accurate. Here let me say that figure 68 in my *British Pewter and Britannia Metal* which stated that several types might have been in either century, contains some examples which are definitely *not* eighteenth century. Mea culpa, my contrite apologies—and my pleasure in having continued to learn.

While it is really surprising how much earlier many styles started than is usually thought, it is equally wrong to give way to the temptation to ascribe the earliest possible date to a piece—particularly if it is one's own. They are more likely to have survived from their bulge of production, and later. A most useful reminder of this is to be seen in a few pewterers' trade cards (advertising handouts), with my gratitude to the British Museum for permission to reproduce. Taken alphabetically (date of striking touch is not necessarily related to date of printing the trade card), we have:

John Alderson (1764–82+), shown here, displays a teapot, sugar caster, tureen with lid, three-legged salt, sauce boat, spouted measure, barrel tankard with 'broken' handle, wavy-edge plate, candle mould, plate, tulip tankard, hot-water plate, very slender baluster. (Best hard-metal quarts were 2s 6d each, common quarts were 1s 9d each.)

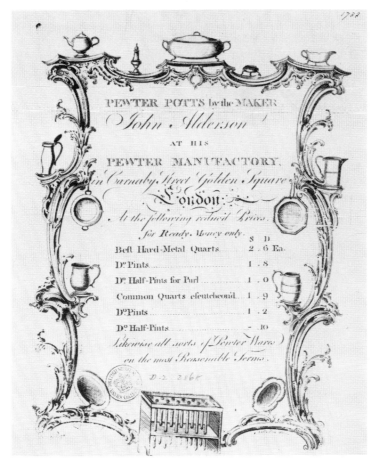

88a

121

88b

R. P. Hodges (1772–1800+) shows a syringe, two cylindrical ink wells, a standish, toy watch, a very neo-classical two-handled lidded cup, and a doll's tea set.

John Kenrick (1737–54+) shows a plain-rim oval dish, a wavy-edge plate, and a heavy lidded tureen.

Richard King (1745–98) shows a dinner service of octagonal flatware.

89a   Left, a 'crank' handle; centre, a 'frisky horn'; right, conventional 'broken' handle. That in the centre is easily recognised as glass bottomed, by its bare lip and multi-reed base.

89b   Good view of an early 'attention', *c.* 1775. Shaped terminal on the pot we call Worcester. On right, sharply trimmed-off terminal. All these illustrations are worth poring over for the many many details to be discerned. These are three good PIPs. Half-pints are more scarce than the larger sizes.

89c   A scutcheon, heavy lip, no fillet, plain base—and not surprisingly, WR crowned. On the right, a rather rare example of GIV crowned—no doubt a perpetuation of the monarch's initials referring to the reign in which the Standard (Imperial) was enacted.

William Life (Cotterell gives *c*.1700 which is obviously an error—should be *c*.1780), shown here, a caster, tulip tankard, footed sauce boats, oval teapot, beaker, cup salt, pot with flattened handle attachment, and cream jug. He accepted 'order, by 1d post, duly executed'.

Robert Peircey (1735–60) shows a picture of a neat pewter shop, visible in which are tea cups, porringer, candlestick, etc.

One would be very much inclined to place most of the items shown in these six trade cards in the nineteenth century.

We know that John Alderson's trade card could not have been later than 1792, (when he is recorded as being in Carnaby Street) when he might have been about 52 years old. Perhaps he had just moved and issued a promotional handout to stimulate his trade. Or perhaps he produced the trade card earlier in his career, and had been at Carnaby Street some while. It would be most helpful to have a tight dating on this card. William Life's true dates and whereabouts are not known, but again, how very interesting it would be if only we had an accurate date for his card—and as previously mentioned if only we knew how accurate the styles depicted were. But the date of the trade cards, someone, *please*.

90 Set of rare Yorkshire pots. The pint particularly looks much earlier than most PIPs, but dating should be conservative, at *c*. 1790–1825.

Around 1795–1810 all sorts of pots appear, new styles emerging and stabilising, shapes which came and died, and one-off made-up pieces. These are what we seek—1770 to 1810. The very great majority of PIPs would seem to be *c*.1815–1825. Records of makers are inadequate, either no mark struck on the piece, or the makers' terminal dates not known. Cotterell's invaluable details in *OP* as to partnerships, insolvencies, changes of address, and recently, M. Boorer's researches, Dr A. S. Law's deductions—all are of great help to piece together firm evidence to elucidate this pewter dark ages.

A rare example is of a squat half pint which must be *c*.1770. It is a plain truncated cone drum, the base of which most unusually sits flush on the table. The handle has a

124

very wide curve, ending in an almost-circular attention terminal. It has a clear mark of a two-handled cup (*OP* 238a), of William Bancks of Bewdley. All that is known of his dating is 'mentioned in a directory of 1790'.

Dating probably from *c*.1790 is a rare type from Yorkshire. This is a truncated cone with a very broad band or fillet round the drum amidships (on the quarts and pints only, not on the half pints). The only six I have seen are verified to the Ridings, and none bears a maker's mark. This is a most attractive style, with an 'early' look. Even more than the broad band and very simple base mouldings, the handle is most

91 A Liverpool pot (see the multi-rings) *MPM*
5767c.

92 An unusual squat truncated cone of *c*.1820, with the border ready for engraving, but never filled; and a good early prototype two band with escutcheon, and the three wee star marks which enclose a minute 'c' in the centre, which M. Boorer has noted is used on pots with escutcheons, and indicates lower-grade alloy, (probably 'c' for 'common'). Gerardin & Watson are the makers. *OP* and *MPM* 1837.

125

distinctive, being 'cranked' (hump topped like a bent thumb), with prominent thumb rest, bold curve to the handle and a particularly long, curved end beyond the attachment, ending in an approximation to a horse's hoof terminal.

It is not always so satisfactory as this, to be able to provide an illustration of the three sizes in a style in PIPs. Mostly they are to be found in quart and pint sizes, the half pint being more scarce.

93 An early inhaler—they are much more attractive without the lid and flexible tube! The handle is perforated at the thumb rest, with vents to the liquid top and bottom, no doubt so that blowing into it will excite the inhalant. *c.* 1780, but similar inhalers were made for a long time, bearing 'Mudge's Inhaler' after his patent in 1778.

What does emerge from the very late eighteenth century which may be encountered? Perhaps a rather squat 'U and fillet'. Perhaps slightly tall and attenuated truncated cones, of which an early feature is a very heavy lip, and sometimes an escutcheon reinforcement where the handle is attached, occurring on lower-grade alloy to obviate the metal tearing, perhaps a Bristol pot (but these seem to be mostly in the States), certainly a possibility of a tulip of the period—and maybe an early glass-bottomed pot.

126

94   Some fine inkstands, the centre an early appearance of the 'loggerheads'. Dating very uncertain, probably c.1790+. (S. Shemmell)

This may surprise a lot of people, but they had started in silver *c*.1770, and I have several examples with marks which prove that they are PIPs, one even in William III wine measure! Their characteristics are a fillet, a multiplicity of rings around the base, but with a most disappointing and unfinished appearance at the lip—there is no bead, just bare and sharp. They are of both superb alloy and craftsmanship. It has usually been assumed that these pots are late—and they do have a long lifespan—so it is well to have a dateable mark.

From Liverpool a charming, rare type appears, with plain body, multiconcave base rings, slightly-flared lip, and the attention terminal is uniquely (I think) diamond shaped. One simplified example I saw recently, with fewer mouldings, looked very much like the birth of the *c*.1840 'concave' type.

In the late eighteenth century or very early nineteenth it became quite common to resuscitate wriggling for the border for a panel on which the innkeeper's or publican's name and other details were engraved. At first these were rectangular, to be hotly pursued by oval and shield shapes. These borders were the work of the pewterer, for very occasionally one pot will turn up with the border void.

Engraving was cursive, rounded at first (to become linear by *c*.1830; and latterly placed under the base).

A small detail is helpful—very often pots of *c*.1815–25 bear the owner's initials elided (for example, ℙ for TP) on the top of the saddle of the handle, to remain visible even when the thumb rests on top.

A word should be inserted here about inhalers, whose bodies are so akin to truncated cones; most often the lid and flexible tube have been lost. The distinctive features are a heavier body, heavy bold handle with three perforations on the thumb rest, and a hole (through the hollow handle) at the top and bottom leading into the body. No doubt you blew into the holes which roughed up the hot balsam, driving off the fumes for you to draw in through the mouthpiece as you recharged the lungs. They run from *c*.1770–*c*.1870, and often are engraved 'Mudge's Inhaler'.

Those with large collections now are in the best position to research and to compare notes with others, and to give opinion—let us hear from you, anyone who has anything to contribute.

10. 1825–1900

Porcelain, pottery, Britannia metal ware, brass, tin-plated and Sheffield-plated goods had successfully beaten pewter to its knees: but the alloy was still pre-eminent in the tavern bar.

Alloy? By now we still had some heavy, cheesy, leaden alloy for the cheaper pots, and some in beautiful hard antimony alloy—all of them cast in the traditional manner. Very often you will see that the lower part of the drum on curved pots has a harder darker oxide than the rest of the body. This is because this half was cast in the hard antimony alloy to give better resistance to denting at its most vulnerable part.

Yes, the pub was the saviour, and the major home, until a further unexpected fillip occurred, when trophies became the in thing for presentation at sporting events. And when this outlet graded off, a few years later, it was found that lead-free pewter was a most suitable medium for Art Nouveau, which wound and wound its way far beyond our period. Although some other uses hung on, and a few more were exploited, the nineteenth century is the great rundown period from the eighteenth century, including its very moulds. It was held together only by the needs of the pubs—measures and tankards.

95 Bristol makers were pre-eminent for their design, quality and craftsmanship in the first half of the nineteenth century. (W. Buckell)

But hold hard, the outlook is far more varied than perhaps I have implied. In writing and illustrating *Let's Collect British Pewter*, it really was most interesting to me to look at this century only, and I was entranced to see what enchanting displays could be made out of solely nineteenth-century pewter—including in it only a few quarts, in a dresser full of thirty-seven different styles of pots, caster, measures and cups. This was intended to be an introduction to pewter, showing what one had a good chance to see and to buy now, but it was also breaking new ground to devote an entity to that century alone.

96   To increase capacity from OEWS (16⅔ fl oz per pint) to Imperial (20oz)
many double volute balusters had their lids ripped off, and a collar added.
This was almost entirely a Suffolk adaptation (R. Bellamy)

This is the period least researched in the whole history of pewter because of the disinterest born of plenty, for plenty there was until a very few years ago. Our exporters have done well, both for themselves and as dollar earners. So the pieces needed for comprehensive and easy research have largely sailed the seas. The eighteenth century

97 Pair of church collecting bowls (placed in the porches). These are particularly late for lead pewter, being dated '1849'. One bears the maker's touch, the other his rose crowned.

has, rather unexpectedly, stolen a little of the thunder of the nineteenth century. The standby of the centuries—balusters—ceased being produced *c*.1820 (except possibly at Newcastle where the lidless appear from their capacities to be post-Imperial). The successor to balusters, the bellied measures, we will deal with a little later, and this was almost the only 'new' style after 1820. Most of the pots and their ancillary parts had been designed and produced by 1800. A few modifications and general standardisation developed. Dishes, plates particularly, survive in large numbers up to about 1820, culminating in the gigantic coronation service of George IV in 1821. Pieces of all

98 A mixed ('harlequin') set of bellied measures. Particularly in the small sizes these are readily found. There are many different capacities below half gill. Very occasionally one might recognise one of the larger sizes as being in OEWS—pre-Imperial. The quart is an early unusual shape.

tableware, including tureens, were pillaged after the feast in a disgraceful exhibition of mob hysteria, and they are now very widely distributed. Many classes of ware turned over to Britannia metalware. Bowls continued, unchanged, and a late pair from a church is dated 1849. Undoubtedly the extra-heavily-lipped quart and pint pots continued to be made, but the type which persisted (even into this present decade in one of its smallest sizes) is the bellied measure, and in considerable numbers. Much stouter in its major diameter than the balusters, it is otherwise of the same conception—but the common English type is (almost always) lidless. Sizes run from the gallon down to half gill, later adding the quarter gill; but in the second half of the century there were about a dozen different authorised and stamped sizes, from 1/10 to 1/32 pint. I even have one which was made by soldering the upper section direct onto the base (so that there is no belly) which holds 1/48 pint! Many of this series bear the Imperial stamp of 1826, and here, one would think, is a design new to the period. Yet once more one can look a few years earlier, for very occasionally specimens exist in OEWS which was abolished in 1826. But we must remember that the old ale measure was, to all practical purposes, the same as Imperial; therefore it is probable that these were in fact produced before 1820. Michaelis has pointed out that a drawing by Hogarth entitled 'Gin Lane' published about 1760 shows a tavern sign depicting almost identically this form.

Since this type of measure is generally thought to be solely of Imperial standard we will take them in this period, with qualifications as to earlier manufacture. Michaelis was the first to sort out their nineteenth-century dating although there may be modifications. As usual, the same difficulties occur in getting an earliest or latest date on any piece, and any estimate of date must be taken as elastic. The verification stamps do not really help, as they could have been put on after manufacture. The maker seldom lived in the district where the stamp was applied. A measure might bear twenty verification stamps (some do) between 1826 and, say, 1900 and later. That does not preclude its manufacture earlier than 1820. However, where GIV or WIV are

99 Michaelis' drawings of the bellied types. Not only the rings but the terminals are most important to dating.

132

stamped, it can be taken that the measure or tankard was stamped at latest before that monarch's death.

There are six main groups of bellied measures, and almost all the bodies could have been made from the same mould (per size, of course). One might for simplicity say that the handles are all the same design between the two points of attachment. We then have only three variables: plain body; rings round the body, and where placed; and terminal to handle. With so few variables, there is little to learn! However, intensified and widespread research tends to throw up fresh facts and to modify dating.

Type 1   Plain body—no rings. Shapes do vary a little, and have not settled down. Handle terminal is a fairly well-formed ball. *c.*1790–*c.*1830.

Type 2   Three or four incised rings above the lower point of handle attachment. Still some variation in shapes. Terminal is a weaker drawn-out ball. *c.*1824–*c.*1830.

Type 3   As Type 2, but with a slightly-thickened band over the seam at maximum body diameter. *c.*1826–50.

Type 4   As Type 3, but no incised rings on the upper curve. *c.*1830–60.

Type 5   Rings on the upper curve only. Stouter handle with no terminal—it fades away almost flush with the body. *c.*1850 onwards.

Type 6   Has a more crude 'feel' and finish. Has a thick, heavy band round the seam, no other rings. 'Terminal' is even less. *c.* 1880 onwards (largely edwardian). (This was also made without the lip.)

The distinctive period details are less clearly definitive in the smallest size. These bellied, or 'bulbous', measures must have been used in very large quantities indeed—until a very few years ago they could be found everywhere. The gallon and half-gallon sizes were always scarce, and it now needs a little patience to make up a set of the six more usual sizes. The variety of types described adds considerably to the interest of the search for them. Occasionally on the earlier type you may come across specimens having an applied plaque bearing GIV crowned.

The squat rather frog-like west country designs are almost the only other nineteenth-century true measures. They are of two types somewhat alike: the West Country—short and squat, similar to copper measures—and the Bristol or Fothergill type (after its principal maker). This is much slimmer and of far simpler lines; while the former are rare, the latter are very scarce indeed. They run from half gill up to very large sizes. Both these may have been made before Imperial measure, too. The Irish 'haystacks' are rather comparable in the essence of design, and reference to the chapter on Irish will clarify the difference. One other type of curious measure is still to be met occasionally—the double-egg-cup, hour-glass shape. One cup is twice the capacity of the other. They are *c.*1830 onwards.

In this period serious-purpose tankards can be taken as always lidless. Some—prizes for competitions, particularly rowing—bear lids, but only for prestige. These trophies of 1860–85 invariably have glass bottoms. Otherwise, from about 1825, the lid was lost.

There is so much to be said of the pots of the period—and much more to be said in the future. They are very collectable, being more or less available are decorative and, occasionally, useful.

Rapidly and increasingly from *c.*1825, the antimony alloy was used for pots. It was already in use. The alloy is so much more serviceable for the clatter and batter of the pub pot. But it is wrong to assume that its use was general. The lead alloy was cheaper.

In this connection, M. Boorer first raised a few points about those pots which dither between pre- or post-Imperial: discs for handle attachments (escutcheons), tend to be

100   A West Country measure compared with a 'Fothergill' (Bristol maker's unique style). Both are now very scarce on the market. (S. Shemmell)

pre-Imperial; these pots bear no quality X. 'Hallmarks' and/or an X on the drum tend to be pre-Imperial, but not exclusively so. I will be a little surprised if you find a poor-quality pot which bears a crowned X (no matter how crude the lettering). Those with an X will be of antimony alloy. Those with no X are softer, and of lead alloy. Yes, do check up—there are so many elementary facts like these to be brought out now.

We have introduced most of the styles in the previous chapter, but now they settle down to rather stereotyped designs. Seeing that the period is comparatively recent research has at best so far been scant. We have allowed pieces to trickle away, untended, unquestioned. There had been an adequate supply of earlier pewter for the great collectors of the 1920s and 1930s, and there was a plethora of nineteenth-century items too commonplace to consider. There has been little attention until the last decade. And, my goodness, now they need only to appear, to disappear. Latterly there have been more marks recorded, in *MPM* and its *Addenda*; but remember that only a small proportion of Victorian pots bears makers' marks. Gradually some detail is percolating, and is dealt with superficially in '*Let's Collect British Pewter*', where there is some crisper information to help the present-day collector. What we need is tighter dating, and more spotlighting of regional types—Newcastle, Wigan, York, Bewdley, Bristol, for instance. No mention of Birmingham, an important centre? Simply because it was good middle-of-the-road ware, by good makers, with practically no obvious distinctive features. Where else? We cannot here illustrate all types and all details separately, but most types are illustrated to show off relevant points.

Changes in the marks denoting the capacity of pots have been worked out by J. Douglas and M. Boorer. It appears that it was not until 1835 that newly made pots had

134

to be stamped with their capacity. In 1841 it was required that all pots in circulation should be so stamped. So normally PIPs were not marked with their capacities. Those made after 1826 often had the capacity stamped in large incuse letters. After 1835 the incuse letters were smaller. Other post-Imperial pots had the words 'Imperial' and the capacity stamped in relief. We should bear in mind that a PIP which continued in service over a long spell of time could have had 'PINT' stamped on it after 1826, and could subsequently have been verified with the county verification stamp and even the post-1878 VR stamp.

Pots are very often inscribed with, not cursive engraving, but linear letters. They are a little difficult to read, but it is easier to scribe than the beautifully curved lettering previous to approximately 1830. The linear engraving as to ownership is very often to be found under the base. This feature tends to be later rather than early. It is noteworthy that wriggling in a coarse hand had been reintroduced—now only for the outline of the area of inscription (see p. 125).

I have never liked pouring lips, for they seem to spoil the line of a piece. They had come on the scene in the early eighteenth century, but only on flagons then (and see the lovely acorn York type). The real moment of glory for these 'spouts' is the first quarter of the nineteenth century. As well as increasing in proportion on flagons, they were adopted occasionally on all types of pot, quart and pint. I think the reason for their existence was that it was quite a custom to have a 'jug' of beer to dispense around those at a table. I heard that this was so in Norwich early in the present century, this being the real use of a quart pot, even without a spout.

Let us go through the main types, in their sequence of seniority. The truncated cone

101 Usually the pouring lip is at the near side. Lipped pots (jugs) are mostly of the first third of the nineteenth century.

135

is the most common type, and is a logical design. One or two localities simplify it into a cylinder. It is now nearly always wearing a cummerbund fillet (except sometimes in Newcastle and possibly Liverpool). Although the truncated cone is of long lineage, the fillet is so commanding that it looks to be a new type. While some quarts certainly of George IV have the broken handle, it is probably safe to say that the later ones are almost alone in being accompanied by the attention attachment. Those from Bristol/Bewdley (between whom there now seems to be great affinity), and perhaps Wigan, are decidedly more cylindrical. Some from Newcastle have no fillet but do have a ball terminal. From all these four centres wider-than-normal bases are a frequent feature. In the earlier pre-Imperial particularly, the thumb rest is a tongue just rising up under the thumb, which then becomes a ridge often with a lazy drooping tongue flopping a little way down the handle, with sometimes a pip beneath the end of the tongue.

102   A variety of truncated cone pots. In the rear, Newcastle with and without fillet (Abbot, *MPM* and *Addenda* 3, and WH, probably W. Hogg, *OP* 2367); and Bewdley. Front, Bristol, Bewdley, Birmingham.

Was the drooping tongue and pip an innovation? Far from it. It was resuscitated with precision from the broken handle of the lovely spire flagons of c.1730–c.1760. Where had it been in those last 60 or so years? I think that these three features will soon disgorge some dating evidence, if someone with sight of a large number will undertake detection work.

The rings round the base—very roughly the fewer and heavier the earlier, the exceptions being Liverpool and glass-bottomed pots. Some years ago the flower-decorating sorority had a run on quarts, which was nice for flowers but not so nice for us, so for a time quarts were rather scarce. All the types run in quart, pint and half pint. All types except apparently the concave, had gills, often engraved for christening (or birth) and these are rather scarce, and seldom verified. The truncated-cone type runs to a rare half-gallon size—even a one gallon. The body type has not died even yet.

Since writing the above I have come across a pint truncated cone of William IV considerably squat, with broken handle, and distinctively bearing the two bands of incised lines which we associate with the two band, and sometimes with the bucket and ridge. This pot, like several others you may well see, bears a significant detail of style with its owner's monogram—in that around and outside the initials there are many 'flecks' and small curved strokes. This was probably a fairly short-lived fashion, so if we can date the flecks we can get a date on the styles of pots, or of details on pots, enabling further referred dating. I consulted Dr Law, and from our combined examples bearing these flecks about thirty percent were pre-Imperial, most others within the next 10 years, the remainder not being closely datable. The result drawn would indicate c. 1824–c. 1835. Perhaps we can coin a phrase and call it 'pre-vic'. The flecks appear on several other types of pot, and footed cups. This is an example of what, retrospectively, should be such an obvious dating clue to have been investigated —but I have never heard it mentioned. This pot is by a previously unrecorded maker, Marshall, stamped in the base, and was verified in Norwich. Also a conventional truncated cone, but with a very wide flat flange round the top (Michael Boorer suggests for dry measure) which again is stamped Marshall in the base, Norwich verified again. Both bear very curious "hallmarks" (double inverted commas!)—see *MPM* 6250— an X in the form of a chair flanked on both sides by a circular stamp of eight radii. Furthermore there is a bucket and ridge half pint with a light sweated-on collar round the top, with the same 'hallmarks' and Norwich stamp. The latter is also very curious, having the lion passing to sinister, which is the wrong direction! (The rounded base could not have been stamped with his mark.) Who is Marshall, and where did he work? In Norfolk there is a saying, 'du different'. Marshall certainly did in so many ways. This is a typical example of the titillation which a 'senior collector' can get from keeping a weather eye wide open on nineteenth-century pieces.

103a This pot shows a happy marriage of the two band and the truncated cone. The unconventional maker is Marshall—see his curious 'hallmarks'. *MPM* 6250.

103b Heavy pewter strengthening rim of *c*.1830. After
c.1850 brass was used as the reinforcement.

An offshoot of the truncated cone, which makes its appearance *c*.1830, has the same body detail, but with a very heavy lip; it is really a measure, but I know it makes a very pleasant drinking pot. Later the pewter lip is replaced by brass, for greater rigidity. Later still the rim is made lighter, and at the same time the base is simplified into two light 'mouldings'—so light that they look to be turned. This type also most surprisingly reverts to a ball terminal to the handle, and on this count I was quite wrong in *BP and BM* in dating it as *c*.1800, for it is *c*.1860. I have not seen a gill in this collared type.

The next hangover type is the tulip, which strangely and conversely with the truncated cone, has lost its fillet. It runs right up to the end of the century, always with the broken handle. It seems to be earlier—shall we say pre 1835—that this handle has a frisky little 'hook', or 'ear' for the thumb to purchase on. This applies with a lesser frequency to other types too. After that the hook goes round the bend a little, to become an uptilted tongue, below which are three or four bars or waves across the handle, for decoration only. The loss of the fillet is very noticeable in aspect.

We will take glass-bottomed pots next, ahead of the U and fillet—probably correctly, but also to keep the U and fillet next to the two band. It is fun trying to guess the original reason for these glass bottoms. There are several suggestions. Take your choice. The press gang chat up a likely young recruit, slip a shilling in his tankard—and he is found to have accepted the King's Shilling. Since the glass bottoms started in about the 1780s, this may be true. Another explanation is to be able to see any hostile movement by your drinking companions. A third—to see if your beer is clear. But I doubt if you will find one of these beautifully-made pots of the eighteenth century. Certainly they are in existence *c*.1820, and probably we may date at least two specimens at least 10 years earlier, maybe 30 years. They run on right through the trophy era to probably *c*.1890 or later. The style of the body—a type of truncated cone—remains very constant, at first with, then without, fillet. The earliest I have seen have a standard handle with shield terminal, next having the attention attachment, then the broken

138

104 A range of glass-bottom pots with marks to help dating. Pint, by Samuel Cocks (1819, no terminal date); half pint by 'T & C'. This mark must have been used by some succeeding partnership, so dating is enigmatic. Half pint by John Edwards, whose date is not precisely known, but whose touch appears to be typically mid 20s; its rectangular handle should place it considerably later. The fourth dated as c.1795, is pre-Imperial by capacity, maker SH 'hallmarks'.

handle, finally the 'rectangular' shape, which comes into use ostensibly considerably earlier than generally thought. One I have bears T & C (Townsend & Compton) but this mark simply must have been in use long after their terminal date of 1817, and at the most optimistic I would not dare to date earlier than c.1840; quite possibly the mark of T & C was used by family successors into the last quarter of the century. Seldom is there dating evidence, but I have only kept those with 'hallmarks', and these bear evidence of pre-Imperial manufacture. The only other dating evidence is on the trophies, with

105 All the main nineteenth century styles of pot except the concave, in the mini gill size, taken to be Christening gifts. Note that the truncated cone and the U and fillet are differently proportioned from their larger sizes. All gills are hard to come by, the barrel exceptionally so.

139

college, sport, date and winner's name. Doubtless the engraved dates are true of the piece's manufacture within a year of shelf life.

U and fillet, like the tulip, stands up from a base. It has settled to a stable shape, from c.1790 to c.1840, after having been rather squat pre-Imperial. Very dignified, although the broken handle is perhaps fussy by comparison with the body. The rare gills are not proportionate, being more squat than even the pre-Imperial examples. S. Shemmell has a rare half gallon.

Two band has exactly the same body and handle as the U and fillet, the bands being formed of several very light turned rings. Again, some, more squat, are just pre-Imperial. The scarce gills are in proportion.

Now we do come to a new style—the bucket and ridge—my name is not too obvious, but better was not forthcoming. It is typical of the scant attention which all these pots had earned that they had no names until I tried to give them a recognisable visual tab. Not erudite, perhaps, but workable. I think this to be the most fascinating WIV to victorian design, and it probably appeared coeval with her coronation. The design seems to me best suited to the pint size. Like most other types, it has the broken handle. About mid century it began to lose its multi rings; and then the fillet, then the ridge around the bottom of the body, finally to drop the body flat onto the table, dispensing with the neck, by which time it had adopted the rectangular handle, to be followed by the tubular handle. The gill is very scarce, the only one I have seen being plain bodied, with a girl's name beautifully engraved. Next, and surprisingly, starting earlier than the foregoing (at least one is known in OEWS, and so is pre-Imperial) is the concave—so popular with the TV props men for plays of any period in antiquity. It is the only other truly nineteenth-century style. I should think it was most popular c.1845–50, and despite what has been written elsewhere, it seems to have been ubiquitous, from Scotland to Thanet and the Lizard. Although we will deal with Scotland in a separate chapter, it is fair to mention here that those sold in Scotland have rather fuller bases

106 I think the bucket and ridge style of pot to be the most attractive. This range shows variations and developments from c.1825 to c.1900.

107 The distinctive concave, showing the long U thumb rest which also appears on some flared footed cups.

than those elsewhere, and the practice of stamping a name which one might well take to be a maker is very often that of a vendor—retailer or wholesaler. This type only (of the pots) has a unique handle, with a long-armed inverted U down the handle; the handle fades rather miserably like the tail of a worm, where it is attached. This type seems to be by far the most popular for the unusual 'barmaids' pots, whose containing plate at the

108 Footed cups. The rather delicately designed double curve strap handles also occur on ale jugs.

141

bottom of the body is set much higher, so that apparently she is drinking up with the customer, but is in fact keeping a clear head, beautiful figure, and the difference in change. We would very much like to hear from anyone who has, or knows for certain, that the concave were ever made in gills, for I have never seen one.

I have at least two other shapes, but which are so rare that we cannot call them types, and so there are probably others as well. One of these is a *half* gill and the other is a sixth gill! Very twee, but the beer held is *too* wee.

Obviously pots for drinking were footed cups, but why, oh why, is the body pushed right up in the air? Very spillable, with such a high centre of gravity. These date themselves as *c.*1830, because the handles most usually seen on them are the 'I'll clasp your wrist, you clasp mine' type, most commonly used on ale jugs, which surely died out *c.*1830 at latest. Some use the same handle as the concave pots, which is distinctive and unusual. Another more cup-like flared-out body has a tongued handle and ball terminal. The majority are in half-pint size. One curious quart, which must have been a type, has a cranked handle and attention attachment, and its base is virtually identical with the last large cup salts; and was used in Southampton. Quite frequently you may find the former types without a handle. But I still wonder why they were made so 'knockoverable'.

The natural sequitur is that eventually the customers wondered why they had to put up with such skittles, for there is a variety of beakers (handleless pots flush on the table, or on a low base). They appear to overlap the footed cups at both ends, and then knock them almost over and out. Probably broadly *c.*1830. That they were concurrent is clear, but I can offer no value as to sequence, and few illustrations. Almost all are outward tapering, or flared, some with no base mouldings, some with wider base, some

109 (a) There are numerous rather similar beakers which break up and enhance a display. The afterthought stamping method of denoting capacity shows the requirement to conform by 1835 latest, more likely *c.*1826–30, which this beaker with no flaring to the base probably is. (b) This beaker is by C. Bentley, *OP* 407, whose 'hallmarks' and circular touch are oft-seen, *c.*1835–40.

142

footed. As far as I know no serious work has been done on these pleasant but disregarded fellows.

The verification marks of 1835–1878, and then post 1878 (see chapter on marks), bring even greater interest to all hollow-ware so marked, and could be a most important factor in any locality research you undertake. For instance, a PIP I have is engraved with the names of the inn, and of the landlord. A county verification and one of post 1878 both put me right on target, and a few minutes in the county library gave me a precise dating of 1822, (due to his taking over the inn, and then dying). Of course, it *may* have been an older pot.

110 Two-handled cups are not unusual in victorian times. That on the left is only partially cleaned—and a very cohesive scale it is.

Two-handled cups. Perhaps these should have followed footed cups, some of the bodies and handles being identical. They are only very seldom engraved, so we have not very much indication as to purpose. Some could be communion cups, perhaps; some for minor social celebration—the loving cup comes to mind—perhaps at weddings. Some are rather squat and solid looking, with pronounced angle of divergence, and flared-out rim, the body surmounting a very high base. These have a ball terminal, and must be from the opening of our period. There are also cumbersome three-handled truncated-cone drinking vessels for passing readily from person to person—each having at least one handle by which to steady himself. Maybe there is some triangle significance. They do not attract me. Quart and pint only, presumably c.1830.

Still on drinking, very frequently you may see rather slim cups on a stem, similar to egg cups—for spirit. Very seldom, if ever, do they bear marks, and while they have appeared only very occasionally earlier dating is extremely vague; probably the better the alloy, the later. Sorting the detail difference awaits your pleasure. Flattish flasks with screw top, too, are not very rare, and may date from c.1770 right through the

111 Spirit cups (like slim egg cups) are not
uncommon—but beware reproductions.

Crimean War. With any screw thread the finer the thread, the later it probably is.
Never a mark do these show.

Funnels, too, are enigmatic. I can only say call them c.1830 with a very wide
tolerance for ignorance. They range in many sizes, and usually bear two bands of
incised lines, very reminiscent of the two-band pots, which is most likely very
significant for dating. But they have a history back at least to the early years of the
eighteenth century, at which time the 'bowl' was conical. As far as I know, after seeing
probably some hundreds, there is only one reference (Cotterell) to one being marked.
We have nothing to go on, apart from the hint of the rings. All I have seen have been
bowl-shaped, leaden, and the great majority must be mid-nineteenth century. Never
pass over an opportunity to inspect every piece of pewter, however commonplace, for
every single piece seems to have some little detail it would like you to appreciate.

Inkwells and inkstands are rather specialised. We all know the 'loggerhead' (cap-
stan) style which was in use in post offices until only about 10 years ago. These are with
or without the very wide stabilising flange, always without a mark. Would someone
please find out when they started? At least we have a terminal date, of our own
observation and experience. The low Treasury type appears to have started by the mid
years of the eighteenth century, possibly earlier. They are really rather plain—and
watch out that you have all the movable containers, with their perforations for sand,
and the inkwell, above which is usually a circle of considerable oxidation, due to the
acid fumes from the ink. Sometimes you may find a mark underneath, or under the lid.
I have seen one japanned—delightful sprays of flowers against a black background. I
do not think there is any opinion as to when the Treasury or the 'wardrobe' type ended.
Let us guess c.1820. Inkwells is one of the many subjects which was taken over by the
sheet Britannia, for apart from the loggerheads and the standish, most others seen are
in that fabrication.

Casters—for pounce, salt, pepper, sugar—is a large subject, and some of the
specimens are most attractive, with their lines and perforations, but latterly they
become very mundane. They make a fine specialised display, and they mingle

144

112 Inkstands we can remember in use in banks and post offices. So far there is no positive
indication of their date of introduction, but this may be earlier than has been thought. Types
other than these loggerheads were almost invariably Britannia-made. (Mrs I. Jackson)

excellently with the more conventional pot and salt shapes, in a row. If you want to get
attention, break up the formality of matching sets. Variation in height and outline
fasten the eye individually. Dating is diabolical, with never a mark, and silver showing
a poor precedent for the range in pewter. Like the spirit bottles, the later neat screw
thread speaks aloud of precise mechanical work.

Another class which so far has not been dated at all satisfactorily is salts. In the
previous chapter we followed them from the early eighteenth century, but confessed

113 Casters can be found, their uses ranging through pounce, salt, sugar. One could happily make a
collection of these alone—and research them. Never a mark!

145

failure to date more accurately than 1770 or 1840. An attempt was made to show a sequence, but while you will sometimes come across specimens, I am afraid that dating still eludes, with scarcely ever a mark to help at all.

Candlesticks would seem to have finished c.1830, and have been dealt with in the previous chapter; but they did continue in the saucered chamberstick style, very soon to turn over to Britannia ware. If you come across one with a mark, shun it, for it will be a repro.

114 This chamber stick illustration cheats a little, for it is in Sheffield plate, but examples in the hard antimony alloy are the same.

Snuffboxes are really more of a 'small antiques' subject, but since they were made in pewter let us have a word. I am not very bright on them (the longer I live the more aware I am of deficiencies, and of how remiss it is to have lost opportunities of observation; yesterday's commonplaces are today's scarcities). Snuffboxes have never been 'strong' in shops which carry pewter, but more to be found in smaller-item shops. Often they depict hunting and sylvan scenes. Earlier they were cast, but now their construction is more suited to Britannia, with the die-stamped decoration. Very charming they are, usually showing evidence of much use.

Spoons and ladles—yes coarse kitchen ware, cast from antimony alloy. Uninteresting styles, but they are homely antiques, often with marks. Spoons are a little difficult to display, but the big ladles can be hung. The heavy round-bowled ones frequently seen are common Dutch spoons, whose style has not changed for about 200 years.

Many other trivia are about—papboats, syringes (used for a variety of purposes from sugar icing to horses' more intimate complaints), bleeding bowls, jerries (both 'Welsh hat' and potty shapes)—no prude I, but I have little use in display for potties or jerries; or syringes—mantel ornaments, pincushion holders, whistles—oh, there are many things you may see, but it would not do to set out one Saturday with one thing exclusively in mind. Keep your mind and options open, and take your opportunities with what pleases *you*.

146

5   A glorious dome-lid in superb hard metal, by William Eddon, *OP* 1503. and most delicately engraved for the
Wool Guild of Norwich, 1747.

6 Fine specimen of a late dome-lid by Gerardin & Watson, with very good 'flecked' monogram. *c.* 1820. *OP* and *MPM* 1837.

115 Snuffboxes are fun, although a rather different class of antique. They are almost invariably in Britannia, and well worn. But that on the left is a fine cast example, probably earlier than our current period.

An enormous subject, almost completely destroyed or dissipated, is that of toy or doll's-house pewter. A prodigious quantity was made in the century under review, and is very fascinating. Some, but not all, is crudely made. Some, ornamented, is stamped out; some is neatly turned. The metal used varies enormously from what seems like chewing gum, to antimony alloy. I think it can be taken that the styles shown in doll's-house pewter were usually decades behind the current fashion.

There seem to be three size ranges—toy, large doll's house, and very small. I have only come across one little set of the latter, very crudely made, in very leaden alloy; plates and pots, these being only about 3/8in high. Although those of us who appreciate fine craftsmanship would not like them, there is a great attraction in the miniature. Does this not touch on one of the main appeals of old pewter—its basic crudeness, often accentuated by wear and oxide—yet so many pieces were of superb craftsmanship and finish; all have come to us through a good life and a hard one.

This mini pewter is surprisingly scarce now, for innumerable tons were made in the nineteenth, and much in the preceding, century. I fear that little sisters had horrible brothers who soon learned the sadistic joy of watching nice little things reduced to a quaking queasy puddle in a kitchen spoon over the gas. I know, from experience!

In the early eighteenth there had been superb large doll's-house pewterware, and the famed Queen Anne doll's houses contain little things we would all covet. To cosset them in one's hands has to suffice. Do not expect to see toy or doll's pewter in 'oak and pewter' antique shops. Sorry to say, there is never a mark on this tiny nineteenth-century pewter.

147

From the wee and twee to much larger containers—tobacco boxes—very pleasant, usually rather tired and well used. The earlier are oval, usually with a mark, the later circular unmarked. The knob of the earlier lids more often than not is a negro head (the emblem of tobacco), and a curious feature is the 'handle' of the lead presser, for it is very often the thumbpiece of a double-volute baluster. I do not think this proves c.1810–20; rather, it is probably making use of the mould later than its period of design (double volutes ceased being made with the coming in of Imperial measure). The later circular boxes have a weak acorn knop, and most often have the familiar two bands of narrow rings, like the two-band pots, and funnels, and are probably contemporary.

Medallions in pewter may attract you. They are often to be found in coin shops and numismatic dealers. They were first produced in the seventeenth century, and are masterpieces of the diemaker's craft, and of the pewterer's in casting them so perfectly.

Communion tokens, too, can be found in the coin shops. Most are Scottish, some Welsh. The eighteenth century ones are more attractive, being hammered, and archaic in appearance; the nineteenth century ones are very formal, and beautifully cast, with New Testament texts.

116 Tobacco boxes were made in pewter c.1780–c.1840, these being c.1810 and c.1820.

While it is just outside the close of our period, it would be as well to mention Art Nouveau. This art form was not confined to pewter, but nevertheless a new demand for pewter was created. In 1899 Liberty's, of Regent Street, London, started to import from Germany the new modern style of sweeping lines in a very wide range of expression. The strong antimony alloy allowed casting the fine swirling designs, and brought them within the price range of a broad contemporary market; and the immediate success brought a boom to those English manufacturers who took it up. Arthur Liberty was responsible for fostering and promoting it, under Liberty's trademark of 'Tudric'. In fact, I think that they might well claim to have injected a rescue act to the trade as a whole at a time when pewter was virtually 'out'. What has happened since then is no concern of this book. In the meantime, alloy and craftsmanship have probably never been bettered. I do not pretend to be enamoured of it, but those who are interested should seek sight of Liberty's centenary exhibition catalogue 1875–1975 in which there is introductory text and illustrations of the whole of their range. In *BP and BM* I wrote '. . . Art Nouveau . . . has not yet caught the eyes of serious pewter collectors'. That is still true of its regard by <u>pewter</u> collectors, but Art Nouveau collectors have moved in . . . Later in this book there is a section on fakes, which you might think would not apply to the nineteenth century. While you may think you bask in an unsullied period, there are one or two words of warning repeated there. I have mentioned marks on late-looking sticks as always undesirable. There are repros of plates, false-style porringers, to the so-called 'African jugs' (which have claimed many a victim). A few years ago out-and-out repros of bellied measures appeared, garish looking, seamed from top to bottom like a bi-valve shell—two halves. Other 'repros', perhaps to give them a euphemistic title, include bellied measures with false verification marks. In any case, repros soon become 'fakes', for in some cases ignorant (?) dealers put high prices on obvious repros, which tend to be accepted as an indication of validity of the piece. (When I say 'dealers', here, I do not, of course, intend to imply the major specialised dealers, who are most ethical and trustworthy. But this should not lead you to be lazy—remember *you* are the guv'nor.)

It is always most difficult to write of the present, and few would want it. There are a great many small manufacturers over the country, and one or two much bigger names long connected with pewter history. Some of their products are approximately replicas of the old styles. Approximately is the critical word and try yourself out in defining the detail differences. Just look in a good gift shop, jeweller or in some tobacconists—and they may produce examples or catalogues.

Now to leave the nineteenth century, repeating some thoughts. It is a most rewarding period for collecting, and one in which you can be active constantly, and lucky. Develop your appreciation of line and detail, then you may spot the earlier ones lurking. Unless you are alert they will not arrest your glance. Develop your judgment, and do correct writers' (including mine, of course) opinions. Here is a very fertile period for research, but already pieces are far from ubiquitous, and recognition by others of the earlier, and less-common, pieces has dawned. Get to know good dealers and other collectors and see, handle and discuss. Amazing how handling generates conversation which sparks off inquisitiveness. Research is urgently wanted over the whole period, on all products, particularly beakers, footed cups, casters, candlesticks, and toy pewter. And do let us narrow the dating on all types of pots.

11. Scottish Pewter—

by P. Spencer Davies

Although Scottish pewter was made to fulfil similar functions to that made in England, it has had a completely separate evolution of styles and forms. Tracing this evolution is now quite difficult since in very many cases, particularly in the seventeenth century but also in the nineteenth, only single examples of some types are known. This is probably because Scotland was a relatively poor nation with a small population, and the total amount of pewter made would have been but a small fraction of that made in England. In addition, tin was not indigenous to Scotland and there may have been a greater incentive to return worn, damaged or outdated articles to the pewterer for melting down. To compound the difficulty, much Scottish pewter was not marked, and identifying such pieces must rely upon provenance, when known, and inspired guesswork.

In the sixteenth and seventeenth centuries, the styles of pewter articles suggest a prevailing influence of France and the Low Countries. During this time there were very strong cultural and trading links between Scotland, particularly Aberdeen and the north-east, and Holland. With the Act of Union of 1707 the rich colonial market, which had previously been England's prerogative, became available to Scottish manufacturers, and commerce boomed. Pewter making was not left out of this surge, but now the balance of trade gradually switched from the east coast to Glasgow and the west. This period saw the introduction of some English influence on the styles of, for instance, baluster measures and plates, but even these retained features which marked them as very distinctively Scottish. With the continuation of the boom into the nineteenth century new styles in measures and tavern pots continued to evolve, and this at a time when English pewter had reached its final decline.

In Scotland, as in England, the pewterers formed themselves into craft guilds. In early medieval times the tradesmen had been members of the powerful merchant guild which was to be found in each of the major burghs. However, continued differences of opinion between the merchants and tradesmen caused the latter to set up their own guilds or 'Incorporations' as they came to be known. With the granting of a Seal of Cause by the magistrates and burgh council, the Incorporations were given official recognition and were able to exercise powers to control the quality of work, the conduct of the tradesmen and so on. The pewterers were members of the Incorporation of Hammermen, which included most of those craftsmen who wielded a hammer: blacksmiths, armourers, saddlers, cutlers, bucklemakers and lorimers.

The earliest-recorded Seal of Cause was that granted to the Incorporation of Hammermen of Edinburgh in 1483. Those of the major Scottish burghs probably date from about the same period or shortly after. Despite rules which stated that certain of the best-qualified persons of the craft would be entrusted to ensure that alloy of the correct composition was used by the pewterers, it is clear that the Incorporations did not manage to achieve this control. Thus, in 1567, an Act was passed complaining of the poor quality of the pewter being made, and stating that forthwith pewter of the first quality was to be stamped with the mark of a crown and hammer, and second-quality pewter was to be marked simply with the maker's name. This is the first reference that we have to the marking of pewter, and there are one or two sixteenth-century items bearing a crowned hammer mark still extant.

During the seventeenth century it appears that standards had slipped again and Acts were passed in 1641, and again in 1663, requiring pewterers to mark their wares with the thistle mark, the Deacon's mark and their own name. No piece of pewter marked in this way has come down to the present day, and it is possible that the Act was largely ignored. However, from about 1600 onwards the Edinburgh pewterers struck a personal touch mark on a touch plate of lead, which was presumably kept by the Incorporation of Hammermen. The two touch plates, which are small in comparison with those of the Worshipful Company of Pewterers of London, measure a mere $12\frac{1}{4}$in long by $4\frac{1}{2}$in wide, and are now in the possession of the National Museum of Antiquities in Edinburgh. With the exception of the first few marks, they all consist of a castle, with the initials of the pewterer on either side and a date below. The date

117 'Castle' mark of Alexander Coulthard 1708, from the neck of a chopin-size tappit hen. This mark is no. 110 on the Edinburgh touch plate, and measures approximately $\frac{3}{8}$in from top to bottom.

151

corresponds to the year in which the pewterer set up shop, and in most cases this is the same as the year in which he became a freeman of the Incorporation. The last mark is that of John Gardner, 1764.

Regrettably the records of the Incorporation of Hammermen do not appear to shed any light on either the initiation or decline in use of the touch plates. This is unfortunate, since these Edinburgh touch marks are something of an enigma. In the early eighteenth century they appear very infrequently on measures but never on flatware. This may be because of an Ordinance, passed by the Edinburgh Incorporation of Hammermen in 1681, that each pewterer should have a stamp bearing his own name. From that date onwards the Edinburgh pewterers' touch marks which appear on plates and dishes commonly consist of a name in a linear punch, or associated with a pictorial device (as with the London pewterers), or associated with a crowned tudor rose. The touch marks used by the pewterers during the eighteenth and nineteenth centuries in the other Scottish towns are similar and often embody the name of the craftsman. During the nineteenth century, not infrequently the maker's mark on measures was cast into the base on the inside or beneath the lid, and was not applied by a punch.

'Hallmarks', equivalent to those used by English pewterers, came into use in the eighteenth century for marking flatware, but these were always applied to the back of the plate or charger. Scottish pewterers emulated their counterparts in the English provincial towns quite often by striking a LONDON stamp below their own touch mark. Whether this was meant to deceive or whether such items were intended for export is not known. The only other type of marks on Scottish pewter consists of verification stamps which appear on measures.

Scottish pewterware can be conveniently divided into that for domestic, tavern, or ecclesiastical use, although there is often considerable overlap. For instance, measures which might be considered mainly for use in tavern or home occasionally appear to have been donated to churches for sacramental use, and large plates and dishes of similar type were used in both church and home.

Domestic and tavern pewter
Very little is known of early flatware. There is but a single plate in existence which may date from the sixteenth century. This has a diameter of $11\frac{3}{4}$in, with a broad $2\frac{1}{4}$in plain-edged rim. Although Ingleby Wood in his *Scottish Pewter-ware and Pewterers* (the only book on Scottish pewter, published in 1907) mentions characteristics of the seventeenth-century plates which coincide closely with those in use in England at that time, I have not been able to trace a single example. However, a small deep dish by George Ross of Aberdeen and a 15in shallow dish by Robert Edgar of Edinburgh, both dating from the end of the seventeenth century, have multiple reeding around the edge of the rim. During the eighteenth century, plates followed those in England with a similar evolution, that is, a single reed round the rim until *c.*1750, and thereafter the edge was plain. Very few plates were made after about 1800 and more often than not those that were do not have hammer marks round the bouge on the underside. A relatively greater proportion of Scottish 9in plates have a deep bowl.

In order to understand Scottish measures to the full, and sometimes to help in dating a particular piece, it may be necessary to use a measuring cylinder and a set of conversion tables. Until 1707 the standard liquid measure was based upon the Scots pint which almost exactly equals 3 Imperial pints. Half a pint (equivalent therefore to $1\frac{1}{2}$ Imperial pints) was termed a chopin and the diminutives, decreasing by one half in each case, were the mutchkin, the large gill, the wee gill and the wee half gill. With the Act of Union of 1707 Scotland was obliged to adopt the standards of England, in other words the Old English Wine Standard. In fact this legislation was largely ignored, and the Scots continued to use the traditional capacities of measure for the next 120 years. Nevertheless, throughout the eighteenth century some measures were made in OEWS capacities and it is almost impossible to distinguish these from the traditional Scottish capacities without the aid of a measuring cylinder. With the introduction of Imperial capacity in both England and Scotland in 1826, a number of new shapes as well as capacity of measure were adopted. Measures in Scottish capacities were allowed to continue in use provided they had stamped upon them the relationship that their capacity bore to the new Imperial standard. Thus one occasionally sees measures stamped on the side $1\frac{1}{3}$S. In 1835 a new Weights and Measures Act was passed which forbade the use of measures of the earlier capacities. There is some suggestion however that Scottish capacity continued in use, in a clandestine manner, for some time after this.

Verification of measures in the eighteenth century came under the jurisdiction of the Dean of Guild in each burgh, who presided over a council drawn from representatives of both the merchant guilds and the tradesmen's Incorporations. It appears, however, that scant attention was paid to this chore and the majority of pre-1826 measures bear no verification marks. In Edinburgh however, the Dean of Guild's stamp, consisting of his own initials over the initials D G, was applied to measures at the time of verification between the years 1801 and 1835, when the responsibility for verification passed to the Weights and Measures Inspectorate. Since the Deans of Guild held office for only 2 years, it is possible to date Edinburgh-made measures of this period quite accurately. Nearly all post-1826 Imperial measures bear verification stamps, punched on by the relevant burgh or county authority and quite often incorporating the coat of arms of that authority. After 1878 standard verification stamps consisting of a crowned VR above a district number gradually came into use, as in England.

Deans of Guild of Edinburgh whose Initials Appear as Verification Marks

The normal 2-year term of office ran from Michaelmas (29th September) to Michaelmas, and therefore extended into 3 years.

*	I I / D G	James Jackson	1799–1801	* T H / D G	Thomas Henderson	1801–1803
*	J M / D G	John Muir	1803–1805	W C / D G	William Coulter	1805–1807
	W C / D G	William Calder	1807–1809	W T / D G	William Tennant	1809–1811
	K M / D G	Kincaid Mackenzie	1811–1813	J W / D G	John Walker	1813–1815
	R J / D G	Robert Johnston	1815–1817	* A H / D G	Alex Henderson	1817–1819
*	A S / D G	Alexander Smellie	1819–1821	J T / D G	John Turnbull	1821–1822
*	R A / D G	Robert Anderson	1822–1823	J W / D G	John Waugh	1823–1825

153

* R W D G	Robert Wright	1825–1827	J H D G	James Hill	1827–1829
* W C D G	William Child	1829–1831	* J S D G	John Smith	1831–1833
* J M D G	John Macfie	1833–1835			

Those marked with an asterisk have been observed by the author;
the others are expected to exist.

The earliest measures that we know of are of the potbellied type, and they date from the seventeenth century to the early eighteenth. Typically they have a domed lid and erect thumbpiece which is almost identical to that found on tappit-hen measures and on certain Dutch flagons of the same period, and the Dutch influence on overall design is inescapable. They were also made without lids, in which case the top of the handle is often somewhat wedge shaped in side view. If they are marked, the maker's mark is

118 Potbellied measures of Scots pint and chopin capacity respectively. The larger has a thistle mark with initials SI on the handle, and is 9in to the rim. The smaller is unmarked and is 6¼in to the rim. Note that the handle and thumbpiece are almost identical to those of tappit hens. Late seventeenth to early eighteenth centuries. (Glasgow Museums and Art Galleries)

154

usually struck on the handle or cast inside the base. All of the identified potbellies were made in the north-east of Scotland—from Inverness to Aberdeen—and they may all originate from that region. They are amongst the scarcest of Scottish measures and to achieve one in a collection must be considered a prize.

The measures most usually associated with Scotland are the tappit hens. The shape is unmistakable, with its combination of straight and curving sections to the body, the domed lid and the simple erect thumbpiece. The handle always has a straight or horizontal top section—a feature which is characteristic also of Scottish baluster measures and most of the potbellies mentioned above. The attachment at the lower end is by means of a short strut, and the handle terminal is sometimes with, sometimes without, a heel. If you look inside the neck of the larger of the pre-Imperial sizes (Scots pint and chopin) you will see a small blob of pewter. This is the 'plouk' (pimple) and indicates the level to which it was filled to achieve the stated capacity. In eighteenth-century Scotland, tappit hens of mulled claret would be taken from the coaching inns to warm and sustain the passengers in the coach outside. The claret would then be poured into a small pewter beaker or 'tassie' for drinking. The tassie was made to fit within the neck of the measure when empty and one can occasionally come across a tappit hen which still has its tassie in situ.

The earliest-known tappit hen has an Edinburgh 'castle' touch mark dated 1669. Unfortunately we do not know when they first made their appearance, but the style remained in use for a considerable period of time, even beyond the changeover to Imperial measure in 1826. (Ingleby Wood suggested that they may date from the sixteenth century on the evidence of a statuary figure bearing a tappit hen which appears on a 'sixteenth-century' fountain in Linlithgow. Unfortunately it transpires that this fountain, having fallen into a state of decay, was extensively restored in the early nineteenth century and the tappit hen is probably only the conjecture of the stonemason who carried out the restoration. The mystery of the origins of the measure therefore remain). Most pewterers however took the opportunity to introduce a change in style at this time. Imperial-capacity tappit hens were but a shadow of their former glory; they were not as heavily cast and relatively few were made. Those in Imperial capacity sometimes have a maker's mark cast into the base, a verification stamp on the neck and an Imperial medallion cast on the top of the lid.

With such a long span of use it is not surprising to find that tappit hens are to be found in capacities ranging from the Scots pint to the Scots half gill, from the Imperial quart to the Imperial half gill and in one or two local capacities as well. A complete set—an almost unattainable goal today—would probably include about eighteen or nineteen different sizes.

By far the most regal of the tappit hens are the crested ones, which bear an acorn knop on the centre of the lid. This seems to add a certain dignity to the piece and probably accounts for their popularity with collectors. They are slightly later than those with plain lids and perhaps first appeared in the middle of the eighteenth century. They were only made in three sizes: Scots pint, chopin and mutchkin, and they were not made in Imperial capacities. The latter two sizes are extremely scarce.

In addition to the lidded forms, tappit hens—as with other measures—were made without lids in and around Aberdeen. These had solid-cast hinge lugs at the top of the handle and are most commonly met with in Imperial sizes.

Tappit hens have always been popular with collectors and there are numerous reproductions in circulation. Nearly all of these can be detected by an experienced eye. It is essential not to be deceived by a nice surface colour and patina—a number of them

119 Tappit hen measures. Left: crested tappit hen of Scots pint capacity with acorn knop to the lid, 9½in to rim. *c.* 1730–1826. Centre: Aberdeen-type lidless tappit hen of one-Imperial-pint capacity, with solid hinge lug. It is marked 'Imperial' and DG (for Dean of Guild) beneath the base; 6in to the rim. *c.* 1826–1835. Right: plain tappit hen of Scots pint capacity, 9½in to rim. *c.* 1730–1826. Both larger measures have a 'plouk' inside the neck, and neither has verification nor maker's marks.

have been in circulation for 50 years or so. Beware of any that bear punched hallmarks at the neck or have a touch mark beneath the base, or have been formed from thin gauge metal. A real tappit hen has a good solid 'feel' and in the pre-Imperial ones the only mark you might find would be an Edinburgh castle mark on the neck to the left of the handle—and these marked examples are extremely rare!

Baluster measures made their first appearance at some time in the eighteenth century but since none of these bears a maker's mark, their origins have to remain obscure. The shape of the body and the flat lid are obviously derived from the styles of the English balusters. However, the Scottish measures have features which make them readily distinguishable. The lid always has a locating flange on the underside, which restricts the side-to-side movement of the lid, so reducing wear on the hinge. This was important because all Scottish measures were made of a soft alloy with a high-lead content and they were never as heavily cast as their English counterparts. In addition, the handle was always slimmer and had the characteristic straight section at the top, noted earlier. However, the most characteristic feature was the form of the lid attachment and the thumbpiece.

The ball thumbpiece was attached to the lid by a rectangular bar thereby distinguishing it from the somewhat earlier English ball-and-wedge balusters. They were made in pre-Imperial Scottish, Imperial and OEWS capacities, mainly in the smaller size range. I have not seen one larger than the half mutchkin, although very similar measures from the north of England were made in the Imperial half-pint size.

The embryo shell baluster has a thumbpiece which is somewhat oval in shape with a

120   Underneath side of Scottish ball baluster lids, showing locating flanges. (H. Myrtle)

V-shaped lid attachment—rather like that seen on English bud balusters. There are several variations in the shape of this thumbpiece. One form, with a pointed top and slight waist below, has been called a spade thumbpiece because of its similarity in outline to a gravedigger's spade. These measures were again made in both Scottish and Imperial capacities, and possibly OEWS also. Those in Imperial capacity cover a wide size range, and I have seen a single specimen with a capacity of half gallon. The difference in size range in which one finds the ball and bar, and the embryo shell balusters, tempts one to speculate that they may have been made for the dispensing of different sorts of liquids. Alas there is no hint of any evidence for this.

The flat-lid balusters appear to have lasted until about 1840. In the preceding years they were gradually being superseded by balusters with a domed lid which probably first appeared in 1826 at the changeover to Imperial measure. Different forms appeared almost simultaneously in Glasgow and in Edinburgh.

The Edinburgh balusters are characterised by a squat body shape, somewhat similar to the English bellied or bulbous measures, but with a more pronounced belly. The domed lid has a concave outer section rising to a flat top. Some measures have a cast 'medallion' consisting of the word IMPERIAL with a crown below it, in the centre of the lid. The fluted thumbpiece is always wedge shaped with four vertical flutes. When a maker's name is present it is usually cast on the underside of the lid. These measures probably ceased when Edinburgh's last pewterer, James Moyes, gave up business in about 1880.

The Glasgow measures kept to the more slender body shape of the earlier balusters. Typically, the lid has a convex dome as on tappit hens. Again, there is an Imperial medallion cast on the centre of the lid and the thumbpiece has radiating ribs, resembling a cockle shell. There are several variations of the Glasgow baluster. The most commonly seen has an Edinburgh type of concave curving lid, but nevertheless has a slender body form and shell thumbpiece. The Glasgow double-dome measures

157

121   Flat-lid baluster measures. Left: embryo shell or spade thumbpiece baluster of half mutchkin or large-Scots-gill capacity. 3½in to rim. c.1750(?)–1826 No marks. Right: ball and bar thumbpiece baluster of one gill OEWS capacity, marked RA/DG on the neck (Robert Anderson, dean of guild in Edinburgh in 1822) 3¼in to rim. Both measures have a locating flange beneath the lid. Although these are both pre-Imperial, the styles were made after 1826 in Imperial sizes also.

are far less common. The lid has two convex tiers and the smooth unribbed thumbpiece is waisted, suggesting an evolution from the embryo shell balusters. The Imperial medallion in the centre of the lid is usually lightly cast and almost invariably some of the detail has been rubbed away during the life of the measure.

Whilst most of the Glasgow balusters are in Imperial capacity, there is a series which has a medallion on the lid bearing the words '4 glass', '2 glass' or '1 glass' respectively. These correspond to the Scottish capacities of half mutchkin, Scots gill and Scots half gill. I am inclined to think that they are pre-Imperial, that is, that they date from before 1826, although they could have been made after that date for use in the kitchen rather than for the dispensing of liquids for sale.

On the east coast of Scotland, and in Aberdeenshire in particular, baluster measures of traditional shape were made without lids. Recent research has shown that there is a range of forms in these, and for convenience I shall call all of them 'Aberdeen' measures. At first sight they may give the impression of being erstwhile-lidded measures which have lost their lids, since the top of the handle still bears a hinge lug. The earliest are pre-Imperial Scottish capacity, and the handle was evidently cast from a mould which had originally been used for lidded measures, the space between the

122 Edinburgh baluster measures, both of half-pint capacity and both have the same squat body shape and the characteristic four-fluted thumbpiece. That on the left has the mark of James Moyes (*OP* 3317) cast beneath the lid which is of typical dished or concave shape. That on the right has no maker's mark, the lid has a slightly-different profile, and a medallion, comprising a crown and 'Imperial ½ pint' cast on to the centre. Both 3¾in to rim. *c.*1840–50.

123 Glasgow baluster measures. Left: dished or concave-lid type of half-pint capacity with typical shell thumbpiece and Imperial medallion on the lid. 4in to rim. *c.*1850 and later. Centre: double-domed lid variety, of gill capacity. The central Imperial medallion is invariably somewhat rubbed and the date beneath the crown—either 1826 or 1835—is not always easy to discern. The thumbpiece is of a plain waisted type. 3½in to rim. *c.* 1826–1850. Right: typical domed lid type with shell thumbpiece and Imperial medallion on the lid. 4in to rim. *c.* 1826–1860. Glasgow measures have a more slender body shape than the Edinburgh ones and very rarely bear maker's marks.

124 Aberdeen-type lidless baluster measures. Left: half pint, Edinburgh body shape, with the hinge lug bored, and verification marks of both Aberdeen County and of Edinburgh. 4in to rim. *c.*1826–1850. Centre: gill, true baluster shape with solid hinge lug, marked 'Imperial' and DG beneath the base. 3½in to rim. *c.*1826–1835. Right: half gill, true baluster shape, with the hinge lug bored, and Edinburgh verification stamp. 2½in to rim. *c.*1826–1850. These 'Aberdeen' measures never bear makers' marks.

slots and in the centre subsequently being filled. The later Imperial capacity measures usually have the hinge slots filled, but the centre is still hollow, as if to take a hinge pin. The latest in the evolutionary series have a completely solid hinge lug. Examples with the bored lug are also found with the Edinburgh measure body shape, and usually bear either Edinburgh or Dundee verification stamps.

The last type of Scottish measure that I want to describe is also the rarest. This is the attractively-shaped thistle measure. The thistle shape is produced by a very pronounced bulbous lower section, which flares out in a straight-sided section above. The measure is raised on a tapering foot section and has a simple elegant handle with a continuous sweep, attached by struts above and below. They first made their appearance in the nineteenth century and those that were still in use in 1907 saw a quick demise following the Weights and Measures Regulations of that year which forbade the use of any measures which did not empty completely when tilted through an angle of 120°. It is doubtful whether the destruction of measures which may have followed this piece of legislation can adequately explain their scarcity today, particularly since very similar measures made from brass or copper are not uncommon. It is difficult to tell how many would be required to make a complete series. The Clapperton collection once contained a graded series of seven measures, the largest being of one Imperial pint. This set has now vanished without trace, and a collector who can track down one or two these days would consider himself lucky in the extreme.

From time to time, measures come to light which apparently have Scottish pre-Imperial capacities but are fashioned in styles which are more clearly English. Examples of this are the double volute, the rare slender ball and the even more rare spray thumbpiece balusters, together with lidless balusters with a double-volute measure type of handle. These usually turn up in the north of England and it is my belief that all of these emanate from Newcastle and perhaps Carlisle and York. This is obviously an area in which further research is desperately needed.

The handsome lidded tankards which were made in both silver and pewter in seventeenth- and eighteenth-century England appear to have had no Scottish counterpart. The earliest drinking vessels in pewter are unlidded tavern pots apparently dating from c.1750–1800. Tavern pots, like measures, were made to conform to the standards of capacity in force at the time, and those of Scots capacity are therefore likely to have been made before 1826. The number of variations in form of the Scottish tavern pots is now known to be very large, and it is quite outside the scope of this chapter to describe them in detail. One of the earliest types has a straight-sided drum flaring slightly at the top and with a skirted foot below. The drum is quite plain and the handle is affixed at its lower end with a strut, terminating in a sharply-forked fishtail terminal. This type is found in both pre-Imperial and Imperial capacities. From Glasgow came the Scottish tulip-shaped tavern pot, a rather more voluptuously-curved variation of the equivalent English type. It has a broken or double-curved handle, and was made in both Scots and Imperial capacities, and when marked usually has the touch of Robert Galbraith of Glasgow.

125   Selection of Scottish tavern pots, all of Imperial-pint capacity. Those on the left and right are by Edinburgh's last pewterer, James Moyes (*OP* 3317). Note the characteristic ball and teardrop handle terminal, c.1850–1880. Second left: Scottish tulip-shaped pot with double curved handle, by Robert Galbraith of Glasgow (*OP* 1802), c.1830–1840. Third left: straight-sided pot with skirted base and 'Scottish fishtail' handle terminal, by J. and H. Wardrop of Glasgow (*OP* 4959), c.1826–1830.

Probably the best known of the late Scottish tavern pots are those made by William Scott and by James Moyes of Edinburgh. These date from c.1840–80 but were heavily-cast and well-fashioned pieces. There are two variations of the body form: one has straight sides with a fillet of incised lines around the centre of the drum and a flared foot, whilst the other has straight sides terminating below in a rib, the whole sitting upon a domed foot. In both examples, the handle is similar and quite unmistakable, terminating in a ball and teardrop.

The number of tavern pots made in these rather well-proportioned styles was probably low, and throughout the nineteenth century the majority of pots, as in England, were of the rather less-interesting concave-sided form.

161

Ecclesiastical pewter

Nearly all of the church pewter still in existence dates from the eighteenth and early nineteenth centuries. The sixteenth and seventeenth centuries were very turbulent periods in the history of the Church of Scotland, with alternating periods of presbyterian and episcopalian forms of worship, until the Presbyterian Church of Scotland became the established church in 1688. It is small wonder that so little has survived.

Whilst England has a legacy of many hundreds of fine seventeenth-century pewter communion flagons, almost nothing is known about Scottish flagons of the same period. This is perhaps partly a result of the disruptions associated with the changes in the form of worship, and partly due to the inherent poverty of the churches. Furthermore, Kirk Session Records of this period rarely make mention of flagons, and far more emphasis appears to have been placed upon the cups or chalices.

Two large potbellied flagons, of a form which is identical to the potbellied measures which I have described previously, were given to the kirk of Brechin in 1680 by 'Walter Jamieson, Bailye and Kirk Master'. Whilst these may have started life in purely secular use, it is more likely that they were the only type of vessel which was available for purchase at that time. Tron church in Edinburgh and Benholme church in Angus both used pewter communion flagons which were gifted to them in 1688 and 1690 respectively. These are straight sided, with a skirted base and raised flat-topped lid, and have something of the style of an English 'beefeater' flagon. Unfortunately, neither of them has a maker's mark, and with so little available to make comparison, it is difficult to deduce where they were made.

In the first quarter of the eighteenth century a form of communion flagon, which was to hold sway for over a hundred years, first made its appearance. The body is straight sided, tapering slightly from the moulded base, and with a single broad moulding around the centre. The lid is not quite flat, but has a slight curvature above and invariably has a flange beneath, like the baluster measures. The early ones had a slight denticulation at the front, but this appears to have been dropped after c.1730. The thumbpiece is always twin lobed. The majority of flagons were about $8\frac{1}{2}$in to the rim, but in the latter half of the century, some of the larger churches used flagons, of the same type but rather more slender in outline, which were some 11–12in to the lip or about 13–14in overall. From about 1790–1800 onwards, spouts were added, but the basic style of the flagon remained otherwise unchanged. At about this time too, some of the spouted flagons were made with an acorn knop in the centre of the lid.

In addition to the flagons, the communion plate comprised large patens for the bread, and cups or chalices for the wine. The seventeenth-century plates, of which several are still in the possession of the churches, all appeared to be of the deep-dish variety with a boss in the centre. Eighteenth-century plates were virtually indistinguishable from domestic dishes and chargers. All of the seventeenth-century communion cups which have come down to us hail from the north-east of Scotland, and are of the simple beaker form which was in common use in the Low Countries at that time. During the eighteenth century a large variety of communion cups appeared, all with the bowl set upon a stem and domed foot. These continued to evolve in style right through to the early nineteenth century when they were gradually superseded by chalices made from Britannia metal.

Quite often Scottish communion plate was engraved with the name of the church, the date and the name of the minister. Apart from increasing the decorative appeal of these pieces, a study of these engravings provides a patchwork history of the prolifera-

126 Typical form of Scottish communion flagon. The lid is slightly domed and has a locating flange on the underside. It is 8½in to the rim and bears the touch mark of William Scott of Edinburgh (*OP* 4160) in the base. *c.*1780–1800.

tion of schisms and secessions which the church in Scotland underwent in the eighteenth century.

Pewter vessels were also used in baptism. Baptismal bowls were deep-sided dishes, usually 9in in diameter, with a narrow-reeded rim—very similar to those used in English churches. Some were made with completely rounded bases, indicating that they were normally inserted in a stone or wrought-iron support. In contrast to all other plates and dishes, the touch mark was almost invariably struck on the *inside* of the bowl. The vessel which was used to bring the water to the baptismal bowl was termed a laver. Much confusion exists over the use of this term. Lavers of silver were smallish vessels with a definite spout at the front, and there was no equivalent style made in pewter. It is not clear whether the communion flagons which I have mentioned earlier were also used as lavers, or whether the laver was not in fact used during the service of baptism in the eighteenth-century church.

An important but often overlooked part of Scottish communion plate was the tokens, most of which were made of pewter. During the seventeenth and eighteenth centuries, communion services were held infrequently, sometimes only once a year or

127 Selection of Scottish communion tokens. The early tokens were made from a high-lead-content alloy, either by striking the impression on to thin sheets of metal, or by casting in a stone mould. The later ones (bottom row) were of hard metal and struck, like medals, under high pressure in a hand-operated die. Those shown are (l. to r. and top to bottom): Brechin, 1678; Campbelltown (Low Kirk), 1737; Carmunnock, 1777—Mr. Joseph Hodgson, minister from 1776 to 1785; Thurso, 1806; Kildrummy, 1810; Edinburgh, Lady Glenorchy's Chapel, nineteenth century, no date; Dundee, St. Paul's Free Church, 1860; Fraserburgh, 1867.

less. They were therefore very important occasions in the life of the kirk and people would travel for miles, often from neighbouring parishes, in order to attend. Only those who had satisfied the kirk elders on their good character and knowledge of the scriptures were issued with tokens, which were therefore highly prized by the recipients. At the communion service admission was gained by surrender of the tokens which were often deposited in a large pewter dish.

The tokens varied in composition from almost pure lead in early times to a high-tin-content hard metal in the latter part of the nineteenth century. Those of the seventeenth and eighteenth centuries have a quaint charm which results from the way in which they were made. The design was either struck onto thin sheets of metal with an iron punch or they were cast in soft stone moulds into which the design had been carved. They are usually about ½–¾in across and either round, rectangular or square. The design may incorporate the initial letter or a contraction of the first few letters of the name of the kirk, and may include the initials of the minister, preceded by the letters M or Mr. Some bear a date whilst others can be given an approximate date if the minister's initials are given. In order to identify these tokens, it is necessary to consult the two main books on the subject by Robert Dick and A. J. S. Brook, now unfortunately long out of print and difficult to come by.

Nineteenth-century tokens have a different sort of attraction. Latterly they were die-stamped from hand-operated presses, like medals, and consequently have great clarity of detail, often including embossed designs of churches, coats of arms or the burning bush. A New Testament text is usually included and identification is no problem, since the name of the church is given in full.

128 Scottish quaich, 5in diameter across the bowl. The two lugs are hollow and have downward-projecting drops at their ends. No marks, *c.*1700. (Glasgow Museums and Art Galleries)

Of the remaining items of pewter, only two come to mind as being exclusively and characteristically Scottish. The first of these is the elegant quaich—the Scottish equivalent of the English porringer. They were made also from treen and in silver, and hallmarking of the latter helped to establish their lifespan as late seventeenth to early eighteenth century. The bowl has two ears or lugs, which may be hollow, and they usually have a downward-projecting tail at their outer edge when seen in side profile. They were probably used as drinking vessels and are extremely scarce.

The final articles are the Stirling dry measures or grain measures. These appear in

129 Stirling grain measure, 7in diameter and 7½in ht., with a medallion on the front bearing the arms of Stirling—a lamb on a rock, surrounded by the words Stirlini Opidum. These have no marks and it is therefore difficult to date them, but presumably they were made at some time in the eighteenth century.
(Glasgow Museums and Art Galleries)

several sizes, are very heavily-cast pieces and always have two loop handles. All of those which I have examined (all too few, since these are very scarce indeed) have a medallion cast onto the front, carrying the arms of Stirling—a lamb above a rock. No-one appears to have made a study of the capacities of these measures, which is unfortunate since this might help in dating them. In the absence of other evidence I am inclined to agree with previous writers, that they date from the eighteenth century. However, it has to be conceded that the rather crude way in which the handles are soldered on, and the general poor finish, does not conform to the usual high standard of workmanship of this period in Scotland. But it may simply be that measures for grain and other dry materials were heavy functional items and may not have merited good finishing. In these, as in many other aspects of Scottish pewter, we still have a lot to learn.

Bibliography

WOOD, L. INGLEBY, *Scottish Pewterware and Pewterers*, Edinburgh, 1907.
BROOK, A. J. S., 'Communion Tokens of the Established Church of Scotland—Sixteenth, Seventeenth and Eighteenth centuries'. Proc. Soc. Antiq. of Scotland. 1906–7, 453–604. (This was subsequently published in book form, same title, Edinburgh 1908.)
DICK, R., *Scottish Communion Tokens other than those of the Established Church*, Edinburgh 1902.

12. Welsh, Irish and Channel Isles Pewter

Wales

There is no evidence of manufacture, unfortunately, at any time for Wales. For such a strongly-nationalistic country this is a great pity; so barren is the subject that it does not arise in discussion. (Since writing this sentence John Douglas has come across a touch in which the name of Stephen Madley appears, *OP* 3052, of Landogar, Monmouth. This is on a pair of plain-rim plates. So here *is* evidence of a truly Welsh maker, and truly Welsh products. The mark is shown in *MPM* 3052. Perhaps this opens the gates.) There is no evidence, either, of makers, or of distinctive types. This constitutes a strong challenge to Welsh collectors—to seek clues in the ancient towns and cities, possibly under a general heading such as 'tin-plate worker', 'white-metal worker', or 'brazier' in records and directories. I have little to help.

A fine flagon is known, which is not in the run of English styles, and is engraved 'Thomas Owen. Clr. Moses Roberts. E. Ellis. Wardens. 1764'. This piece, to judge by lid, thumbpiece and body, is *c*.1710. The mark is illegible save ' . . . ONDO . . . ' (part of 'London', which does *not* prove London manufacture). The names are, all three, a very strong clue to its provenance, but it is perhaps wishful to think we have found a purely Welsh style.

It should be added that the type of thumbpiece is not unique, and certainly it emanated (if only thence) from Wigan. Not far from Wigan to the Welsh border. But it is possible that the three Welsh names were all displaced persons, all worthy pillars of some English church.

It has been suggested by Mr R. Mundey that the 'spray' baluster may be a Welsh type, and in that he has native support. But I know that they have turned up in the north-west of England, so once again—Wigan or Chester? They could have been so easily sent to both the north, and to mid-Wales. I remember, too, that Bert Isher sketched for me from memory a delightful slim baluster (of *c*.1700 at the latest), which he thought to be a Welsh type. It had a ball thumbpiece, but the ball was flattened amidships, to leave the top flat. I wonder if any reader has an example, and any ideas as to provenance.

The third is not evidence, only custom—in Wales, and I think probably just over the Marches, it was the custom to stand plates face to the wall on the dresser, and to clean the exposed underside. Constant recurrence of a maker of bright-bottomed plates could faintly suggest that he was a Welsh maker.

In the absence of facts I think we must take it that supply was forthcoming from the ring of manufacturing centres, Wigan, Liverpool, Chester, Bewdley, Worcester, Gloucester, Barnstaple, and Exeter, plus others including London of course.

Ireland

That pewter was made and used in Ireland is certain, and from very early times. Cotterell quotes a reference to a delivery to an abbey in 1344, of twelve saucers, twelve dishes, twelve plates, and twenty-four chargers. No doubt treen was used, if anything, by the lower orders. Nice thought, twenty-four dishes! Perhaps it was within the next 200 years that some bumpy-bottom dishes excavated about 3 years ago in County Armagh were made. The makers' marks are wild, and show what I take to be gaelic-influenced art. They are recorded in *MPM* nos 6180, 6181, 6182, 6183.

By the mid seventeenth century pewterers are recorded in a guild of silversmiths, and of hammermen. Like Scotland, Ireland was poor, and could not support a Company. The makers banded with other crafts of hammermen. From this time onwards there are references to poor alloy (thereby cheating both the customer, and the revenue man). At the end of the century it was enacted that pewter was to be as good as that of London, and marked too. However, nowhere is there any record of a piece bearing the well-known English secondary mark, the rose crowned—at any period. There are very few references to early pewter (perhaps wills might help), but that of the seventeenth

130 Magnificent Irish flagon of the latter seventeenth century, by a London maker, David Heyrick. *OP* 2292a. Apart from the top of the lid it is very similar to a beefeater. (D. Peatling)

168

131 Excellent examples of the Irish chalice and flagon of *c.*1765–80. Note the 'coiled spring' handle. 9⅛in to lip. (W. Allen)

century we do hear about and can see some very rare flat-lidded flagons, and some communion cups.

In 1713 there is a reference to 'dishes, plates, porringers, tankards, quarts, and spoons' (no doubt 'quart' = pot). It is noteworthy that some of their magnificent flagons were made by London makers. And if a fellow had moulds for one flagon, he must have been confident of making many.

There are some church flagons with body and lid forms similar to the beefeater, but the features are mixed. The handle is a wide 'S', like a spring, with fishtail terminal and the body carries a spout; one feature of *c.*1670, one of *c.*1710 and one of *c.*1760; say *c.*1725. This body shape, with extremely wide base and the same handle, is carried on through the century, a dome lid supplanting the previous lid. The eighteenth-century chalices, too, are easily identified, having nearly-parallel sides of a rather narrow cup, and very stout stems.

169

We have no trace or sight of hollow-ware of the eighteenth century (other than the flagons and communion cups), but plates and dishes in the conventional single reed, and plain-rim English styles do turn up from time to time. 'Hallmarks' arrived in the middle of the eighteenth century, 120 years after appearing in England. These 'hallmarks' often incorporate a harp in one shield. The use of the term 'English block tin' sounds like a foreign country, but in Ireland alone this term was used.

In the early nineteenth century we run into the really delightful and distinctive haystack measures—probably made for Imperial measure in 1826. Note that they are still made today! These ran from one gallon to half noggin (a noggin being equal to a gill). There is a strong similarity of line to the West Country measures. Finally there is the series, again being reproduced today, called 'noggins'. They are obviously sired by the baluster, but have neither lids nor handles, and run from half pint to quarter noggin; the latter size has a concave aspect. I once owned one of an earlier variety, but now regret having passed it on. It was of half pint, taller, slimmer neck but wide lip, and the belly was carried rather lower. It had a definite air of bud, and was, I suppose, late eighteenth century or early nineteenth.

132 Comparison of the Irish haystack and the English West Country measure. Haystacks are reproduced to this day.

Recently Dr P. Spencer Davies had one not dissimilar, a little later looking, but its contents were nearer Scottish measure than OEWS or Imperial. It may have been *the* standard, or it may have been a local standard.

N. Brazell notes the alternative spelling of 'naggin' and the occasional use of 'glass', which here equals half a gill. He is also inclined towards Dublin and the east as the source of noggin measures, and the haystack from Cork and the south. I do regret that no further information is forthcoming. Is there an Irish collector who has more to tell?

133   A pint Irish pot of probably *c.*1860.

Channel Isles

If you have any pieces of Channel Isle pewter you should get, or at least see, *Pewter of the Channel Islands*, a truly masterly and completely exhaustive study of what appears at first sight to be only two types. It must be by far the most thorough book on any aspect of pewter yet. Stanley Woolmer and Charles Arkwright were the collaborating

134   Half-pint, gill and half-gill 'Noggins' (A noggin is also a capacity of one gill.) The quarter gill is straight sided, with wider collar and base, giving a concave aspect. (Mrs. M. Dring)

171

135   The now very popular Channel Isle flagons, left, Jersey, plain-bodied and no flare-out at base, by the famous (and sometimes faked) John de St Croix, c.1760. The Guernsey, with rings round the body, and with pronounced shaping at the base. Note the pointed heart-shaped lid with twin-acorn thumbpiece, neither found on the British mainland.

authors; perhaps they had the ideal combination of their two personal attributes, a small type range to investigate, few makers, the accessibility to a not-indigestible number of specimens, and the entré to distant collectors for their specimen details.

We must pass over the pewter from the islands' mere 75 square miles rather rapidly, because first the Channel Isles are not strictly part of Great Britain, and secondly the restriction of styles leads one either to admire rather superficially, or to delve deep, to bring out all they have to say of themselves.

136 An interesting range of lidless Jersey measures, showing variations of handles and blind hinge boss. Quart to half gill, of which the three smaller are earlier, having solid handles. Curiously, the half pint measures 9 fl. oz. From Edward VII onwards each reign has had a different stamp. The complications are admirably discussed in Woolmer and Arkwright's *Pewter of the Channel Islands*.

The products known and actually made by Channel Isles makers, islanders who mostly worked in London, and probably most of whose products were made for the isles, are confined to Guernsey flagons, Jersey flagons and measures, plates, dishes and porringers. The plates and dishes are like the conventional English single reed and plain rim. The porringers, extremely rare, are also conventional. So to the flagons, which are far more indicative of continental style than English, and there is no English counterpart. The Guernseys, tall, feminine, baluster-like, but with pronounced foot, bear attractive encircling rings round the neck and belly. The Jerseys are plain, low-hipped, heavy-looking, squatting on the table. And to Jersey only belongs the similar conception but mostly slimmer, pretty, lidless measures.

In form these flagons owe all to the south of the Channel. The Guernsey would seem to have been inspired either by Dutch design, or perhaps by one or two types in the northern regions of France, Falaise in particular. The Jersey has a strong affinity with the rather dumpy Normandy flagons. Their onset would seem to have been about 1700.

There are several sub-types in both islands, which have been identified and classified as the result of observation of minute detail, the dating being confirmed by research into the makers and other records and parallels. While the lidded flagons are, not unnaturally, more common in the larger sizes, the similar lidless (measures) are generally scarcer and reasonably appear only in the smaller sizes. These measures appear to have run from c.1780–c.1900. As for capacities, the rarer ones are rather a jungle, certainly demonstrating both islands' different standards, and possibly both Old English Wine Standard and Old Ale Standard, finally to home in on Imperial. Wear and tear, initial inaccuracies, induced inaccuracies and the possibility of the intrusion of French measures make certainty of analyses of measurements very nebulous indeed. Woolmer, a Jersey man himself, points out how very strongly individualistic and close knit the islanders are both as a whole, and per island, giving many instances pertinent to this distinctive pewter. What is common in both types is the approximate similarity of outline, the heart- or leaf-shaped lid, the (continental) twin-acorn thumbpiece and the solid handle. But there are many fascinating details, even down to the decoration on the hinge pin, which are important to dating and maker—and speak volumes on Woolmer and Arkwright's work.

The Jersey measures alone (and nearly all do) bear verification marks, of which the majority are GR crowned, perpetuated from about 1727 (George II), right through until ER (Edward VII). Then a reversion to GR crowned, with J or G underneath, for Jersey and Guernsey respectively. These were used through George V and George VI reigns. And now we have EIIR. Since the flagons were not measures, only a few (accepted as such) bear verifications, but those of Guernsey which did, used two stamps—a five-petalled rose and a sheaf fleur-de-lys—both of which were applied to the same pieces. This is rare, and probably dates from 1832. The modern GU (Guernsey) stamp probably dates from 1917.

13. British Pewter in New England
by Ian D. Robinson

This chapter is intended to provide a survey of the British pewter likely to be found in the United States today. It is based on the writer's collecting experience, primarily in the last 10 years in New England. New England was, with nearby New York and Philadelphia, the most heavily-populated region of colonial America in the seventeenth and eighteenth centuries. This survey deals primarily with makers and forms, assuming that the reader has access to *OP* and *MPM*. At the end of the chapter the bibliography provides key references for those who wish to dig more deeply.

Origin of British pewter in New England
Pewter made in the British Isles forms a large proportion of all the antique pewter found in the United States today. This includes American (and colonial) pewter, along with smaller quantities of 'continental' pewter of the late eighteenth and nineteenth centuries.

Judging from the working dates of the British pewterers whose wares are found most often in New England today, British pewter came to North America in large quantities from the late seventeenth century to about the war of 1812. Certain makers' wares are so frequently seen that there is little doubt that they could be classified as 'export' makers. In addition, smaller quantities of British (and continental, particularly French) pewter were also brought as family possessions by British and European immigrants in the seventeenth, eighteenth and nineteenth centuries. Since the Second World War, American antique dealers and collectors have brought over additional pieces, many of which are now in private collections and museums. Thus, the pieces which are found today could have arrived by any of these routes. Against this, judging from the advertisements in the colonial newspapers, much of the early domestic pewter was sold to local pewterers for melting down and fabrication into new pewter.

The makers and their marks
Today, if one compares the antique British pewter found in Great Britain with the British pewter found in the United States, the distribution of makers is not the same. Nearly all the British pewter found in the United States has marks of eighteenth century pewterers, with a very few from the late seventeenth century and with some nineteenth-century makers, especially James Yates pots and measures, and James Dixon's Britannia. Approximately ninety makers account for over ninety percent of the British pewter in the United States. Furthermore, nearly all the marks on this pewter are attributable to known makers, with several notable exceptions which will be discussed below. Pewter by makers listed in *OP* or *MPM* from no. 5374 onwards is

quite scarce in the United States, unlike Great Britain. In the United States, however, there are quite a few marks of *known* British makers unrecorded in *OP*. Many appear to be marks only used on 'export' pewter. The fact that these are not recorded in *OP* suggests that most of these were never seen by Cotterell. The inclusion of many of these in *MPM* and *MPM Addenda* has gone a long way to correcting this deficiency. The collector in America, therefore, has a much shorter list to consider when seeking to identify the maker of a piece of British pewter. This list is based on pewter which I have seen in antique shows, auctions, collections and museums in New England in the past 10 years.

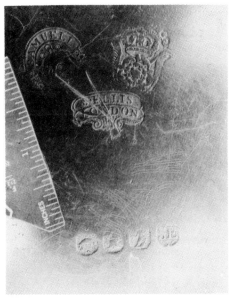

137a   On an 8¼in single-reed plate by Samuel Ellis. Note one dot in name with London label. Also note the mould defect in the word London which appears in some but not all pieces with this mark. *c.*1721–64 or 1754–86.

137b   On an 8½in single-reed plate by Samuel Ellis. Note two dots in name with London label. Recorded under *OP*1547. *c.*1721–64 or 1754–86.

In the case of those makers who struck their touch mark on the London touch plate the date of striking is used in my list as the beginning-working date. In many cases, the ending-working date is not certain. Subsequent research, chiefly by Cotterell himself and Ronald Michaelis, has provided rather more information about the working dates than *OP* gives, and this has been used on the list. Note the large proportion of Bristol makers, who account for perhaps twenty-five percent of the British pewter found in New England.

Frequently there was more than one maker of the same name, often father and son. Among those are Samuel Ellis and Richard King for whom the correct attribution of the marks of these particular export makers is, I feel, a little uncertain. Care should be taken in assigning dates to pieces by these and any other makers with the same names. For example, some of the marks assigned in *OP* to Richard King Jr may have been used

176

by his father. Illustrated is one of the problems with two different Samuel Ellis London labels, only one of which is recorded in *OP*. Furthermore, 'hallmarks' do not necessarily indicate the maker of a piece, although this is normally so. This is particularly troublesome in the case of the Samuel Ellis 'hallmarks', which are found not only with the touch marks of Samuel Ellis, but also with those of Thomas Swanson, and Fasson and Sons. The S. Ellis mark of *MPM* 1547 is probably a correct assignment to *OP* 1547 as it has been found with the 'hallmarks' of Robert Iles (*OP* 2522) who died in 1735, and also on a spire flagon dated 1743.

Another problem of special importance to collectors of British pewter in the United States is the assignment of the working dates of John Townsend and his successors. John Townsend struck his touch in 1748 but entered into a series of partnerships of somewhat uncertain working dates before his death in 1801. The partnership with Thomas Compton alone probably accounts for ten percent of all the marked British pewter to be found in New England today. Hence the dates of this partnership are of special interest. The dates of the partnership with R. Reynolds (*OP* 4797), which is reported in *OP* as 1766–77, seem credible but the dates in *OP* for his other partnerships with Thomas Giffen and his son-in-law Thomas Compton have been questioned.[1] I have used the proposed dates even though they are not consistent with information in *OP* which states that Townsend and Giffen were working in 1793. It is possible that John Townsend had several simultaneous partnerships. Townsend & Giffen used the Fenchurch Street label also recorded in *OP* for 4795 and 4800. The issue is somewhat further clouded by the listing of a second John Townsend (*OP* 4796) and a Mary Townsend (*OP* 4798), who may have been the daughter of John Townsend and the wife of Thomas Compton. John Townsend was in the United States for 2 years beginning in the summer of 1785.

One other maker whose dates are now in question, due to the use of the marks by others, is James Yates whose mark is now known to have been used 1860–95 instead of 1800–40.

138 On a 16½in single-reed dish with no maker's name but with Bush and Perkins 'hallmarks', London label spelt with a Q, and waisted rose-and-crown marks. (Note attribution to Robert Bush Senior or Robert Bush & Co. in *Addenda*.) The same marks have been seen on a 9in single-reed plate but without any 'hallmarks'. *c*. 1770–80.

Some of the makers in this list are not nearly as common in Great Britain as in the United States. Among these are Edgar Curtis and Co., George Grenfell, Alexander Hamilton, Philip Matthews, Townsend & Giffen, W.S. (*MPM*5962b) and 'sheaf of wheat' (*MPM* 6245).

British pewter 'hallmarks' are usually found with a maker's touch mark struck on the piece. However, a significant number of plain-rimmed and single-reeded plates and dishes are seen without touch marks but with a 'waisted' rose-and-crown mark, usually double struck, in combination with the 'hallmarks' of four different Bristol makers or

177

only with a London label. Although they are usually only on flatware, I have seen these marks on an inkstand. These combinations are seen today on both sides of the Atlantic. These makers account for perhaps five percent of the eighteenth-century flatware found in New England and the reason for the lack of the touch mark has not been suggested. The 'hallmarks' found so far include: Ash & Hutton, Burgum & Catcott, Bush & Perkins and T. & W. Willshire (*OP* 5203). The collector of British pewter in the United States should be aware of the use of the rose and crown on colonial pewter until the time of the revolution. Such pewter commands a healthy price in America. I am *not*, however, suggesting that the dishes with the waisted rose-and-crown marks were made in British America.

139   On a 15in single-reed dish with no maker's name but with London label in a serrated rectangle, and waisted rose-and-crown marks. *c*.1760–90.

The chart shows the working dates of the makers in the check list, plotted in order of initial working dates. (Makers with only a single known date are excluded.) This bar graph is useful, in combination with the diagrams in the chapter '1710–1825', to isolate quickly the probable makers of a piece found in the United States. It will be seen that the number of frequently-found makers reached a peak of about thirty around 1750 or 1760 and declined after that until the early nineteenth century. During the period of decline, there was a simultaneous build up in the output of colonial and American pewterers.

Check list of makers of British pewter most frequently found in the United States
(In date sequence)

Name	Location	Approximate working dates	OP/MPM Number	Relative abundance
John Cave I	Bristol	1650–1690	857	Scarce
Daniel Ingole	London	1658–1691 (died)	2538	Scarce
William Withers I	London	1655–1678 (died)	5242	?
Erasmus Dole, Sr	Bristol	1660–1682 (died)	1409	Scarce
Erasmus Dole, Jr	Bristol	1680–1697	1410	Scarce
Col John Shorey I	London	1683–1721	4262	Scarce
William Withers II	London	1685–1725	5243	Scarce
IF	—	*c*.1690–1730	(Laughlin 585/*MPM* 5595)	Scarce
William Eddon	London	1690–1745	1503	Common
Edward Leapidge I	London	1699–1727	2893	?
James Hitchman	London	1701–1736	2340	Common
John Cave II	Bristol	*c*.1705	858	?

7 (a) Five PIPs (pre-Imperial pots) — Bewdley, Bristol, London and East Riding being represented. All *c.* 1800-1820.

(b) Rather dramatic display of presumably late nineteenth century die-stamped dolls house tea set (the d'oily is 9 inches in diameter).

8 (a) Inkstand — very rare in 'full colour'. The japanning has crazed a little. Unidentified maker. c. 1825.

(b) Two of the later, excellent Scottish measures, Edinburgh and Glasgow respectively, showing the design credit to the bellied and baluster inspiration. These were made mostly through the last threequarters of the nineteenth century.

Name	Location	Approximate working dates	OP/MPM number	Relative abundance
John Shorey, Jr II	London	1708–1732	4263	Common
Henry Sewdley	London	1709–1740	4193	Scarce
Spackman & Grant	London	1709–1758	4435	Scarce
Timothy Fly	London	1712–1737	1704	Scarce
Richard Going	Bristol	1715–1766 (dead)	1909	Common
William Hulls	London	1718–1768 (died)	2460	Scarce
Thomas Stevens	London	1720–1750	4513	Scarce
John Langford I	London	1720–1757 (died)	2823[a]	Common
George Lowes	Newcastle	1720–1765 (died 1774)	3001	Scarce
Samuel Ellis I	London	1721–1764 (died 1773)	1547	Extremely common
Richard King III (father)	London	1722–1757 (died)	2749	Common
John Watts I	London	1725–1765 (died)	4991	Common
Edward Leapidge II	London	c.1728	2894	Scarce
Alexander Hamilton	London	1728–1755	2098	Common
Robert Sadler	Newcastle	1730–1780	4088	Scarce
John Fasson I	London	1731–1769	1635	Common
Edward York	London	1733–1776 (died)	5358	Scarce
Henry Maxted	London	1735–c.1760 (?)	3150	Common
Stephen Cox	Bristol	1735–1754 (died)	1189	Scarce
John Dolbeare	Ashburton	1735–1761 (died)	1408	Scarce
Philip Matthews	London	1736–1755	3135/ (5952a)[b]	Scarce
Henry Little	London	1737–1764 (died)	2948	Scarce
John Shorey III	London	c.1738	4264	?
Francis Piggot I	London	1738–1773	3682	Very common
Henry Joseph	London	1736–1786[c]	2686/5668c, 5706, 5706a, 5747a, 5747ei	Very common
Benjamin Blackwell	London	c.1740	437a	Scarce
Samuel Duncomb	Birmingham	1740–1780	1466	Common
Ash & Hutton	Bristol	1741–1768 (Hutton died)	118	Scarce
Francis Piggot II	London	1741–1784 (died)	3683	Very common
Allen Bright	Bristol Colwell	1742–1763 (died)	574	Common
Richard King, Jr IV	London	1745–1798 (died)	2750	Very common
Sheaf of Wheat	?	c.1745–1800	6245	Common
WS	?	c.1745–1800	5962b	Scarce
John Fasson II	London	1745–1792	1636	Scarce
John Townsend I	London	1748–1766 (died 1801)	4795	Very common
Burford & Green	London	1748–1780	698	Very common
Joseph Spackman	London	1749–1764	4440 (5936g?)	Very common

Name	Location	Approximate working dates	OP/MPM number	Relative abundance
John Watts II	London	1749–1780	4992	?
Henry Appleton	London	1750–1771	98	Scarce
Samuel Ellis, Jr II	London	1754–1786	1548	?
Robert Bush, Sr I	Bristol Bitton	1755–1785	737	Very common
George Grenfell[d]	London	1757–1775 (died 1784)	1994	Very common
William Fasson	London	1758–1800	1639	Common
WN	?	c.1760	5821 (3374?)	Scarce
Thomas Swanson	London	1760–1783 (died)	4593	Very common
No name Rose and Crown	Bristol?	c.1760–c.1790	see text	Very common
William Hogg	Newcastle	1760–1810 (?)	2367 (5694c/d)	Common
Robert & Thomas Porteus	London	c.1762	3732	Scarce
Stephen Maxwell	Glasgow	1763[h]–1800	3153	Scarce
Burgum & Catcott	Bristol, Littledean	1765–1779 (dissolved)	708	Common
Robert Bush & Richard Perkins	Bristol, Bitton	c.1770–1780 (?)	740	Common
John Hudson	London	1771–1829 (died)	2440	Scarce
Richard Yates	London	1775–1807	5344	Very common
Graham & Wardrop	Glasgow	1776–1814[i]	1943	Common
John Townsend & Thomas Giffen	London	1777–1779 (or 1793)	4801/ Laughlin 599	Common
Nathaniel Barber	London	1777–1788 (bankrupt)	250	Scarce
John Townsend II	London	c.1778	4796	?
William Scott III (father)	Edinburgh	1779–1805	4160	Scarce
John Langford II	London	c.1780	2824	Common
Robert Bush & Co. (Robert Bush, James Curtis, and Preston Edgar)	Bristol	1780–1793 (dissolved)	739	Very common
John Townsend & Thomas Compton	London	1780–1801 (John Townsend I died)	4800	Extremely common
Ingram & Hunt	Bewdley	1780–1820	2540a/5708/	Common
I and TF	London?	1783–1797[j]	Jacobs 139	Scarce
Thomas Willshire	Bristol	1785–1825	5202	Scarce
Henry & Richard Joseph	London	1787–1815	2687 (OP only)/5747ei	Common
Edgar Curtis & Co.	Bristol	1793–1801	1266a /1508	Very common
Carpenter and Hamberger	London	1794–c.1817[c]	812	Common
William Scott IV (son)	Edinburgh	1794–c.1826	4161	Scarce
Robert Bush, Jr II	Bristol, Bitton	c.1796–c.1816[f]	738	Scarce
Fasson and Sons	London	1797–1810	1640	Very common
Stephen Maxwell & Co.	Glasgow	c.1800	3154	Scarce

Name	Location	Approximate working dates	OP/MPM number	Relative abundance
Thomas Compton	London	1801–1817 (died)	1063	Common
Thomas and Townsend Compton	London	1801–1817	1064 (hm of 4800)	Very common
Edgar & Son	Bristol	1814–1850	1510	Common
John Yates	Birmingham	1808–1852	5340a	Common
Joseph Austen & Son	Cork	1828–1833 (father died 1845)	153	Common
James Yates	Birmingham	c.1860–1895[g]	5338	Very common
Munster Iron Co.	Cork	1833–1905	3334	Scarce
J. Wylie	Glasgow	1825–c.1850	5323	Scarce
Hale & Sons	Bristol	1800–1850	2070	Scarce
J. Moyes	Edinburgh	c.1850	3317	Scarce

Notes to the checklist of makers

a The I:L mark, frequently found in the United States, has been found with the touch mark of *OP* 2823. See Ronald Michaelis, *P.C.C.A. Bull.* **6**, 211 (1972). It is illustrated in Laughlin (882) where it is erroneously attributed to an American maker.

b See also TS mark on p. 226 of *A History of American Pewter*, by Charles F. Montgomery, Praeger Publishers, 1973.

c Date given by Michaelis but Henry Joseph is known to have worked in partnership with at least one of the Francis Piggots, the second of whom died in 1784. See fig 159b for additional marks of Henry Joseph.

d I have recorded the use by George Grenfell of the Grace Church Street label, recorded in *OP* for Robert and Thomas Porteus (*OP* 3732), successors to Richard King (possibly Richard King IV since Robert Porteus struck his touch in 1762).

e At 25 Haymarket in 1817.

f Partner with William Bush, Jr (*OP* 743) until 1816.

g Listed in 1895 London directory but not 1900.

h On Argyle Street in 1814.

i A freeman in 1763.

j John Fasson (*OP* 1636) and Thomas Fasson (*OP* 1638) have been suggested by Michael Boorer.

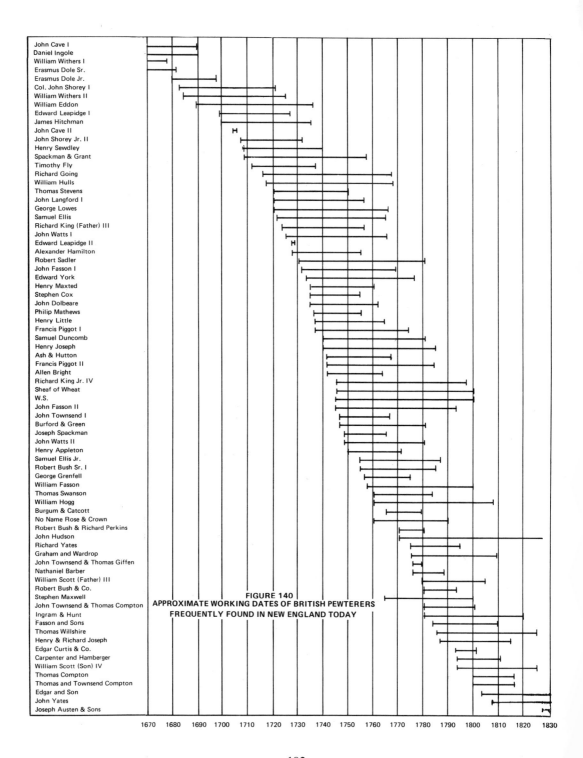

John Cave I
Daniel Ingole
William Withers I
Erasmus Dole Sr.
Erasmus Dole Jr.
Col. John Shorey I
William Withers II
William Eddon
Edward Leapidge I
James Hitchman
John Cave II
John Shorey Jr. II
Henry Sewdley
Spackman & Grant
Timothy Fly
Richard Going
William Hulls
Thomas Stevens
John Langford I
George Lowes
Samuel Ellis
Richard King (Father) III
John Watts I
Edward Leapidge II
Alexander Hamilton
Robert Sadler
John Fasson I
Edward York
Henry Maxted
Stephen Cox
John Dolbeare
Philip Mathews
Henry Little
Francis Piggot I
Samuel Duncomb
Henry Joseph
Ash & Hutton
Francis Piggot II
Allen Bright
Richard King Jr. IV
Sheaf of Wheat
W.S.
John Fasson II
John Townsend I
Burford & Green
Joseph Spackman
John Watts II
Henry Appleton
Samuel Ellis Jr.
Robert Bush Sr. I
George Grenfell
William Fasson
Thomas Swanson
William Hogg
Burgum & Catcott
No Name Rose & Crown
Robert Bush & Richard Perkins
John Hudson
Richard Yates
Graham and Wardrop
John Townsend & Thomas Giffen
Nathaniel Barber
William Scott (Father) III
Robert Bush & Co.
Stephen Maxwell
John Townsend & Thomas Compton
Ingram & Hunt
Fasson and Sons
Thomas Willshire
Henry & Richard Joseph
Edgar Curtis & Co.
Carpenter and Hamberger
William Scott (Son) IV
Thomas Compton
Thomas and Townsend Compton
Edgar and Son
John Yates
Joseph Austen & Sons

FIGURE 140
APPROXIMATE WORKING DATES OF BRITISH PEWTERERS
FREQUENTLY FOUND IN NEW ENGLAND TODAY

1670 1680 1690 1700 1710 1720 1730 1740 1750 1760 1770 1780 1790 1800 1810 1820 1830

The forms

Naturally, the forms one expects to find today are those of the eighteenth century. Thus, one rarely finds forms of the seventeenth century such as broad-rimmed dishes, flat-lidded tankards, seventeenth-century style candlesticks and flagons, knopped spoons or pewter with wriggled engraving. However, there are numerous examples of seventeenth-century British pewter with a history of being in North America in the seventeenth century. For example, the pewter recovered[2] from the sunken city at Port Royal, Jamaica, contains many examples of seventeenth-century British pewter.

141   Porringer by Joseph Pickard, London (*OP* 3665). From a well adjacent to the present Williamsburg, Virginia post office. Discarded about 1725. Note the unusual decorated bracket. Bowl diameter 4¾in.
(Photograph courtesy of the Colonial Williamsburg foundation.)

142a   On an 8in plain-rim plate with the mark of W.S. (*MPM* 5962b) and unrecorded London label. *c.* 1745–1800.

142b   On a 7¹³⁄₁₆in plain-rim plate with unusually clear mark of 'sheaf of wheat' (*MPM* 6245), with unrecorded London label in a serrated rectangle. *c.* 1745–1800.

English seventeenth-century pewter porringers have been recovered[3] from an Indian grave in Rhode Island. Colonial Williamsburg[4] own a porringer, recovered from a well at Williamsburg, Virginia, with the touch of Joseph Pickard (*OP* 3665), who struck his touch in 1693 on the London touchplate. The Museum of Fine Arts in Boston owns[5] a $21\frac{3}{8}$-in broad-rimmed dish (with the maker's mark of *MPM* 6000e) once owned by the inhabitants of Plymouth Colony. The late Percy Raymond described[6] a number of late seventeenth-century and early-eighteenth-century pieces with known Massachusetts provenance. Household inventories showed[7] that there was significant ownership of pewter in the homes of the Virginia Colony. The same source details a 1696 shipment of 'Tinn Wair' to Virginia.

For the pewter collector in the United States I will point out some of the similarities and differences between British and American forms. Although most eighteenth century British pewter forms were also made by American pewterers, there were some forms made by American nineteenth-century pewterers that were not made by British makers. For example, sundials and nineteenth-century whale-oil lamps are relatively common in New England, being of local origin.

Sadware

Sadware (or flatware) is the general term for plates, dishes and basins. Plates run from 7–10in and dishes are over 10in in diameter. Although dishes 18in and over are called chargers in British usage, dishes over 13in are commonly called chargers in New England today. In the case of the following makers in the list, I have seen only sadware: John Dolbeare, Fasson and Sons, Alexander Hamilton, Spackman and Grant, Thomas Swanson, John Watts, WS and 'sheaf of wheat'. The New Hampshire Historical Society owns a bedpan by Thomas Swanson.

Among the makers who appear to have exported only hollow-ware are Carpenter and Hamberger, Philip Matthews and William Scott. William Eddon and William Hogg really belong in the list of hollow-ware makers even though they made a few pieces of flatware, of which I have seen none in New England.

Unlike nearly all the American pewter, British sadware is invariably hammered on the bouge. However, sadware in British America was also hammered. The size of British sadware that I have found in the United States ranged from a $7\frac{1}{4}$in plain-rim plate by Samuel Ellis to a 22in single-reed charger by John Shorey. There are very few larger examples in private collections and museums but most of these probably arrived in the twentieth century. The most common British pewter plate sizes found in New England are $7\frac{5}{8}$in, $7\frac{7}{8}$in, $8\frac{1}{4}$in and $9\frac{3}{8}$in. Dishes are most frequently $11\frac{3}{4}$in, $13\frac{3}{8}$in, $14\frac{7}{8}$in, $16\frac{3}{8}$in, $18\frac{1}{4}$in and $20\frac{1}{4}$in. The largest-size charger usually encountered in New England is $20\frac{1}{4}$in, frequently with 'hallmarks' on the front of the rim indicating that the piece was probably made before about 1735, as a high proportion of the large ones were. Colonial and American pewterers seem not to have made chargers over 20in which is consistent with the fact that most surviving chargers over 22in were made before 1735. Most British flatware found in New England has a single reed but ten or twenty percent have plain rims. One occasionally finds triple-reed chargers and, rarely, a broad-rim charger. Wavy-edged plates of the late eighteenth century also appear but they are more frequently continental than British.

Broad-rimmed seventeenth-century baptismal bowls are a great rarity but an example by Erasmus Dole is illustrated in Laughlin[8]. The eighteenth-century British pewter basins, with their characteristic narrow rim (about $\frac{1}{4}$in), are decidedly more common in New England than in Great Britain. In the past 3 years, I have seen basins by twenty-five makers in the list, including nearly all of the eighteenth century makers designated as very common or extremely common. They were certainly used as baptismal bowls as well as for food and washing. Although John Shorey is recorded[9] as having sold basins in 1723, the earliest marked British narrow-rimmed basin seems to be a 3-pint basin by Adam Bancks (*OP* 222A) and the latest is by Thomas Compton.

John Townsend and his successors account for about one third of all the marked basins in New England. In the case of the Townsend and Compton partnership alone, there are at least eight sizes, including $7\frac{7}{8}$in, $8\frac{1}{8}$in, $10\frac{3}{8}$in, $10\frac{1}{2}$in, $10\frac{7}{8}$in, $11\frac{5}{8}$in, and $11\frac{3}{4}$in. The capacities, measured to the top inside of the bowl (not the outer edge of the rim), usually range from $1\frac{1}{2}$ beer (or ale) pints (a $7\frac{5}{8}$in diameter basin by Robert Bush and Co.) to 9 beer pints (a 13in diameter basin by John Townsend). The smallest that I own is a beer pint ($6\frac{1}{2}$in by Robert Bush) and the largest recorded is a $14\frac{1}{4}$in basin in the collection at Colonial Williamsburg by Richard Foster (*OP* 1733), dated 1768. The Bristol makers generally seem to place their touch in the well and the London makers usually place theirs on the back. There are, however, exceptions to these generalisations. As in the case of other sadware, British basins can usually be distinguished from their American cousins by the hammering of the bouge. The 6-in diameter basin is relatively common in American basins of the nineteenth century but previously unrecorded in British pewter.

Among the basin makers seen in New England are the mysterious WS (*MPM* 5962b) and 'sheaf of wheat' (*MPM* 6245). Both marks are unfamiliar to collectors in Great Britain. However, all the sadware by these makers that I have seen is hammered, suggesting that they are British. The WS mark is recorded on $10\frac{3}{8}$in (marked on the outside bottom) and $11\frac{5}{8}$in basins and on a $7\frac{5}{8}$in plain-rim plate. I have seen the sheaf-of-wheat mark on $6\frac{7}{8}$in and $10\frac{1}{4}$in basins (marked in centre of well), plain-rim plates ($7\frac{13}{16}$in, $8\frac{1}{8}$in) and on a $8\frac{9}{16}$in single-reed plate and a $16\frac{1}{2}$in single-reed charger. The lack of 'hallmarks' on the front of the plates suggests, if British, that they were made after 1735.

Drinking vessels
Although it has been usual in Great Britain to refer to a tankard as a drinking mug or pot with or without a lid, I shall use the term tankard to refer to drinking vessels with lids only and limit the term pots to drinking vessels without lids.

Although there are a small number of British pewter flat-lid tankards in private collections and museums in America, nearly all were brought across the Atlantic in this century. One is most unlikely to encounter a flat-lid tankard in New England today. However, there is a flat-lid tankard wriggled with a portrait of William III by William Eddon which is stated[10] to have an early-eighteenth-century Massachusetts provenance. The only other maker of flat-lid tankards in the list is Erasmus Dole. There is a flat-lid tankard by this maker in a private New England collection. I know of no example by this maker in England.

One is much more likely to see dome-lid tankards and pots by many of the makers listed. Many of these tankards were used in place of flagons in New England communion services as well as in taverns and homes. Illustrated are two fine dome-lidded tankards, typical of the British tankards found in New England today. The first has the PM London mark (*MPM* 3135), now attributed to Philip Matthews of London, as well as a WR crowned mark. The other popular style of tankard, the tulip shape, is by Ash and Hutton. Both forms were made by a large number of London and Bristol 'export' pewterers, judging from the number that have survived in New England.

143 Flat-lid tankard with wriggled portrait of William
III, *c.*1695. First three h.m.'s on lid are those of William
Eddon. Indistinct touch and fourth h.m. Owner's initials
may be those of John Worthington, of Springfield (Mass.)
First Church. Thumbpiece replaced. Overall height 7¼in.
Base diameter 5¼in. (Photograph courtesy of the Colonial
Williamsburg Foundation.)

William Eddon and Richard Going are also particularly well represented among the
twenty-five or so makers of dome-lid tankards often found in New England. Very
likely some were used as communion flagons. Some had banding around the base,
designed to give the pieces importance.

Pots and beakers were often used in place of chalices in communion services. For
example[11], U-shaped pots by William Eddon, dated 1742, belonged to the communion
service of the First Church of Springfield, Massachusetts. Pots by Robert Bush were
also part of the same service. Beakers by the John Townsend partnerships, often found
in New England, were also probably used for this purpose. Many of the British pewter
pots found in New England today are twentieth-century imports, chiefly of the James
Yates tapered drum (usually called truncated cone in Great Britain) variety. However,
there are many desirable pre-Imperial pots to be found. I recently acquired two
eighteenth century U-shaped pots in New England which are illustrated. Both have a
WR crowned stamp. The half pint, which came from New Hampshire, has the
'hallmarks' of Philip Matthews, who worked until about 1755. The pint, without a

144 Dome-lid tankard with the mark of Philip Matthews, London (*MPM* 3135). Height to lip 5½in *c.* 1736–55.

145 Tulip-shaped dome-lid tankard with circular lamb and flag touch of Ash and Hutton. Height to lip 8⅛in. *c.* 1741–88.

146 Pair of dome-lid tankards with touch and 'hallmarks' of Townsend and Compton, probably made for use as communion flagons. Overall height 7¾in. *c.* 1780–1801.

visible maker's mark, is identical to the William Eddon pots mentioned above. This appeared on Cape Cod, at a very modest price. Note the early use of the ball terminal on a pot.

More common than eighteenth-century U-shaped pots are those with a tapered drum such as the plain-bodied quart by Townsend & Compton. This has the same WR crowned mark seen on all Townsend & Compton pots. I have the same WR crowned mark on a pint pot by Thomas Compton, suggesting that this was applied by the maker. Another of the same type by William Hogg but without a WR crowned mark is shown. The hollow-cast single-curved handles on both quarts have a 'tongued' thumbrest and an 'attention' terminal. As in Great Britain, British eighteenth-century pots with ball terminal (sometimes called 'bud' in America) handles are scarce. Usually these are tapered-drum pots by Robert Bush, Edgar Curtis & Co., Graham & Wardrop, and William Hogg. Examples of tapered-drum pots with a ball terminal are also found by the nineteenth century maker Thomas Holdgate (*MPM* 5687).

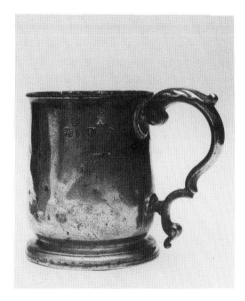 

147 Half-pint U-shaped pot with 'hallmarks' of Philip Matthews and WR crowned mark. No mark on inside bottom where TS relief-cast initials (Laughlin mark 595) are usually found on these mugs. Notice early use of acanthus leaf on a pewter handle. Height to lip 3½in. *c.*1736–55 if maker is Philip Matthews.

148 Pint U-shaped pot with WR crowned mark. No visible maker's mark but identical to examples by William Eddon. Found in Massachusetts. 4½in height to lip. *c.*1740.

The third form of eighteenth-century British pots occasionally seen in New England is the tulip shape. An example by John Townsend is illustrated in an article [12] on this maker. I have seen other tulip-shaped pots by Samuel Ellis, Robert Sadler, and Ingram & Hunt. Finally an example of Scottish pots which are to be found in New England is shown. Note the unusual hollow handle. This one is by Graham & Wardrop and is lacking a WR crowned mark. As far as I know, the WR crowned mark was not used on

149 Quart pot by Townsend and Compton with
WR crowned mark. 6in height to lip. *c.*1780–1801.

150 Quart pot with WH mark (*MPM* 5694 c,d) on
body, probably William Hogg. 5¾in height to lip.
Half-pint pot with same mark on inside bottom and
Cumberland verification stamps. No WR crowned
mark on either. *c.*1760–1810.

151 On quart pot.

American pewter pots but is found on many of the eighteenth-century British pots
found in New England. Although the mark was used on drinking vesels in Great
Britain until about 1825, its use on 'export' pots after 1776 may have declined. It seems
to be absent on 'export' pots by makers who worked outside London after the
American revolution but more research is needed on this point.

It is worth mentioning that most surviving American pots made in New England
have tapered-drum bodies dating from about 1780 until well into the nineteenth
century. There are only a few examples of the tulip-shaped body made in the last half of

189

the eighteenth century in America. There appear to be no American pots of the U-shaped form which were made in England around 1740 (and again about 1810–20). We do not find English barrel-shaped pots in New England (they are scarce in England) but an American-made example is known.

152 Pint pot with partial touch, shown under *MPM* 739 but possibly 737 or 738. No WR crowned mark. Height to lip 4½in. *c.*1780–93.

153 Pint pot by Graham & Wardrop. Height to lip 4½in. *c.*1776–1814.

Porringers

English porringers are decidedly more scarce in America than in England. The few that are seen, usually have bouged and guttered bowls typical of American porringers. They also have a triangular bracket, whereas American porringers vary. The most common handle (or 'ear' as it is known in Great Britain) on British pewter porringers in New England is the 'coronet'. This type is known as a crown handle[13] in America and was also made by a number of American eighteenth and nineteenth century pewterers. It is difficult to say on which side of the Atlantic the coronet handle originated but this handle has been seen on a porringer in England with a flat-bottomed bowl which dates *c.*1690–1720. Most British examples seem to be by mid-eighteenth-century Bristol makers including Allen Bright, Burgum & Catcott, Robert Bush, Stephen Cox and Richard Going. However, an example by Ingram & Hunt of Bewdley is also recorded. Most surviving examples are by Robert Bush. One of a pair by Richard Going is illustrated.

Porringers by Edgar Curtis & Co., with a handle of the type known[14] as 'flower-handle' in America, are found from time to time. This type was also made by American pewterers, particularly in Rhode Island, in large quantities in the second half of the eighteenth century. A rare English example is illustrated, showing a very fine handle. It is by Adam Bancks (*OP* 222A) who died in 1716.

The third type of British pewter porringer handle seen in New England is the geometric-handled[15] porringer, known as 'crescents and crosses'. These are usually by John Langford Senior.

A few English commemorative pewter porringers have been found in the United States with histories of lengthy ownership.[16]

154 Coronet-handled porringer by Richard Going. Bowl diameter 4¹³/₁₆in. c.1715–66.

155 Rare flower-handled porringer by Adam Bancks. Bowl diameter 4⅞in. c.1690–1716.

Measures

Although English pewter lidless bellied measures of the nineteenth century are relatively common in New England, most were probably brought from England in the twentieth century. Considerably more interesting are the eighteenth century lidded baluster measures. Most are double volute but there are a few buds by Thomas Matthews (*OP* 3138/5800) and IF (Laughlin 585). Many of the double-volute measures have incised stamped initials CM or PM without a maker's touch mark. These same initials are found repeatedly, but others are found as well. These marks seem to be rare or absent on double-volute measures found in England. These may be capacity seals such as Colony (or Commonwealth?) of Massachusetts or Province of Maine (until 1820). There is only a small number of makers of double-volute measures, all British. Among the makers I have seen in New England are John Fasson (*OP* 1635), William Fasson and Thomas Stevens. (As far as I know, the only form that I have seen by Thomas Stevens is double-volute measures.) The double-volute measure is certainly one of the finest forms in British pewter.

Perhaps because of the large number of nineteenth-century Irish immigrants, a relatively large number of nineteenth-century Irish measures are found in the Boston area. These include the popular haystack measures and the lidless balusters. In addition a few nineteenth-century pots by Joseph Austen & Son and Munster Iron Co. of Cork are found.

Scottish measures, particularly tappit hens, are very scarce in New England. Probably most were brought over by immigrants or in the twentieth century.

191

156 Half-gallon bud baluster measure with touch of I.F. (Laughlin *585/MPM* 5595). Note pip on thumbpiece. Found in the Ashley River below Dorchester, approximately 30 miles northwest of Charlestown, South Carolina. Overall height 11⅛in. *c.*1690–1730. (Photograph courtesy of the Colonial Williamsburg Foundation.)

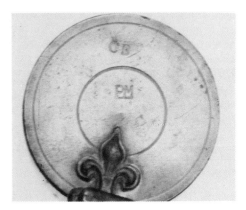

157 CM and PM stamps, frequently found on English lidded baluster measures in New England, in these cases on double-volute measures found in New England, *c.*1740–1800.

158 Pint double-volute measure by John Fasson (*OP* 1635). Found in Massachusetts. Overall height 6in. *c.*1731–69.

Teapots

Pear-shaped and drum-shaped pewter teapots made by a large number of eighteenth-century English makers exist in private collections in New England. They are scarcely ever seen in England, suggesting that they were primarily made for export. Generally,

159a Drum-shaped teapot by Henry Joseph. Wooden lid finial not original Height overall 5⅛in. *c.* 1740–85. (Collection of William O. Blaney.)

159b Touch of Henry Joseph on drum-shaped teapot. This shows coronet and crowned × over the HJ mark shown in *OP* 5747A. Must be a later touch than *MPM* 5706 (transferred to *OP* 2686 in *Addenda*).

193

in addition to the maker's touch mark, a crowned quality mark is found stamped on the outside bottom. Among the frequently-seen teapot makers are Robert Bush, Bush & Co., Edgar Curtis & Co., Samuel Ellis, William Fasson. George Grenfell, Ingram & Hunt, Henry Joseph, Francis Piggot, Joseph Spackman, John Townsend, and Townsend & Compton. Recent research[17] on the forms and marks of Henry Joseph reveals at least eight different teapots by this maker alone.

160   Pear-shaped teapot by John Townsend. *c.* 1748–66.
(Collection of Oliver Deming.)

Communion flagons
One rarely sees seventeenth-century English pewter flagons in New England. Instead, eighteenth-century spire flagons by London makers are relatively common. The inscription on the spire flagon reads: 'SCITVATE NORTH CHVRCH OF CHRIST

161   Inscription on spire flagon with 'hallmarks' of Carpenter and Hamberger (*OP* 812) but probably by Thomas Carpenter (*OP* 811), *c.* 1760. (Collection of Oliver Deming.)

1760' indicating that this one was in use at the peak of the export trade to the colonies. Scituate is a town near Boston. The 'hallmarks' are probably those of Thomas Carpenter (*OP* 811) of London.

Among the British pewter communion pieces in the collection of the New

Hampshire Historical Society[18], there are spire flagons by Carpenter & Hamberger, Richard Yates, Pitt & Floyd (*OP* 3695), and Samuel Ellis. I have seen other spire flagons by John Shorey, Henry Joseph and WN, (*MPM* 5821 possibly *OP* 3374). There is also a Britannia flagon by James Dixon and Son in the collection. All of these New Hampshire pieces have documented ecclesiastical use. There seem to be few marked examples of English chalices in New England although there are examples by Edgar Curtis & Co. and they are known to have been made by William Eddon.[19]

Spoons

British-made spoons, both pewter and latten, can be found quite often in New England. However, pewter spoons with knop-decorated stems which are prior to 1660, are not usually seen. Latten spoons have been dug up in numerous sites in New England, primarily in Massachusetts. Among the types found[20] are seal tops, puritans, and trifids.

There are a very large number of unmarked pewter wavy-end and round-end spoons to be found in America. Most may be of modern origin. Bronze spoon moulds for these types of spoons appear much more frequently in New England than in Great Britain. I have seen a number of round-end spoons by Richard King and Samuel Ellis. However,

162 7¾in round-end spoon
by Samuel Ellis (*MPM* 1547),
probably *c*. 1721–64.

163 7¼in round-end spoon
with a caricature of 'Farmer'
George III. No maker's mark
but cast initials IH. *c*. 1810.

195

one is more likely to find fiddleback round-end spoons and ladles by nineteenth-century Birmingham makers, especially John Yates and Thomas Yates (*OP* 5346). In New England one also sees round-end spoons and ladles by Thomas Menut of Montreal, *c.*1810, who seems to be the only identified Canadian pewterer.[21] A delightful round-end spoon is illustrated with a caricature of 'Farmer' George III, one of several seen recently in New England.

Other forms

There are a number of other British forms which one sees repeatedly in New England but space does not permit detailed discussion. Among these are forms known as broth bowls by makers such as Henry Joseph, Richard King, John Langford and John Townsend. It has recently been suggested[9] that the eighteenth-century term for this form was butter basin, judging from an invoice of Samuel Ellis to the London Company of Clothworkers.

164 2¼in long snuffbox with wigged man on lid, probably 'Farmer' George III, *c.*1810.

165 Inhaler by Carpenter and Hamberger. Overall height 5in. *c.*1794–1817.

Mention should be made of the number of pewter snuffboxes found in the United States. Although many may have been imported in the twentieth century, the large numbers suggest that they were exported to the United States in the early nineteenth century; some are French. Dating is, of course, difficult because of the rarity of marked examples.

A fine pewter inhaler by Carpenter & Hamberger is illustrated in this book. American-made examples of the late eighteenth century have been illustrated in books on American pewter but, until now, inhalers have not appeared in the books on British pewter. This example was found in New England.

Fakes

Fakes of British pewter are chiefly of seventeenth-century forms and not of the eighteenth century which constitutes most of the British pewter in the United States. Probably the most frequent fakes of British pewter in the United States are Irish

196

haystack measures and an occasional tappit hen with Bush & Perkins 'hallmarks'. There has been significant faking of American marks, however, and it is amazing that so many collectors in America have chemically overcleaned their pewter, including their British pewter, resulting in what is known as the American finish. The removal of all traces of the metal oxides results in the loss of one of the most important clues to authenticity.

Bibliography

1 SWAIN, CHARLES V., 'Townsend & Compton', *Pewter Collectors Club Bulletin*, **6**, 288–89 (1973).

2 SPENCER DAVIES, P. 'Seventeenth Century Pewter from the Sunken City of Port Royal, Jamaica', *Connoisseur*, January, 1975.

3 MICHAELIS, RONALD F., 'Back from the Dead, English Pewter Porringers from a Red Indian Grave in Rhode Island, USA', *Apollo*, October, 1950.

4 HUME, IVOR NOËL, 'The Wells of Williamsburg', *Williamsburg Archeological Series No. 4* (1969).

5 FAIRBANKS, JONATHAN, *American Pewter in the Museum of Fine Arts Boston*, (1974).

6 Catalogue of Harvard Tercentenary Exhibition, July 25 to September 21, 1936, (Cambridge, Mass.; Harvard College, 1936).

7 BAILEY, WORTH, 'Notes on The Use of Pewter in Virginia During the Seventeenth Century', *William and Mary Quarterly*.

8 LAUGHLIN, LEDLIE IRWIN, *Pewter in America*, Vol I, pl. 244, Barre Publishers (1969).

9 HOMER, R. F., 'Clothworkers Pewter', *Pewter Society Journal*, Spring 1977.

10 RAYMOND, PERCY E., 'Ancestral Pewter', *American Collector*, August 1947.

11 HOWE, FLORENCE THOMPSON, 'Some Early New England Church Pewter', *Antiques*, September, 1932.

12 MONTGOMERY, CHARLES F., 'John Townsend, English Quaker with American Connections', *Pewter Collectors Club Bulletin*, **5**, pp. 23–26 (Dec., 1964).

13a WOLF, MELVYN D., 'Crown-Handled Porringers—A Method of Identification', *Pewter Collectors Club Bulletin*, **7**, 54–65, (1975).

13b RAYMOND, PERCY E., 'Crown-Handled Porringers', *Pewter Collectors Club Bulletin*, **39**, 144–9 (1958).

14 RAYMOND, PERCY E., 'American Pewter Porringers with Flowered Handles', *Pewter Collectors Club Bulletin*, **40**, 1–9, (1959).

15 YOUNG, M. ADA (STEVIE), 'I : L—Again!', *Pewter Collectors Club Bulletin*, **6**, 166–8, (1971). *See also* Ledlie Irwin Laughlin, *Pewter in America*, Vol. III, pl. 882, Barre Publishers, (1971).

16 MICHAELIS, RONALD F., 'Royal Portraits and Pewter Porringers', *Antiques*, January, 1958.

17 HILT, WAYNE A., 'Henry Joseph—Master Pewterer', *Pewter Collectors Club Bulletin*, **7**, 293–300, (1978).

18 CARTER, WINTHROP L. AND ROBINSON, IAN D., 'British Pewter Forms: 1600's to 1930', Catalogue of an exhibition at the University of New Hampshire, 1976.

19 SUTHERLAND-GRAEME, A. Capt., 'William Eden, Master Pewterer', *Connoisseur*, April, 1938.

20 RAYMOND, PERCY E., 'Latten Spoons of The Pilgrims'. *Antiques*, March, (1952).

21 RAYMOND, PERCY E., 'Montreal Pewter Spoons and Ladles', *American Collector*, April 1948.

14. Recognising European Pewter

by D. A. Mundill

Hon. Librarian, The Pewter Society

It may seem unusual to include a chapter on European pewter in a book about British pewter, but many collectors have pieces of continental origin and are unable to ascribe these pieces to a particular country, let alone to a maker, or perhaps they are not very interested in these pieces and cast them aside as 'foreign'. Also it may help to differentiate the provenance of some pieces which might be taken as British. These notes cannot hope to solve the problems collectors may have, but only to whet their appetite to seek further, to kindle more interest and also to encourage them to collect continental pewter with pleasure.

The subject of European pewter covers such a vast area and so many different ethnic habits and traditions that the variety of shapes and styles to be found will perforce also be vast. The numerous marks encountered will also be perplexing and may demoralise the collector unless he has some guide to help him.

The pewter craft developed in Europe very much along the same lines as it did in Britain. It is very difficult to say who started first and where and when pewter making was revived during the early Middle Ages. One fact that we must bear in mind is that the regulations of the craft were governed by hundreds of guilds as opposed to the situation in our country where there was one very powerful company and only a few provincial ones.

The main pewter-producing countries in Europe have one type of ware which we do not find in Britain and that is the manufacture of 'noble pewter' — 'edelzinn' in the Germanic group of countries and 'Orféverie d'Etain' in France. These pieces were of such extravagant design and craftsmanship, usually relief cast, that they were made by pewterers more akin to the silver and goldsmiths craft. The principal makers during this period, mid sixteenth to mid seventeenth century, were François Briot, Caspar Ederlein and Isaac Faust.

It is unlikely that such pieces would be found in the antique shops where collectors would hope to find a bargain, so let us consider the type of pewterware that one might come across.

Sadware or flatware, (plates, dishes and suchlike) are perhaps a good place to start, because some continental plates are similar to English plates, and this could cause confusion. British plates as a rule are hammered around the bouge and although the hammer marks are always removed to a certain extent by the use of the lathe, when looking at the under surface of the plate and playing the light upon it, the hammer marks are still discernible. On the other hand continental plates are moulded only and completed on the lathe. Also the rims of continental plates differ from their English counterparts, latterly curving more in the horizontal section.

The manner in which owners marked their pewterware may on occasions give us a clue in differentiating. English plates of the period *c.* 1690–1750 often bear the well-known triads, for example, D $\overset{\text{M}}{\text{A}}$ whereas the continental counterpart would be A W—D M the 'W' being the maiden surname. The wavy-edged plates, which in my opinion originated from and were very popular in Europe, did not last long when introduced into England, but notice the bouge, the owners' initials, if any, and the touch mark distribution.

Continental drinking vessels do not seem to compare with British tavern mugs and tankards. Lidded tankards abound in Germany in particular and in other northern countries, but were used much more frequently as commemorative and presentation pieces, particularly as 'shooting prizes', rather than just drinking vessels in hostelries where earthenware mugs would have been used, some perhaps with pewter lids. There appears to be a lack of similar articles in France where wine was the main beverage and for this purpose glass vessels would have been used.

The north-western towns in Europe produced some very attractive lidded tankards demonstrating many of the pewtering skills, such as relief casting and punch-work

166 Showing the similarities between a Guernsey measure and the measure of Falaise.

199

decoration. Many tankards have thumbpieces with a ball on top and this usually indicates that they originated from ports in the Hanseatic League.

Although France was not prolific in pewter tankards, the wine measures from which wine was dispensed deserve special mention. These measures, as that is what they really were, could be described less coldly as flagons. Before the metric system was introduced every town or district had a measure of its own and the shape of these measures and capacities varied from place to place. It is possible to make a substantial collection of these measures alone.

The Channel Islands, due to their close proximity to France, used similar measures which could be confused with French measures. The measure of Falaise is very similar to that of Guernsey and at times the Normandy measure has been confused with the Scottish tappit hen.

The metric system
The introduction of the metric system in France and the rest of Europe unfortunately did away with the use of the individual shapes of flagons and these were replaced by the rather plain cylindrical measures which were not only used in France but in many other continental countries.

The metric system was introduced in 1793, but merchants and shopkeepers would not comply with the new regulations until new laws, compelling them to do so, were eventually introduced in 1840. The previous measures or pichets remained in use unofficially and were still being manufactured, but they were no longer marked by weights and measures officials.

167 A group of metric measures showing (a) with collar and lid outside the collar. (b) with collar and lid inside the collar. (c) with collar and no lid. (d) plain-rimmed top.

The metric measures are to be found in the following shapes: plain-rimmed top; plain-rimmed top with a lid; with a collar; with a lid inside the collar; with a collar and a lid outside the collar.

The lidded types have slightly-dished lids and erect thumbpieces. The handles are rectangular and the measures are to be found in the following sizes: double litre; litre; demi litre; double décilitre; décilitre; demi décilitre; double centilitre; centilitre.

The Germanic countries did not conform to the former sizes but used a series which divided into half and quarter litres.

The various continental countries using the metric measures have different methods of verification. In France a different letter is used each year and is always a Roman capital letter; in Belgium a Greek capital letter is used and in Holland the capital letters are in script. Variations of handles and shapes make these measures interesting and collectable. They were used as late as the first quarter of the twentieth century and are still to be found at reasonable prices.

Flagons

Flagons in central and eastern Europe seem mainly to have served as presentation and commemorative pieces. Many flagons were made individually for particular customers. These flagons are very elaborate, incorporating some relief work, and are usually mounted on three feet in the shape of spheres or brackets. The lids very often have cast figures holding a large scroll upon which details of the presentation are engraved. These flagons invariably have some connection with guilds, corporations or societies.

In the south and south-east, the flagons are usually plainer and very often the body is slightly concave. Bulbous or pear-shaped flagons are usually found in northern France and the Low Countries. In Holland and northern Germany these flagons are also used for ecclesiastical purposes.

Marks

The marks to be found on European pewter are numerous and no rules apply, that is to say, that the crowned rose, the angel and the hallmarks are to be found in almost every country. The quality marks were usually the pewterer's hammer (sometimes crowned) and this eventually gave way to a crowned rose or to the angel mark; the hammer mark in some cases was reserved for second class pewter.

A crowned rose was originally used to put on pewter articles which were imported from England in the hope that the public would buy the pewter manufactured locally since the imports were having an adverse effect upon trade. As the imported pewter was considered of superior quality, the crowned rose became a mark of quality and also became the standard mark of the pewterers who placed their initials outside the device, and many years later the initials were placed inside the crown. This type of touch can be found in most European countries but was extensively used in Flanders.

The angel mark originated as a pun of the words 'engels' (meaning angels) and 'English'. This was also used as a quality mark sometimes including the town mark as well as a pewterer's mark all in one.

The crowned X mark has its origin in Nuremberg where the standard composition was ten parts of tin to one part of lead. This became a sign of quality to be used all over the continent and was known as 'test pewter'.

The town mark is sometimes used on its own or in a combination with the pewterer's touch mark to make one mark. In Germany it is the custom to use three marks to denote good quality pewter and in this case one mark would be the town mark, and the other two marks, which could be identical, would be the pewterer's initials or touch, and so the three marks together denoted quality.

The 'hallmarks', that is, four smaller marks in a row, to simulate silver marks, are to

168 Three German marks denoting quality. Showing the town mark of Lubeck and the pewterers' mark of Johan Gottfried Hutting and 33 for 1633, the date of the ordinance stating the quality of pewter to be used in Lubeck.

be found in most countries and are usually slightly larger than the English pseudo 'hallmarks'.

Labels are also used to indicate the provenance of the tin used or the quality of the pewter. Examples of these are as follows:

Fein Zinn	Germany
Engels Block Zinn	Germany
Engels Hard Tin	Holland
Estain Fin	France
Etain Fin	France
Etain Sonnant	France

169 Three Austrian quality marks showing the angel mark of quality. An unusual version of a rose and the name of the pewterer Joseph Danzl of Vienna, c. 1820.

Other marks indicating quality are the large crowned F which is used in Switzerland and also in France, where it has palm leaves on either side. The single C or double C back to back and a date would denote pewter conforming to an ordinance of that date, and also that a tax had been paid; examples are to be found in Paris and other provincial cities in France.

A date in the touch mark can mean the date of becoming a master pewterer, which is the same as receiving the Freedom in England. The date could also mean that all pewter made in a town conforms to a decree of that date. An example of this is Geneva where all good pewter bore the date 1609 in the touch.

170 The crowned rose used extensively in the Low Countries with the pewterer's initials in the crown. The town mark of Antwerp showing the castle walls and two hands. The mark of Jan Van Antwerpen, c.1850.

171 Modern reproductions are still being made today and can easily be recognised by the inferior metal containing no tin at all, although some manufacturers are using first-class lead-free metal. Some of the modern marks are illustrated. These marks are mainly found on plates and cylindrical measures.

Town marks are very important in continental pewter collecting because they are so frequently used, and they enable us at least to say that a particular piece came from this or that town. We may not be able to go further than this due to lack of research and due to the fact that records were lost, particularly in Belgium and northern France due to the wars, and so the actual pewterer may remain unknown.

These town marks usually consist of part of the coat of arms of the town, or represent some folkloric connection with the town. The following illustrate this point: Antwerp—Castle walls and two hands; Malines—Bishop holding shield with arms of town; Brussels—St Michael and the devil; Amsterdam—Coat of Arms; Rotterdam—Coat of Arms: Augsberg—Pomegranate.

Touch marks
The individual pewterers' touch marks on continental pewter are to be found in the following books:

Sweden. *Tenngjutare I Sverige* by Birger Bruzeli (1967)

From 1754 to 1912 the marking of pewter in Sweden was controlled by the state. The marks during this period included the quality mark, town mark, pewterer's mark and

172 An Austrian chocolate pot made by Joseph Phillipp Apeller of Innsbruck *c.*1770. The handles of these pots are usually bound with rattan to insulate the handle.

204

the date mark. In some instances, although unofficial, touches incorporating the angel and the crowned rose were used as supplementary marks, and tend to hinder the situation rather than help. This book gives the touches of all the Swedish pewterers during this period as well as their total output by weight of pewter manufactured.

Germany. *Die Deutschen Zinngiesser und Ihre Marken* by Erwin Hintze (1921–26).

The author divided the country into seven sections, thus giving seven volumes. Many areas of central Europe are also included such as parts of Switzerland, Hungary and Austria.

173   A small Flemish measure with spout at front and shell thumbpiece. No maker's mark. *c.*1850.

Switzerland. *Die Zinngiesser der Schweiz und Ihre Werk* by Dr. G. Bossard (1920–34)

France.

The reference work of this country is known as 'Tardy'. This book is well illustrated and has a great number of touch marks which, although useful to determine the area of provenance, are not attributed to any particular maker.

Holland. *Tin en Tinnegieters in Nederland* by B. Dubbe (1979).

This book covers the history of Dutch pewter and includes about 1,500 pewterers and illustrates about 600 touch marks.

A considerable amount of reproduction and false pewter articles have been made and are still being manufactured in European countries. These pieces are in the style of the original pewterware and many are found in Britain. They could have been made some 50 years ago and brought to this country as souvenirs and gifts and frequently appear in provincial auction rooms.

174 A German shooting trophy engraved with wrigglework and made by John Gottfried Hutting of Lubeck. Marks as in fig. 168. *c.* 1829.

Marks which bear the words Fein Zinn in an angel mark with a date 1730 and *no* initials or town mark are to be avoided as well as the crowned rose with initials ND and the town mark of Brussels.

It is hoped that collectors who have found these notes of interest may wish to seek further and look upon their pieces of European pewter with interest and delight.

There is nothing better than seeing pewter and the Victoria and Albert Museum will be found to be of great interest as many fine pieces are displayed there.

In these days of easy travel, a visit to some continental museums could be of benefit. The following museums show a general collection of pewter: Cologne—Kunstgewerbe-museum; Paris—Musée des Arts Décoratifs; Rotterdam—Museum Boymans—Van Beuningen; Ghent—Museum Bijloke.

Some examples from the collection of MM Charles and Philippe Boucaud follow.

175   Flagon from Normandy, with twin acorn thumbpiece. Caen, eighteenth century.

177   Flagon from Austria. Very typical. Eighteenth century.

176   Porte-diner, for workmen in the fields. Paris area, eighteenth century.

178   Drinking cup—to be found all over Europe. Nineteenth century.

179 Flagon typical of eastern France, Germany and Switzerland. This example from Wurttemburg, eighteenth century.

180 One type of Swedish flagon. Nineteenth century.

The books which are particularly worth consulting to get an overall picture of European pewter are:

Les Etains by Philippe Boucaud and Claude Fregnac, Office du Livre, Fribourg, Suisse.
Zinn by H.U. Haedeke, Klinkhardt and Bierman, Braunschweig, Germany.
National Types of Old Pewter by H. H. Cotterell, Adolphe Riff and R. M. Vetter, The Pyne Press, Princeton, USA.

15. Britannia Metal—Its History, Alloy and Manufacture

by Jack L. Scott

The relationship between the wares made by the Britannia metalsmiths and those produced by the earlier pewterers may be much closer than heretofore realised. The efforts of eighteenth-century pewterers to produce a better and harder metal are now well documented. To gain hardness many makers added antimony (rather quietly, one would suspect) to their best grade of pewter. A small amount of copper was also added

181 Candlestick, unmarked, c.1795. Although the top and the base are cast, the column is heavy sheet-metal stock, and a vertical seam can be seen.
(Sheffield Museum)

on occasion. Additionally, the eighteenth-century London pewterers advertised their best wares under standard trade descriptions, the most popular being 'French pewter' and 'white metal'. One authority attributes the beginning of 'French pewter' to James Taudin. Thomas Chamberlain of London struck his touch in 1734, and was elected Master in 1765. His trade card advertised 'superfine White Metal called French Pewter'. George Holmes, who began working in 1743, produced 'best fine white ware metal dishes and plates called French Pewter'. A label mark used by John Jupe on his

209

wares advertised his superfine French Metal. Others who advertised white metal included John Kenrick and William Sandys.

It will be seen then, that the development of the Britannia metal trade did not arise as the result of any singular discovery, nor was the vast industry which grew from its introduction in the eighteenth century based on new techniques or manufacturing innovations. A blend of circumstances involving social reform, economic growth and the application of known manufacturing methods resulted in an industry that touched nearly every home in the nineteenth and twentieth centuries.

182   Teapot by Dixon & Smith, *c.* 1812, with bright cut engraving.
The construction is mainly of stamped parts.

The early quarter of the eighteenth century saw the beginning of economic and social growth which was to have a far reaching impact on England and the world. The wealthy class grew, as did the merchant class which eventually became the new middle class. By early nineteenth century the Industrial Revolution had given cities and towns a working class as well, each with buying power, even if limited in the instance of the working class.

As buying power increased, the potters, located primarily in Staffordshire, turned out great quantities of wares aimed at all levels of society. The market turned to Staffordshire for the colourful and relatively inexpensive 'china', and the long-established traditional pewter industry went into decline.

Silver remained out of reach of the middle class and most likely out of the fondest dreams of the working class, yet their enlightenment and desire for better things was satisfied by two closely-related Sheffield-originated industries: the making of Sheffield plate and Britannia metal.

In spite of the wars with the American colonies, France and Spain during the final years of the eighteenth century and the early years of the nineteenth century, the Industrial Revolution moved ahead, increasing economic growth. Total public expenditure in England rose from £27,500,000 in 1792, to £173,500,000 in 1815. The new prosperity continued to bring greater social awareness.

Even those with a limited purchasing power looked for a touch of elegance in their home life. This factor prepared the way for the Britannia metal industry. The question may be raised as to why the long-established pewterers could not supply the need for elaborate tea services and tableware at modest cost. By the end of the eighteenth

210

century the pewter industry had been reduced to the limited production of plates, tankards and measures. Collectors of eighteenth-century traditional pewter will point to many exceptions to the previous statement, but that is exactly what they are — exceptions.

183   Covered sugar by Dixon & Sons, 1823–29. The body is made of two stamped halves, and the lid is a single stamped piece. Casting was used for the knob, handles and feet. A special feature is the gadroon edge which was cast separately and applied in the same manner as Sheffield plate.

Late eighteenth-century trade cards of London pewterers clearly illustrate teapots, canisters, cream jugs, and other related items, yet few of these were made and very few have survived. The pewterers recognised the market potential but couldn't produce the goods. The concept of pewter making had always been exclusively one of casting. In fact other methods of fabrication, such as spinning, had been expressly forbidden in antiquity by the Pewterers Company. All parts were cast in moulds, soldered together and finished on a lathe or by hand.

As the pewter industry was in a state of continuing decline, the investment of very expensive moulds for new products proved to be too speculative. Of greater importance was the fact that casting produced a thick and heavy product which did not achieve the feeling of elegance the market demanded. Another contributing factor was that pewter was no longer in general use in the home, the only extensive use being in inns and public houses. Heavy pewterware was thought to be old-fashioned and out of vogue.

In 1769, James Vickers took up residence and shop on Hollis Street in Sheffield, amidst a large colony of silversmiths and platers. This date is given in a traditional story related by Charles Dixon, an early nineteenth-century manufacturer and amateur historian from Sheffield. The story, in part: 'about the year 1769, a person was taken very ill, and Mr Vickers visited him in his sickness. This person was in possession of the recipe for making white metal. Mr Vickers bid him 5 shillings for the recipe, and the offer was accepted'.

The date is further confirmed by the fact that James Vickers first appears in the Sheffield rate (tax) books for that year. Dixon's story also relates that Vickers borrowed 10 pounds sterling to make his first items, which were cast spoons. He took them to London where they were well received and quickly sold. From this modest beginning rose the vast world-wide Britannia metal industry of the nineteenth century and the lead-free pewter industry of the twentieth century.

211

The alloy used by Vickers was not of his own discovery, but was made from a formula obtained and possibly used by an unnamed person. The 'recipe' was similar to that used by the pewterers in London for their best metal, except that the small amount of lead was omitted entirely, the tin was increased slightly and the antimony was increased to about six percent. About two percent copper was also added; the same as many London makers had done. It must be kept in mind that there was no standard formula for pewter and the alloy varied from maker to maker, from wares to wares, and from part to part.

184 The canoe or boat shape first appeared about 1810, having evolved from similar but more rectangular silver patterns of the 1800–1810 period. The design remained very popular until 1830.

James Vickers described his wares as being made of white metal just as the competition in London had been doing for years. His initial success with spoons was due to the fact that they were better than the London-made goods. Not only were they stronger but they were of a better colour.

Vickers, surrounded everywhere in Sheffield with rolling mills and sheet metal, very quickly discovered that his alloy, unlike tin-lead pewter, was very well suited for rolling into sheet stock. Utilising the resources, knowledge, work skills, available rolling mills, stamps, dies, engravers and techniques allied to the silver and plated trades, Vickers began to make products in white metal in the same manner and style as the silversmiths and platers. They were sold, of course, at a substantially lower cost than the products which they copied.

The market was then covered. The buying public had a complete choice of products and cost; including silver, Sheffield plate and white metal.

From the beginning of the trade, emphasis was placed on craftsmanship and quality, as well as good design. The range of goods made by Vickers during the first years is not known, but his advertisement in the directory for 1787 is interesting in that it reads, in part, 'He makes also measures, teapots, castor frames, salts, spoons, etc.'.

It was during the latter years of the eighteenth century that the descriptive name of the products was changed from white metal to Britannia metal.

The first hint of the change is given in the directory for 1792, when five firms are listed as makers of Britannic metal. The use of the spelling Britannic is curious. The

Sheffield Courant included an item in November 1793 advertising a sale of cutlery, crockery, glassware and Britannia metal tea and table spoons. The directory for 1797 uses the term Britannia metal for all entries.

Those familiar with Franco-Anglo history may support the theory that Britannia was a commercially advantageous move to patriotism, used to compliment anti-French feeling and may have been directed towards the 'best French metal' advertised by the London pewterers. An important point is to be made here. It is entirely logical that the Sheffield makers would have turned to a trade description for their wares. What better choice than Britannia!

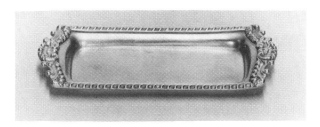

185   Snuffer tray of heavy sheet stock with cast edges applied in the manner of Sheffield plate. Dixon & Son, 1823–29.

Whatever the reasons, the new name was successful and remained in use throughout the nineteenth century and well into the twentieth.

It would appear that James Vickers was the only producer of white metal wares in Sheffield until 1790. The rate books confirm that Richard Constantine began in business in 1792. Hancock and Jessop were makers of Sheffield plate who also made Britannia metal. Their partnership dates from 1790. Two other firms were Broadhead, Gurney, Sporle & Co., and Froggatt, Coldwell & Lean, both of whom made both wares. Their partnerships date from about 1792. It is interesting to note that the three latter partnerships were very short lived.

About 1800, the manufacture of wares under the name of Britannia metal was first introduced in Birmingham and by 1805 experiments had begun in America. The trade was taken up in Birmingham by the pewterers who added Britannia metal wares to their pewter trade. John Yates, Thomas Yates, Abel Grove, Thomas Millward, Richard Sturges, and Yates, Birch & Spooner, among others, produced both pewter wares and Britannia metal goods. Those Birmingham men retained their pewter trade while, at the same time, joining in with the Britannia metal market for tea and other domestic wares.

It would seem also, that by the year 1820 nearly everything which was made in Sheffield plate was also made in Britannia metal with the exception of knives, forks and elaborate candelabra which were not suited for construction in the softer Britannia metal.

The industry grew hand in hand with the plated trade. Large factories, utilizing steam and water power, employed hundreds and, eventually, thousands of workers to turn out products of exceptional quality.

Unfortunately, this knowledge of large factories often comes as a severe blow to the collector who, in cherishing a favourite item, had envisaged a little old craftsman alone at his small workshop. It is true that a large part of the work utilised hand

213

186 Three-piece covered hot-water steak dish made of stamped and hand-formed sheet stock excepting the cast handles and Japanned wooden feet. Dixon & Son, 1823–29.

craftsmanship, but much of it received assistance from power machinery, and goods were turned out by hundreds of such craftsmen working for the factory owner whose name appears on the bottom of the articles. One can be reasonably assured that the three industries of silver, Sheffield plate and Britannia metal, in most instances involved large productive factories. James Dixon had built a new factory for the manufacture of Britannia metal goods in 1822, and by 1846 there were 400 employees at work there; 50 years later the number of workers at this one factory had more than doubled.

187 Bachelor-size teapot with a body of upper and lower stamped halves, by Joseph Wolstenholm, c. 1825–30.

214

In the early years of the nineteenth century, the Britannia metal manufacturers continued to duplicate the designs of earlier and contemporary silver and plate. Often the very same dies were used. As the Sheffield plate designs became more and more ornate (*c*.1830–45) the most popular Britannia metal designs remained those of clean lines and traditional forms. The Britannia metal trade unknowingly continued the long-standing tradition of the earlier pewterers of producing wares of good taste, fine proportions and simple lines.

Collectors have a difficult time developing a satisfactory definition of Britannia metal. The Pewter Society (of Great Britain) accepts that Britannia-metal wares by any process come under the general heading of 'pewter'. (See below.) Yet there is a feeling among the British pewter lovers that those wares made by the cold processes should (at least in part) receive a special designation. While wares of cast-tin alloy are considered to be specifically pewter, those which were constructed of sheet stock in the late eighteenth and the nineteenth century are specifically designated as 'Britannia metal'. The official opinion of the Pewter Society has been quoted in the Introduction.

188   The flower petal type of wooden knob was used almost exclusively on teapots from 1830 to 1840. Their use continued into the 1840s with various metal knobs which were first introduced in 1840.

In America no such official definition exists but the traditional feeling of the American antiques dealers, auctioneers and collectors has been that all wares of tin alloy are called pewter. The American definition would then be:

'Britannia Metal: All those pewter products of the eighteenth century and the nineteenth century which were at that time produced and sold under the trade description of Britannia Metal.'

Much of the discussion among collectors centres around the construction methods used by the makers of pewter wares of bygone years. Vickers introduced the technique

215

189a Cast candlestick with gadroon decoration, c.1800-30. Unlike tea wares where the gadroons were applied, in candlesticks the gadroon design was part of the casting.

189b Cast Candlestick, c.1830-40. Unmarked.

of rolling the metal into sheets, which were then cut into appropriate sizes and shaped by hand or formed by the drop-stamping method requiring a pair of steel dies, one in cameo, the other in relief, between which the sheet of metal was shaped. The relief die, with several hundred pounds of added weight and raised several feet over the cameo die and accurately guided by steel shafts was dropped with great force, forming the metal between the dies. To prevent damage in the instances of large pieces the metal was taken down to the die, a little at a time, requiring several droppings. Obviously a different pair of dies was needed for every part to be stamped. This method became the principal method for forming parts for wares made in the late eighteenth century and the entire nineteenth century.

By mid nineteenth century many pieces were formed by pressing in lieu of stamping. Large steam presses exerted much greater pressure than stamping and forms could be shaped in one movement.

Casting played an important role in the making of wares. Feet, collars, pedestal bases, knobs, handle mounts, hinges, knob pegs, and so on, were all cast in bronze or brass moulds before being added to ware made of sheet stock. Although the use of rolled sheets brought new and welcome dimensions many items were entirely cast in moulds. This sentence spotlights the important divergence of view of what is encompassed by 'Britannia metal'. This was especially true in the instances of tankards, measures, candlesticks. pepper pots, spoons, ladles, and such like. During the period from about 1835-45 some items, including coffee pots, which had been made primarily

216

of sheet metal were at this time made entirely of cast pieces. The antimony was always increased to give greater hardness to cast pieces and parts.

About 1825, spinning was introduced to the Britannia metal trade. A sheet of metal was placed on a lathe revolving at high speed. With special tools the spinning metal was pressed against a wooden chuck to give the desired shape. This process could be accomplished in very short time, often less than a minute for simple patterns. While it is true that the round-shaped bodies were often spun, spinning was a more important factor in making parts such as teapot collars, rim bases and small items such as salts and mustards.

190 Dish cover, one of a set of six. The design was formed by drop stamping, or by steam powered press. A special feature is the filled silver handle. The design was registered by James Dixon & Sons on 6 September 1848.

191 Tobacco box with spun body and applied decorative edges, and cast knob. Richard Sturges, Birmingham, c. 1850.

For the most part, the fabrication of wares required great craftsmanship involving many processes, each demanding special skills. A typical coffee pot of c. 1835 would very possibly be made of four main body parts (stamped), spout of two pieces (stamped), upper pedestal part (spun), pedestal base (cast), collar (cast), two-part hinge (cast), hinge pin (cast), lid rim (cast), lid (stamped), knob peg (cast), handle mounts of four pieces (cast), grate (hand formed) and a japanned wooden knob handle.

In putting the parts together, the solder was of a formula and melting point so close to that of the wares that the responsibility for final assembly was left to a master craftsman whose number or mark was often placed on the base of the wares along with the maker's mark.

Upon completion of the wares, all seams were hand burnished to render them smooth and invisible. Steam-driven leather buffs were then used to produce a silver-like shine. The final steps of hand cleaning and inspection were usually done by women employees.

Hence we have a coffee pot, hand crafted of many processes, all for the wholesale price of 12s 6d.

The Sheffield makers took care to mark their goods, nearly everything receiving the makers' name with the exception of candlesticks. In Birmingham, production was not equal to that in Sheffield and marked wares from that city are not frequently found.

The marks are usually stamped incuse by hand but numerous intaglio or marks in

217

192b Mustard with glass lining, copied from a georgian silver design, popular throughout the 19th century. Philip Ashberry & Sons, 1856–1860.

192a Soap box by Thomas Yates of Birmingham, c.1850.

193 Coffee pot, c.1860. It would seem that those who bought and used Britannia metal wares in the 1860s often rejected the ornate victorian designs issued by the electro-plate trade. Many pear shapes, of good proportions and utilising similar unobtrusive rim bases and plain handles were also widely used.

relief were also used. The first mark used by James Vickers was intaglio, as was the mark used by William Parkin. James Dixon and Sons used intaglio marks on occasion and nearly all spoons and ladles were similarly marked.

Although occasional trade marks appeared from about 1861, the use of trademarks was not frequent. Marks in the style of touch marks were never used on Britannia metal goods in the eighteenth and nineteenth centuries although examples do exist of wares cast by existing pewterers using the Britannia metal formula and receiving the pewterer's regular touch.

During the years of 1842–45, events took place in Birmingham and Sheffield which had a profound effect on the industry.

On September 25, 1840, Elkington's of Birmingham was granted patent no. 8447 for electroplating silver on a base metal. This patent was preceded by less-definitive patents and followed by improving patents, but Leader (R. E. Leader, *The Early History of Electro-Silver Plating*, London, 1919) considered the 1840 patent to be the master patent for electroplating. The original purpose of Britannia metal had been to provide a substitute for silver and Sheffield plate. The electroplating process brought it closer to its original intent. Britannia metal plated very well and required no changes in production other than adding the plating process.

194 Teapot, probably spun, with clean traditional lines. James
Dixon & Sons, *c*.1860.

The market for unplated Britannia metal slipped into a steady decline beginning about 1870, as the plated trade replaced more and more of the market. Yet it would be safe to say that the production of Britannia-metal goods, which were unplated, and sold as such, retained their quality until 1914, when production stopped entirely with the beginning of the First World War. When it restarted, nearly all Britannia metal firms produced their wares under the new trade description—"English Pewter".

219

16. Notes on Fakes and Repros

I found it difficult—impossible—to write this chapter containing so many facts so tenuously connected, in a flowing manner, without it appearing to me to be padded up with detergent-like verbiage. So let us keep it pithy, although staccato. So please accept it as the title says—'Notes on. . .'. Back in the 1920s and 30s collecting had come to stay. The Society of Pewter Collectors (now the Pewter Society) had been formed in 1918, and erudite wealthy professional men, and a woman, were keen collectors. Based on Massé's pioneering and book, and two or three others, notably Hilton Price's *Old Base Metal Spoons*, interest was sparked off. It is extraordinary how well and thoroughly they garnered for their collections. How uncared-for pieces were channelled to antique shops, and how these pieces came to their notice it is hard to imagine. Certainly workmen on building excavations were approached, successfully. Huge, these collections were. When faking started neither I nor they knew. But it is quite certain that in their keenness to acquire rare early pieces a new surreptitious supply arose—fakes. It was let known what individuals wanted, and hey presto — soon they were offered such pieces—pieces often to make up sets of, for instance, very rare baluster measures.

Many well-known illustrations in the older books are known to be fakes. Beautifully made, and in impeccable technical detail of manufacture. Makers', and housemarks, the more to glamourise, wear and tear, repairs, and scale—they had every appearance of age. Some were magnificent, superb pieces, in first-class condition. All had evidence of authenticity which passed unwary scrutiny. Metal showing many signs of removal of 'oxide', too—metal pitted in a simulation of the surface after chemical treatment. Unsuspectingly, unchallenged, these pieces were eagerly taken up. Doubts appear to have been totally absent, and criticism was neither sought nor given.

Fakes are 'made to deceive'—specious—and deceive they did. In the mid thirties I guess that doubt did dawn, and when it did, it was still rather tolerant. Hence there are now a great many fine, 'early' pieces which are not true, widely distributed, in the UK and in America; even, in fact, in museums (to whom collections had been bequeathed). I do not for one moment suppose that many, if any, have been destroyed; rather they are cherished. (The Pewter Society has a small collection of excellent examples in its 'chamber of horrors'—pieces which have come to be recognised for what they are, and have been donated.) I have been examining a very fine collection in a museum, and at a guess, about twenty to twenty-five percent are fakes, some so well produced that present knowledge is not capable of certainty about them—particularly the very small pieces. There are many pieces in which a part appears to be acceptable, and perhaps the reverse side of that part unacceptable. A curate's egg. One has to remain humble and

195 A typical fake baluster of the 20s or 30s, from the Pewter Society's collection of Awful Warnings. See the over-imposing hammer thumbpiece. It is difficult to appreciate the spurious surface texture in the remoteness and haze of a reduced screened black and white illustration, but often tell-tales are distinguishable. (The Pewter Society)

openminded, and not give in to the temptation, when turned to as an authority, of a decision which is not fully justified, where the mind and conscience are not fully at ease. In some ways experience can make one decisive; in others, of the awareness that 'the more you know, the more you know you don't know'.

An awareness of 'something not quite right' is a danger signal which should initiate close inspection. If you handle a piece and become faintly uneasy, try to analyse what is the cause of the unease. A good modern pewterer who knew the technical detail could cast them quite inexpensively in plaster moulds taken from originals. It is very easy to be taken in by clever fakes, for on seeing a rarity available, one's desire wells up, suppressing discrimination and discretion. I expect all collectors have had them, and not only in their earliest days. Price is no criterion. At a major sale pieces may be detected by the majority—they may probably not fetch the full market value of true pieces. But they are to be seen fully priced in shops probably unrecognised by the vendor. Having been made some 40 years ago they may well have acquired some true

221

196 Close-up of house marks on a fake 'wedge' baluster. The detail is invariably inferior to genuine dies.

dulling oxide. They were treated, battered, repaired, and are at their 'best' when dusty and dirty, and, complete with dents, scratches, nicks, tears, half-struck marks, and inscriptions, these pieces can be very misleading, particularly so in poor light.

On the other hand, consider these pieces when lightly cleaned—and compare with several true pieces completely cleaned—the differences then are widened. Some fakes have an indefinable smoothness. This touches on the difficulty of conveying in words the many almost-imperceptible and very difficult-to-relate clues. Many very experienced collectors will tell you that they cannot put their finger on points, or describe them, yet show them a piece and their judgment will be instantaneous; even sometimes from a photograph. In cases of doubt, usually living with a doubtful piece for a few days, picking it up and putting it down, will bring the realisation and decision. So if you can, get it on approval!

The difficulty of describing features succinctly which appear in fakes will be appreciated, and also the reluctance to give too much away to any would-be faker, but some notes may be of help.

Many fakes carry an unnatural appearance of corrosion. They are speckled, too regular and too widespread. Compare a suspicious piece with several known genuine pieces, in as near similar condition as possible, and the differences become noticeable. A dull, solid, leaden, almost greasy impression is sometimes given. But who is to say that all fakes were made by one man, or by one technique? Do not overlook the likelihood of different sources and different treatments. There may also be methods of accelerating the formation of oxide, but it is usually taken that any oxide which is not of the utmost hardness and brittleness is suspect. One may need to prod the scale in an inscription, or scratch the scale on the base. Confusingly, true pieces which have had chemical treatment in partly removing the oxide can be left with a rather soft skin. Furthermore, one must consider the varying handling and storage conditions over the ages; that some pewterers may have made perhaps unmarked pieces, crudely. Some

222

197 Some more fakes which were garnered unquestioned by the early collectors. Technical detail is remarkably punctilious as far as manufacture goes, but sometimes well-copied marks are in the wrong places, or, say, a spoonmaker's mark is used on a flagon. Not impossible, but a very suspicious piece of evidence.
(FitzWilliam Museum, Cambridge)

198   It is well to study the appearance of the 'corrosion' in this and other examples against true pieces.
(FitzWilliam Museum, Cambridge and the Pewter Society)

199 A close-up showing first the incongruous fit of the thumbpiece wear on the handle; and next, on a true piece—how the thumbpiece nestles into the wear. (The Pewter Society)

may have made wares from moulds not designed for that purpose and size (lid, thumbpiece, handle).

Sometimes the glamour is overloaded, such as adding interesting house marks to a baluster, to make it the more irresistible to induce even the suspicious to take a chance. Look for true scratched wear on bases, and the bruising of the thumbpiece on the handle—and that it 'fits'.

Very often there is some foolish error, such as a mark lifted from a specialised maker, a spoon-maker's for example, applied to a baluster. If a maker is known only, say, for his marked flagons you should be very wary if this mark appeared on, a 'stick', or on dishes. The placing of the mark is important. It varied in many wares with the times. Be careful if a mark is out of place or out of era. On baluster measures, the more usual true position is on the right of the handle, on the lip; less frequently on the lid, (although this is quite a usual place on buds). I have it there on hammerheads and buds, as well as on two very rare types (not fakes, I hasten to add!). If you find a baluster with the mark on the left of the handle (although some true ones are marked on that side,) or worse—in or on the base—think twice, and thrice! I had a beautiful French broad-rim plate once, with a spurious English spoonmaker's mark on it.

Recently I have found that there may appear to be evidence that at least some fake balusters are appreciably oversize, since those tested averaged about ten percent over the average capacity of similar-date true balusters. Spoons with badly cast bowls are invariably wrong—the frequent horned head-dress fakes, and other styles (acorn and others). Badly-made dies for house marks, and touches, almost certainly condemn a piece out of hand. Some pieces have marks which would almost certainly not be marked. Some are over glamourised—perhaps 'hallmarks' when there would have been none. Some may be just plainly anachronistical. Perhaps the most common faking is not as bad—the piece is perfectly true, but has acquired an 'old' mark 250 years after its manufacture—there is many a piece in this category, an earlier type than the known date of the maker's striking. Likewise, and worse, an inscription or wriggling has been added.

Continental pieces, from the days when they were not wanted here or at home, were adorned with English marks (as related above). So often a true piece has a new part added—lid, handle, thumbpiece—made, or treated, to deceive. Most fakes have their surfaces heavily treated to deceive, with acid treatment to etch irregularly—but the appearance of these has, loosely, two recurring features. The small 'corrosion' is too regular and 'speckled', and the large patches look 'different' from true heavy corrosion. But here I must plea not to pigeonhole such statements as either inclusive or exclusive—they are very inadequate attempts to convey a start to recognition. Sometimes desirable features are accentuated, such as oversize thumbpieces on spurious hammerhead balusters purporting to be of $c.1650–c.1700$. The range of products which come to mind is primarily wedge, ball and hammerhead balusters, then seventeenth-century salts, candlesticks, flat-lid tankards, spoons, broad-rim dishes, communion cups, and early flagons. And on some items, remember, only the mark may be fake. Recently I saw a new class of 'fakes'. But they certainly were not fakes, because they resembled nothing else whatever in pewter. They were dreamed-up styles, very crudely made, and had been treated to an 'oxide' consisting of a very heavy black greasy 'goo' which could be scraped by a thumbnail. One piece was made incorporating the top half of a bellied measure. They would not fool any collector, except perhaps the tyro who would like to collect real oddities. A thought as to values shows that awareness and discrimination can save many hundreds of pounds.

(a)

(b)

200 (a) There are far too many of these ill-cast bowls of spoons, with very credible knops. True spoons were excellently cast. Beware these horned headdress, acorn and maybe others, probably maidenhead. (b) This, mentioned in 'Marks', seemed to be a very rare survivor of condemnation showing the arrow—until inspection showed it to be fake.
(Anon.)

227

An extension of pieces made with under- or oversize parts is those made up from parts of different, true pieces. Marrying a lid to an item of hollow-ware is an obvious example. But it can go much further, where perhaps a late salt bowl is placed on a 'stick' base; or contrarywise, a footed plate has lost its foot. Thumbpiece replacement is an obvious likelihood, and sometimes very difficult to detect. A clay or plastic mould can so easily be taken from a true piece. One may well feel that an old, scaly, battered piece would look daft with a pristine piece added, so the latter is stained tastefully—*some* treatment is called for. How far one accepts dents, scratches, distressing, warping, nitric acid dulling, and so on, can, I suppose only be decided by the next buyer. *He* wants it to look 'right' (in both senses), and the vendor has a real interest that it should look 'right'—and so swiftly will restoration become accepted as genuine. How can one implement a code of practice on the many professional and amateur restorers?

Two ethical answers, alas, appear not to be favoured by the majority of restorers, nor by purchasers. One is that every replaced part should be stamped deeply with a die, just as Massé used a minute die with his distinctive initials HJLJM bitten in incuse on every single repair he made. (One I own has it four times, so small that they are barely visible.) This is currently being done by at least one very ethical dealer, skilled in repair. But even so, owners/purchasers may resist the treatment. Answers to this suggestion are—'stable door', 'spoiling the look', 'I don't want it to show, because the value will drop'. I can only say that these additions are made to deceive. A repair is legitimate, but added parts . . .? These parts, such as thumbpiece, or lid, can so easily pass muster, made by a really skilled craftsman. I know that it is a challenge to the craftsman to be able to deceive other people, but we should distinguish true from false for posterity's sake.

The other answer, which is, I believe, standard museum practice, is to make the missing part in a plastic substance, coloured to match, approximately; or perhaps I should say to tone, yet to remain easily distinguishable. This is not so much fun for the real pewter-working man, for he likes to pursue the craft, and to give rein to, and to challenge with his expertise. Since the former practice is the more popular, I can only fear for future generations.

I leave you to range over the many answers when an ingénue says 'what does it matter if the owner does not know?'! Let us leave fakes by saying, not only do you judge a piece as a whole, but every part, detachable or fragile, must be scrutinised. If one part is suspect, or replaced, redouble the scrutiny on the remainder. Some fakes are wholly fake, some partly so. Some faking is confined to the addition of marks, or wriggling, onto true pieces. In your private catalogue—be honest with whatever you record, and if possible, see that the catalogue is available after you, and I, are. And if you are a newcomer big-pocket collector, do not be in too much of a hurry.

The dividing line between fake and repro. They merge, likely as not. There are probably only a few fakes of the eighteenth century, but from the latter part of the century, there are many repros. Certainly there are repros of sixteenth and seventeenth century items, but there is usually a slight difference in detail in nearly all styles of whatever period. But not always. Fakes set out to deceive, but repros merely aim to look old! Since a large quantity were made before the Second World War, many have gained some oxide, on top of the chemical discolouring. They are smooth, smoother than true oxide. When scratched, metal immediately shines. But the passage of time allows true oxide to form, and in a very short while these will be accepted as genuine— little single-reed plates of 7in diameter approximately, and 9in porringers with two

201 A really unconvincing plate, bearing four lion passant 'hallmarks'. Smaller such plates with three 'hallmarks' can sometimes be seen in antique shops being used as ashtrays. Another shot of the 'wedge' (fig 196). (The Pewter Society)

spindly handles, rectangular-based 'sticks', tappit hens, and others, all bearing marks, many of which are direct and true copies of old makers' marks. Many are the repro pieces I have seen at antique fairs in the past—despite their vetting panels. It amazed me!

I have heard that a few years ago a foreign salesman went the rounds of likely shops —'any style, any marks!' I do not know if any orders were taken, nor what the products looked like. Another fake or repro trap which I have not seen is of bellied measures purporting to be mid or later nineteenth century, complete with spurious verification marks. I guess that both were hoping to deceive. Not likely to deceive are bellied measures made like bi-valve shells, in two halves, seamed top to bottom, and exceedingly crude they are—but they could be tidied up by a good craftsman—or collector.

202 A really fine fake beefeater. It is just too cylindrical to be normal. The owner writes 'Fake. "St Mark 1664" with Adam and Eve engraving and typical mottled fake finish to surface.' (Anon.)

Until last I have kept detailed mention of fake marks on fakes and repros. Inspect the marks of any suspect piece very carefully. Twice recently I have had reason to do so. In both cases it was fortunate that, as is often so, the true maker had struck his mark on the London touch plate, large photographs of which appear in Cotterell's *Old Pewter*. Comparisons with these showed minute differences. In one there was one less 'pellet' surrounding the circular mark; in the other were minute but detectable differences of spacing of letters and the device. Of course, the maker *may* have had two dies, very similar 'duplicates'. You cannot be overconfident—but in these pieces there was already a doubt.

230

203 None of my acquaintances collects repros, so illustrations are hard to come by. Here are quite common examples. Plates abound, particularly with Bush & Perkins, and Samuel Duncombe 'hallmarks'—and others. (Anon.)

Much can be gained from the way marks have been struck. There are some repro/fakes the mark die of which purports to have been struck on the tilt, so that one edge bites in deeply to fade away, as was frequently and truly the case. I daresay that you have seen instances of the phoney die showing the sharp edge where it has been too deeply struck; instead of fading away, a sharp line appears all along the fade-away position!

Marks which have been found and recorded of fakes and repros had not hitherto been published. But in *MPM* and in *Addenda* over sixty (between the two books) are published, noting also on what items they have been seen, not, of course, claiming to be comprehensive. Many of these were the result of the work of Michaelis. One paragraph he wrote privately is quoted: 'It must not be supposed that all pewter bearing one or another of these marks is necessarily a fake; the marks themselves are, in the main, copies of genuine old pewterers' touches, mostly to be found on the London touch plates, and they have been selected by the fakers either because they have been found on genuinely-rare pieces, or simply because the mark may bear a date which is thought to give some added embellishment to a piece which already appears to be desirable or rare'. The marks which are on repros are almost entirely *confined* to repros, excepting notably Bush & Perkins, and Samuel Duncombe.

When it comes to fakes and repros, prices are no criterion or guarantee and are often dictated by bluff or ignorance by the vendor. Ten years ago (and for several years) there was an obvious repro stuck in a shop in a glamour area at the going rate for a genuine example. Fortunately it did stick. In one month, in a holiday area, I saw two identical flat-lid tankards, not in the least convincing, not even to be flirted with; in fact, so obviously to be eschewed. One was priced at the going rate of the time as genuine; the other was at the ex-catalogue price. So, to end sententiously, quoting the final paragraph of *British Pewter and Britannia Metal* as valid as when written:

> Let your knowledge and experience grow by handling and reading as much as possible, and let your collection grow in step, both in number and value, with your knowledge most certainly including something of fakes. You may consider it worth while to own one or two duds for reference. You need to take bold decisions—let them be bold through knowledge, not rash chances.

May I add another line? Start with nineteenth-century pieces, and get to know the feel of the subject.

Appendix I
Where to see pewter

Museum and National Trust displays, mediaeval onwards
United Kingdom
Alcester, Coughton Court
Barnstaple, Arlington Court
       Museum
Birmingham Art Gallery
          Weoley Castle
Broadway, Bretforton, The Fleece
Calstock (Cornwall), Cotehele House
Cambridge, Fitzwilliam Museum
Chastleton House (Nr Stow-on-the-Wold)
Cheltenham Museum
Claverton Manor, Bath. (American pewter)
Dublin, National Museum of Ireland
Durham, Washington Old Hall
Edinburgh, National Museum of Antiquities
          Royal Scottish Museum
Glasgow, Kelvingrove Art Gallery and Museum
           Hunterian Museum, University of Glasgow
London, Museum of,
       Pewterers Hall (see end of Appendix)
       Victoria and Albert Museum
Newcastle, Wallington Hall
Salisbury, St Ann Street Museum
Stirling, Smith Institute
Stoke-on-Trent, Little Moreton Hall
Truro Museum
Walsall, Mosely Old Hall
Welshpool, Powys Castle
Wigan Museum.

Many other Museums have some very good pewter, some of which may be on display, with more held in store.

There is a very fine collection indeed at the Pewterers Hall, London (which is not a museum). It may be seen, by prior arrangement, if convenient.

The Pewter Society's collection of fakes is also housed at the Pewterers Hall, and may be seen as above.

Overseas
Auckland Museum, New Zealand
Boston (Society of Preservation of New England Antiques)
        Museum of fine arts
Cape Ann, Massachusetts, White Ellery House
Deerfield, Massachusetts
Guernsey, St Peters Port, Lukis, and Guille Alles
Jersey, St. Helier, Museum of the Societe Jersais
Manchester, New Hampshire, Currier Gallery
New York, Metropolitan Museum of Art
Newark, New Jersey.
Shelburne Museum, Vermont.
Sturbridge Old Village, Massachusetts
Sydney, Art Gallery of New South Wales
Weston, Vermont, Farrar-Mansur House
Williamsburg, Colonial, Virginia
Winterthur, Delaware

UK Romano-British (Some on display, some in store)
Bath
Bury St Edmunds
Cambridge University (Department of Archaeology and Ethnology)
Devizes
Elveden (Nr Thetford)
Ipswich
London, British Museum
        Museum of London
Northampton
Oxford, Ashmolean
Reading
Taunton

Appendix II

Short Bibliography

BOUCAUD, P. & FREGNAC, C., *Les Etains*, Office du Livre, Fribourg, Switzerland, 1978.

COTTERELL, H. H., *Old Pewter, Its Makers and Marks*, Batsford, London, 1929. Reprinted 1963.

COTTERELL, RIFF AND VETTER, *National Types of Old Pewter*, Pyne Press, Princeton, 1972.

GASK, N., *Old Silver Spoons of England*, Herbert Jenkins, 1926.

HATCHER, J. AND BARKER, T. C., *A Short History of British Pewter*, Longman, London, 1974.

HOMER, R. F., *Five Centuries of Base Metal Spoons*, Homer, 1975.

HOW, G. E. P., *Ellis Collection of 16th and 17th century Provincial Spoons*, How of Edinburgh.

HOW, G. E. P. and HOW, J. P., *English & Scottish Silver Spoons (Mediaeval to Late Stuart)*, in three Vol., How of Edinburgh.

KAUFFMANN, H. J., *The American Pewterer, His Techniques*, Thomas Nelson Inc., Camden, New York, 1970.

LIBERTY'S (OF LONDON), '1875–1975' Exhibition Catalogue (p. 72 to p. 79).

MICHAELIS, R. F., *Antique Pewter of the British Isles*, Bell, London, 1953.

British Pewter, Ward Lock, London, 1969.

Chats on Old Pewter (revised from Massé), Benn.

The Pewter Collector (revised from Massé), Barrie & Jenkins, London, 1971.

PEAL, CHRISTOPHER A., *British Pewter & Britannia Metal*, John Gifford, London, 1971.

Let's Collect British Pewter, Jarrold, Norwich, 1976.

More Pewter Marks, Peal, Norwich, 1977.

Addenda to More Pewter Marks, Norwich Print Brokers Ltd., Norwich 1977. 1978.

PEWTERERS' COMPANY. *A short history of the Worshipful Company of Pewterers of London and a Catalogue of the Pewterware in its Possession.* Worshipful Company of Pewterers, London, 1968.

Worshipful Company of Pewterers (London) Supplement to its Catalogue of Pewterware 1979, Pewterers' Company.

PRICE, F. G. HILTON, *Old Base Metal Spoons*, Batsford, London, 1908.

VICTORIA & ALBERT MUSEUM, *British Pewter*, H.M.S.O.

WOOD, L. INGLEBY, *Scottish Pewterware and Pewterers*, Geo. A. Morton, Edinburgh, 1907.

WOOLMER, S. AND ARKWRIGHT, C., *Pewter of the Channel Islands*, John Bartholomew, Edinburgh, 1973.

Journals are published twice a year by both the Pewter Society and the Pewter Collectors Club of America. Distribution is to members only in each case.

Some articles in antiques magazines

COTTERELL, H. H., 'Dating the Pewter Tankard', *Connoisseur*, April, 1932.

'Scottish Pewter Measures', *Connoisseur*, May, 1931.

GASK, N., 'Mediaeval Pewter Spoons', *Apollo*, December, 1949.

GRAEME, A. S., 'Pewter Church Flagons', *Connoisseur*, October, 1950.

'Pewter Spoons', *Connoisseur*, December, 1947.

HOMER, R. F., 'Unique Medieval Pewter Spoon', *Connoisseur*, April, 1973.

MICHAELIS, R. F., 'English Pewter Porringers', *Apollo*, July, August, September, October, 1949.

'Royal Portrait Spoons in Pewter', *Apollo*, June, 1950.

'Decoration on English Pewterware', *Antique Collector*, October, 1963, February, 1964.

'Capacity Marks on Old Pewter Measures', *Antique Collector*, August, 1954.

'Royal Occasions', *Antique Collector*, August, 1966.

'Pewter Tankards & Tavern Pots', *Discovering Antiques*, Issue 35.

'Pear-shaped Flagons', *Antique Collector*, October, 1971.

MINCHIN, C. C., 'A Berkshire Pewter Collection', *Apollo*, April, July, 1946.

'Pewter Flagons & Tankards', *Antique Collector*, February, 1952.

'Some Uncommon Examples of Old English Pewter', *Antique Collector*, February, 1971.

PEAL, CHRISTOPHER A., 'Pewter Salts, Candlesticks and some Plates', *Apollo*, May, 1959.

'Notes on Pewter Balusters', *Apollo*, January, 1950.

'Tankards, and Housemarks', *Apollo*, April, 1949.

'Notes on Pewter Flagons', *Apollo*, May, 1950.

'Romano-British Plates and Dishes', *Proc. Camb. Antiq. Soc.* Vol. LX, 1967.

'Latten Spoons', *Connoisseur*, April and July, 1970.

'An English Pewter Collection', *Antiques (of America)*, August, 1969.

'Britannia Metal IS Pewter', *Antique Finder*, October, 1971.

'British Pewter', *Australasian Antique Collector*, 17th ed., 1976.

'19th Century, Pure & Simple', *A.D. and Collectors Guide*, September, 1973.

'Rule Britannia', *A.D. and Collectors Guide*, January, 1973.

'18th Century Pewter', *Antique Collector*, June and July, 1973.

'Pewter in the 18th Century', *A.D. and Collectors Guide*, March, 1977.

'A Great Collection Dispersed' (Michaelis), *Antique Collector*, 1974.

'Pewter 1650–1700', *A.D. and Collectors Guide*, October, 1978.

'The English Pot', *Antique Collector, and Antique Finder*, April, July, 1978.

SPEIGHT, H. W., 'Verification Marks on Old Pewter Measures', *Antique Collector*, December, 1938.

Appendix III

Localities of known makers with marks.

This is an aid to research into regional type establishment.

It is confined to recorded makers with marks, not names only per locality, of which there are very many. First date only given. London, and Edinburgh plain castle mark (as being too early and rare), are omitted. Post 1650 only.

There are many more makers with marks whose location is not known, or is only suspected. There are many more marks for many of the *OP* numbers in *MPM* and *Addenda*.

The south and west form a separate batch.

There are some huge gaps in the localities represented, where there must have been activity.

Dates are taken from *OP*, where no other evidence has come to light.

England

Banbury
| | 4860 | Usher, Thomas, 1739 |

Bewdley
Bewdley	227	Bancks, I & Co, *c*.1800
	238a	Bancks, Wm, *c*.1790
	1197	Crane, J.C., *c*.1800
MPM	2540a	Ingram & Hunt, *c*.1780
		(*OP* 5708)

Birmingham
	430	Birch & Villers, *c*.1774
	1465	Duncombe, J. *c*.1706
	1466	Duncombe, S. *c*.1740
	4876	Villers & Wilkes, *c*.1808
	5338	Yates, James, *c*.1860
	5340a	Yates, John, *c*.1820
	5346	Yates, Thomas, *c*.1808
	5347	Yates & Birch, *c*.1840
	5348	Yates Birch & Co ?
	5349	Yates Birch & Spooner *c*.1829
MPM	3104a	Mason, Harry, *c*.1875
MPM	4844a	Tutin, ?, *c*.1780

Brighton
| *Addenda* | 3736a | Postlethwaite, G. *c*.1860 |

Bristol
118	Ash & Hutton, *c*.1741
295	Batcheler, John, *c*.1676
385	Bennett, Thomas, 1761
386	Bennett, T, *c*.1720
574	Bright, Allen, 1742
708	Burgum & Catcott, 1765
737	Bush, Rbt. Sr., *c*.1755
739	Bush, Rbt & Co, *c*.1780
740	Bush & Perkins, *c*.1770
813	Carr, John, *c*.1750
857	Cave, John, *c*.1690
859	Cave, Thos, Sr., 1684
1095	Cooke, Wm., 1795
1189	Cox, Stephen, 1735
1260	Curtis, James, *c*.1770
1266a	Curtis & Co, *c*.1800
1410	Dole, Erasmus, 1679
1411	Dole, John, 1699
1511	Edgar & Son, 1814
1561	Embris, Edm., *c*.1720
1740	Fothergill, M. 1793
1776	French, John, 1784
1909	Going, Rich'd., 1715
2001	Gregory, Edward, *c*.1694

2002	Gregory, Edwd, 1705	
2021	Griffith, John, 1747	
2841	Lansdown, Wm. 1740	
2843	Lanyon, Thos., 1715	
2899	Lee, Benjamin, c.1780 ?	
2952	Llewellin, Peter, 1840	
2990	Lovell, J. Jnr., 1725	
2992	Lovell, Rbt., 1752	
3128	Matthews, Jas., c.1740	
3289	Morgan, Joseph, 1807	
3314	Mower, George, 1687	
3478	Page, Thomas, 1737	
3523	Parnall & Sons, 1820	
3617	Perkins, Rch'd., c.1770	
3618	Perkins, Wm., c.1750	
3924	Rich, Wm., c.1835	
4539	Stiff, Wm., 1761	
4981	Watkins, Wm., 1728	
5200	Willoughby, Roger, 1680	
5202	Willshire, Thomas, 1785	
MPM 328	Beaker, Richard, c.1650	
MPM 1409	Dole, Erasmus, c.1660	
MPM 1508	Edgar, Curtis & Co. c.1820	
MPM 2951	Llewellin, c.1830	

Chester
222	Bancks, Adam, c.1760
5223a	Wilson, Ralph, c.1690

Coventry
425	Billing, Samuel, c.1675

Darlington
2946	Lister, John, c.1750

Gainsborough
4938	Walmsley, John, 1712

Kendal
MPM 1100a	Cookson, Wm c.1675

King's Lynn
MPM 4169	Seegood, Henry, c.1670

Leeds
Addenda 2794b	Labron, ?, c.1800

Liverpool
2368a	Holden, Richard, c.1740
2924	Leatherbarrow, Jas 1710
2925	Leatherbarrow, Thos 1690
MPM 1968a	Green, Robert, c.1765
MPM 2417a	Houghton, I., c.1750
MPM 2738b	King, George, c.1820
Addenda 2370a	Holdgate, Thos c.1820
Addenda 2925b	Leatherbarrow, Thos., 1790

Newcastle
2367	Hogg, William, c.1760
3001	Lowes, George, c.1720
4088	Sadler, Robert, 1730
4216	Shaw, John c.1760
5234b	Winship, Thos, c.1760
MPM 4215a	Shaw, ?, c.1740

Norwich
3192	Melchior, John, c.1690
MPM 412a	Berry, Chris., 1701
MPM 3191a	Melchior, Corn., c.1705
MPM 3192a	Melchior, Thos, c.1660
MPM 5369a	Young, Matthew, c.1650

Oxford
MPM 3484a	Paine, I., c.1690

Penrith
1243	Crowley, Abr'm., c.1720

Petersfield
917	Churcher, Adam, 1690

Sunderland
35	Alder, William, c.1700

Whitehaven
1723	Forde, Thomas, c.1695

Wigan
89	Anderton, James, c.1700
210	Baldwin, Christopher, 1690
212	Baldwin, Robert, c.1690
228	Bancks, James, c.1705
505	Boulton, Thomas, c.1760
2136	Hardman, John, c.1690
MPM 4214b	Sherington, Nich. 1694

Winchester
MPM & 5132a	Widmore, Thos., c.1710
Add.	

Windsor
Addenda 1757a	Franklin, ?, c.1730

Wolverhampton
MPM 3486a	Pallisers, ?. c.1680

York
2161	Harrison, J.Jr, 1693
2162	Harrison, John, 1720
2437	Hudson, Francis, 1756
3755	Poynton, Toundrow, 1735
4004	Rodwell, Thomas, 1704
4697	Terry, Leonard, 1700
5076	Wharton, Arthur, c.1735
MPM 1086	Cooke, John, 1652
MPM 1931	Gorwood, Joseph Sr c.1750

MPM	1932	Gorwood, Joseph Jr *c.*1780
MPM	5210	Wilson, Edward,1715

South and West
Ashburton
	1408	Dolbeare, John, ?*c.*1730

Barnstaple
	2902	Lee, Samuel, *c.*1720
	4233	Shephard, Nicholas, *c.*1745
	5015	Webber, Alexander, *c.*1710
	5016	Webber, John, *c.*1655
	5017	Webber, John Jr., *c.*1680

Bideford
	4099	Sanders, Simon, *c.*1700
	5165	Williams, A., *c.*1730

Bridgewater
	748	Butcher, Jas.Jr., *c.*1700

Chard
	989	Clothyer, Robt., *c.*1670

Dorchester
MPM	2919ai	Lester, Edward, *c.*1670

Exeter
	944	Clarke, Samuel, *c.*1725
	1326	Daw, Robert, *c.*1680
	1586	Evans, Humphrey, *c.*1730
	1659	Ferris, John & Co., *c.*1780
	1754	Foy, Philip, *c.*1725
	1824	Gauls, ?. *c.*1810
	2839	Langworthy, Lawrence, 1719
	3132	Matthew, Nath'n'l., *c.*1850
	3302	Mortimer, J, *c.*1760
	4678	Taylor, William, 1780
MPM	661a	Bryant, Edward, *c.*1695
MPM	4678	Taylor, W.., *c.*1780

Falmouth
	4807	Tregelles, I.., *c.*1725

Launceston
	2416	Hoskyn, Henry, *c.*1680

Liskeard
MPM	5118b	Whitford, George, *c.*1670

Plymouth
MPM	1000a	Cockey, M.., *c.*1750

St Austell
MPM	3015a	Luly, S.., *c.*1750

Tavistock
	2488	Hutchins, W., *c.*1680
	3607	Pennington, John, *c.*1680

Tiverton
	2356	Hodges, Sampson, *c.*1707
	2357	Hodges, Thomas, *c.*1720

Totnes
	1001	Cockey, W., *c.*1740

Truro
	2417	Hoskyn, John, *c.*1750
MPM	1294	Daniel, Jacob, *c.*1750

Scotland
Aberdeen
	5882	Ross, George (*OP.*4037) 1664

Edinburgh
	75	Anderson, Adam, 1734
	196	Bain, Alexander, *c.*1826
	218	Ballantyne, Wm., 1749
	1144	Coulter, Alex., *c.*1720
	1694	Fleming, William, 1717
	1808	Gardner, John, 1764
	1941	Gourlay, David, 1794
	2277	Herrin, James, 1692
	2473	Hunter, William, 1749
	2529	Inglis, Arch., 1732
	2537	Inglis, Thomas, 1719
	2761	Kinnear, Andrew, 1750
	2765	Kinniburgh, Robt. 1794
	2766	Kinniburgh & Son 1823
	2768	Kinniburgh & Scott *c.*1800
	3317	Moyes, J., *c.*1850
	3817	Ramage, Adam, *c.*1810
	4160	Scott, William, 1779
	4161	Scott, William, 1794
	4364	Smith, John, *c.*1730
	5130	Whyte, Robert, ?1805
	5292	Wright, Alex., 1732
	5295	Wright, James, *c.*1773
MPM	5130	Whyte, Robert, *c.*1835

Glasgow
	994	Coats, Arch & Wm. *c.*1795
	1446	Drew, William, 1794
	1802	Galbraith, Robert, *c.*1828
	1943	Graham & Wardrop, *c.*1776
	2999	Lowe, C., *c.*1850
	3054	Maitland, James, 1715
	3153	Maxwell, Stephen, *c.*1763
	3889	Reid, H., *c.*1850?
	3890	Reid, H. & J., *c.*1845
	3894	Reid, W., *c.*1800
	4959	Wardrop, J. & H., *c.*1810
	5323	Wylie, J., *c.*1825
	5521	Connell, Mathew (*OP.*1069) *c.*1780

MPM 3168a McPhail, ?., *c.*1850
MPM 4161a Scouler, D., *c.*1816
Addenda 78a Anderson Bros., *c.*1900

Inverness
    1288 Dallas, James, *c.*1750
    1289 Dallas, Lachlan, *c.*1700
Inverurie (Aberdeen)
    1477 Durie, ?., *c.*1800

Paisley
    2366 Hogg, John, 1794
  MPM 1794b Fullerton, A., *c.*1860

Perth
    6033a Young, David (*OP.*5361)
         1750

Ireland
Belfast
    791 Campbell & Co. *c.*1850

Cork
    152 Austen, Joseph, *c.*1795
    153 Austen, J. & Son, *c.*1826
    3334 Munster Iron Co., *c.*1833
    3524 Parr, Norton, *c.*1740
    3748 Powell, Robert, *c.*1725
    4203 Seymour, W & Son, *c.*1820
  MPM 2364a Hogg, James, *c.*1830

Dublin
    716 Burroughs, Edmund, *c.*1745
    1719 Ford, Roger, *c.*1730
    1836 Geraghty, John, *c.*1815
    2114a Hamphie, Alexander, 1719
    2242 Heaney, John, *c.*1765
    2736 King, Anthony, *c.*1740
    3163 McCabe, Owen, *c.*1750
    3207 Merry, Lawrence & Richd.,
         *c.*1850
    3208 Merry, Martin, *c.*1820
    3444 Ormiston, John, *c.*1765
    3794 Purcell, Laurence, *c.*1800
    3983 Robinson, Chris., *c.*1730
    4125 Savage, Silvester, *c.*1785
    4259 Shirley, James, *c.*1815
    5490 B., W., 1698
  MPM 1515a Edmonds, WG. & Co. *c.*1840
  MPM 4297a Simpson, W.., *c.*1730
  Addenda 1515b Edmundson & Co, (Brit.
         Metal)
  Addenda 1751a Fox, J. & Co, *c.*1900
  Addenda 1823c Gatchell, S & Sons, *c.*1885
  Addenda 2679d Jordan, H & Co, *c.*1900

Limerick
  Addenda 1924a Goodwin & Co, *c.*1900

Waterford
    925 Clark, Charles, 1790
    5282 Woods, Samuel, *c.*1820

Index

Note: (m) = maker; italicised numbers denote bibliographical reference

Burgum & Catcott (m), 178, 180, 182, 190, 237
Burroughs, Edmund (m), 240
Bush, Robert, Jr. (m), 180
Bush, Robert, Sr. (m), 180, 182, 185, 186, 188, 190, 194, 237
Bush, Robert & Co. (Robert Bush, James Curtis and Preston Edgar) (m), 180, 182, 185, 194, 237
Bush, William, Jr. (m), 181
Bush & Perkins (Robert Bush and Richard Perkins) (m), 51, 177, 178, 180, 182, 197, 231, 232, 237
Butcher, James, Jr. (m), 239
buttons, 17
B.W. (m), 240

Campbell & Co. (m), 240
candle moulds, 17
candlesticks: 16th c., 77; early 17th c., 14, 85; late 17th c., 92, 93; 18th–19th c., 110–11; Britannia metal, 209; chamber sticks (19th c.), 146; marks on, 63
capacity standards, 67, 68
Carpenter, Thomas (m), 194
Carpenter & Hamberger (m), 180, 182, 184, 194, 195, 196
Carr, John (m), 237
cartouches, 65, 202
casters, 26, 30, 103, 144–5
castle (mark), 151, 155, 156
caustic soda, for cleaning, 40
Cave, John, I (m), 178, 182, 237
Cave, John, II (m), 178, 182
Cave, Thomas, Sr. (m), 237
chalices, English, 195; Irish, 169
Chamberlain, Thomas (m), 13, 51, 209; and Hopkins, 51; wavy-edged plates, 103, 104
chamber sticks, 146
Channel Isles pewter, 171–4
chargers, 21, 168, 182
Charles II period pewter, 21, 95
Churcher, Adam (m), 238
church(es), pewter in, 32, 47; medieval, 73; 16th c., 77; 17th c.flagons, 81–3, 162; 18th–19th c. flagons, 105–7, 169, 186, 194–5; chalices 169, 195; collect-ing bowls, 131–2; Irish, 169, 170; Scottish, 162–6
cider jugs (see ale jugs)
Clark, Charles (m), 240
Clarke, Samuel (m), 239
cleaning pewter, 33–43; objections to, 34–8
Cleeve, Bou(r)chier (m), 51
Cleeve, Richard (m), 51
Clothyer, Robert (m), 239
CM (mark), 191, 192
Coats, Arch. & William (m), 239
Cockey, M. (m), 239
Cockey, W. (m), 239
Cocks (Cox), Samuel (m), 9, 139
coffee pots, 217, 218
collecting pewter, 23–32; European, 198
communion: cups, 107, 108, 162, 169, 170, 186; flagons, see flagons, church; tokens, 148, 164–5

Company, The, see Worshipful Company of Pew-terers
Compton, Henry (m), 52
Compton, Thomas (m), 52, 177, 180, 181, 182, 185, 188
Compton, Thomas and Townsend (m), 181, 182
Connell, Mathew (m), 239
Constantine, James (m), 213
Cooke, John (m), 238
Cooke, William (m), 237
Cookson, William (m), 238
coronation ware, George IV, 131–2
corrosion, 37, 77; and fakes, 222, 224, 226
Cotterell, Howard Herschel, 3, 6, 7, 27, 28, 31, 38, 46, 47, 50, 59, 64, 84, 103, 124, 144, 168, 176, 230, 235, 236
Coulter, Alex (m), 239
Coulthard, Alexander (m), 151
Cox, Stephen (m), 179, 182, 190, 237
Crane, J. C. (m), 237
'cranked' handles, 120, 122, 126
Crowley, Abr'm (m), 238
crowned X (mark), 64–5, 134, 201
cruets, medieval, 73, 74
cups: European drinking, 207; footed, 141; spirit, 144; two handled, 143
Curtis, Edgar & Co. (m), 177, 180, 182, 188, 190, 194, 195, 237, 238
Curtis, James (m), 180, 237
Curtis, John (m), 105

Dackombe, Aquila (m), 108
Dallas, James (m), 240
Dallas, Lachlan (m), 240
Daniel, Jacob (m), 239
Daniel, Joseph (m), 202
dating problems, 103, 105, 134
Daw, Robert (m), 239
decoration, 76, 85, 94–5, 97
dents, tapping out, 41
Dixon, Charles (m), 211
Dixon, James (m), 175, 195
Dixon & Smith (m), 210
Dixon & Son(s) (m), 211, 214, 217, 218, 219
Dolbeare, John (m), 179, 182, 184, 239
Dole, Erasmus, Jr. (m), 178, 182, 237
Dole, Erasmus, Sr. (m), 178, 182, 184, 185, 238
Dole, John (m), 237
doll's house pewter, 147
dome-lids, 96, 98, 105; Eddon, 103; flagons, 105, 106; tankards, 96, 98, 103, 113, 185, 186, 187
Donne, J. (m), 99
Drew, William (m), 239
Duncombe, J. (m), 237
Duncombe, Samuel (m), 179, 182, 231, 232, 237
Durie (m), 240
Dutch pewter, 205

Eddon, William (m), 178, 182, 184, 185, 186, 188, 195

242

'edelzinn' (noble pewter: Germ.), 198
Ederlein, Caspar (m), 198
Edgar, Preston (m), 180
Edgar, Robert (m), 152
Edgar & Son (m), 181, 182, 237
Edinburgh baluster measures, 157, 159, 160
Edmonds, W. G. & Co. (m), 240
Edmundson & Co. (m), 240
Edward IV, 12
Edward VII verification marks, 174
Edwards, John (m), 139
"EG" (m), 82, 84
electroplating, 219
Ellis, Samuel, I (m), 52, 176, 177, 179, 182, 184, 188, 194, 195, 196
Ellis, Samuel, II (m), 180
Elmslie & Simpson (m), 52
Embris, Edmund (m), 237
emery paper, for cleaning, 40–1
Emes, John (m), 8, 89, 90
engraving on pots, 128, 135
epoxy resins, 43
eruptions, 36–7
escutcheons, 120, 123, 125, 126
European pewter, 198–208; books on, 208; flagons, 201; marks, 201–4; metric system, 200–1; museums displaying, 206; touch marks, 204–8
Evans, Humphrey (m), 239

fakes, 87, 93, 95, 149, 172, 196–7, 206, 220–32; and repros, 228–32
Fasson, John, I (m), 179, 182, 191, 192
Fasson, John, II (m), 179, 181, 182
Fasson, Thomas (m), 181
Fasson, William (m), 180, 182, 191, 194
Fasson & Sons (m), 177, 180, 182, 184
Faust, Isaac (m), 198
Ferris, John & Co. (m), 239
fillets, 98, 113, 115, 118, 125–6, 136, 138, 140, 161
'fine metal', 17
fishtail terminals, 117, 161
Five Centuries of Base Metal Spoons, 74, 79, *235*
flagon(s), 8, 44; Romano-British, 96; 16th c., 75, 78; early 17th c., 81–3, 84, 162; late 17th c., 89–90, 96, 162–3; 18th–19th c., 105–7, 110, 194; beefeater, 89–90; Channel Isle, 172, 173; church, 17, 81–3, 89–90, 105–7, 162, 163, 185, 186, 187, 194–5, 201; Cromwellian, 16; dome-lidded, 105, 106; Eddon, 116; European, 201, 207, 208; flat-lidded, 105, 169; handle touches, 58; Irish, 168–70; knops, 82–3; marks on, 62–3; muffin-lidded, 82–3; Scottish, 162, 163; 'spire', 105, 136, 194, 195; Welsh, 167; York, 105, 107
flat-lids: flagons, 105, 169; tankards, 95–98, 185, 186, 226, 232
flatware, 16, 184, *see* plate(s)
Fleming, William (m), 239
Fly, Timothy (m), 179, 182
Ford, Roger (m), 240
Forde, Thomas (m), 238

Foster, Richard (m), 185
Fothergill, M. (m), 237; measures, *see* Bristol measures
Fox, J. & Co. (m), 240
Foy, Philip (m), 239
Franklin, ? (m), 238
French, John (m), 21, 237
French pewter, 205; reproduction, 26–7; white-metal, 209–10
Froggatt, Coldwell & Lean (m), 213
Fullerton, A. (m), 240
funnels, 26, 103, 144

gadrooning, 15, 92, 93, 98
Galbraith, Robert (m), 161, 239
Gardner, John (m), 152, 239
Gaskell & Chambers, 55
Gatchell, S., & Sons (m), 240
Gauls (m), 239
George III, 195, 196
Geraghty, John (m), 240
Gerardin & Watson (m), 125
German pewter, 205
Giffen, Thomas (m), 177
GIV (marks), 67–9, 123, 132, 133
Glasgow baluster measures, 158–9
goblets, 85
God, John (m), 18
Going, Richard (m), 179, 182, 186, 190, 191, 237
Goodwin & Co. (m), 240
Gorwood, Joseph, Jr. (m), 239
Gorwood, Joseph, Sr. (m), 238
Gourlay, David (m), 239
GR crowned (mark), 174
Graham & Wardrop (m), 180, 182, 188, 190, 239
Great Fire of London, 20, 46, 48
Green, Robert (m), 238
Gregory, Edward (m: *c*.1694), 237
Gregory, Edward (m: 1705), 238
Grenfell, George (m), 177, 180, 181, 182, 194
Griffith, John (m), 238
Grove, Abel (m), 213

Hale & Sons (m), 181
hallmarks, 61–3, 84, 90, 93, 96, 134, 137, 139, 152, 170, 177, 178, 201–2, 226, 229
Hamilton, Alexander (m), 177, 179, 181, 184
Hammermen, Incorporation of (Scottish), 150–2
Hamphie, Alexander (m), 240
Hancock & Jessop (m), 213
handles: porringer, 190; pot, 118–20, 125; broken, 105, 120, 122, 136; crank, 120, 122, 126; styles, 115; tongued, 120
Hand(s), R. (m), 97
Hardman, John (m), 238
'hard metal', 17
Harrison, J., Jr. (m), 238
Harrison, John (m), 238
Heaney, John (m), 240
Henry VII, standards, 68, 69

Reid, W. (m), 239
repairing pewter, 31, 43–5
reproduction pewter, 26–7, 149, 203, 206; and fakes, 228, 230–2
research, need for, 20, 105, 134, 149
Reynolds, R. (m), 177
Rich, William (m), 238
Robinson, Christopher (m), 240
Rodwell, Thomas (m), 238
'Romano-British Plates and Dishes', 73
Romano-British pewter, 5, 46, 71–3; museums displaying, 234
rose (mark), 202; and crown, 63–4, 177, 178, 180, 182, 201, 203, 205, 206
rosewater dishes, 108
Ross, George (m), 152, 239

Sadler, Robert (m), 111, 179, 182, 188, 238
sadware, 16, 184, *see* plate(s)
St. Croix, John de (m), 172
salts, 30, 35, 63, 77, 85, 91–3, 103, 109–10, 145–6, 226; marks on, 63
Sanders, Simon (m), 239
Savage, Silvester (m), 240
scale, removal of, *see* cleaning pewter
Scattergood, Thomas (m), 52
Scott, William, III (m), 161, 163, 180, 182, 184, 239
Scott, William, IV (m), 180, 182, 239
Scottish pewter, 150–66; domestic/tavern, 152–62; ecclesiastical, 162–6
Scouler, D. (m), 240
secondary marks, 50–5, 60–70; crowned, 64–5; hallmarks, 61–3; hR, WR, GIV, WIV, 67; House marks, 65–6; labels (cartouches), 65; owners' initials, 66–7; rose and crown, 63–4; verification marks, 50–5, 68–70
Seegood, Francis (m), 84
Sewdley, Henry (m), 42, 179, 182, 238
Seymour, W. & Son (m), 240
Shaw, John (m), 238
Shaw (m), 238
Sheaf of Wheat (m), 177, 179, 182, 183, 184, 185
Shephard, Nicholas (m), 239
Sherington, Nicholas (m), 238
Shirley, James (m), 240
Shorey, Col. John, I (m), 178, 182, 184, 185, 195
Shorey, John, II (m), 179, 182
Shorey, John, III (m), 179
Simpson, W. (m), 240
Smith, John (m), 239
Smith(e), Samuel (m), 54
Smith, Thomas (m), 96
snuff boxes, 26, 30, 146, 147, 196
snuffer tray, 213
soap boxes, 218
Society of Pewter Collectors, *see* Pewter Society
soldering, 43–4, 217
Spackman & Grant (m), 179, 182, 184
Spackman, Joseph (m), 179, 182, 194
Spackman, Joseph & James (m), 54

'spire' flagons, 105, 136, 194, 195
spirit cups, 143, 144
spoon(s), 18, 25, 26, 30, 46, 47; medieval, 73, 74, 75; 15th c., 76; 16th c., 78–80; early 17th c., 87–8; late 17th c., 91; 18th–19th c., 110; 19th c., 146; fake, 226, 227; marks, 58, 63; New England, 195–6; racks, 25
spouts, 135–6, 162
Stevens, Thomas (m), 179, 182, 191
Stiff, William (m), 238
strawberry dishes, 104
Sturges, Richard (m), 213, 217
sugar, covered, 211
Swanson, Thomas (m), 52, 177, 180, 182, 184
Swedish pewter, 204–5
Swiss pewter, 205

tankards: 16th c., 76; 17th c., 95–8; 18th–19th c., 112–17; Cromwellian, 16, 84; depicted in touch mark, 59; development chart, 114–15; dome-lid, 96, 98, 103, 113, 185, 186, 187; Eddon, 116; European, 199–200; fakes and repros, 226, 232; flat-lid, 95–8, 185, 186, 226, 232; lidless, 113; marks on, 63, 67, 68, 96; New England, 185–90; Queen Anne, 15; Scottish, 161; as trophies, 133, 199; 'tulip', 113, 117, 118, 161, 185, 187; *see also* pots and tavern pots
tappit hens, 154–6
tassie (beaker), 155
Taudin, James (m), 209
tavern pots, 17, 47, 90, 96, 98, 99, 161
Taylor, W. (m), 239
Taylor, William (m), 239
teapots: Britannia metal, 210–11, 212, 214, 215, 219; New England, 193–4
tea services and tableware, 210–19
terminal styles, 115
Terry, Leonard (m), 238
thistle mark, 151, 154
thumbpiece styles, 115
'tin pest', 36, 37–8, 77
Tin Research Institute, 3
tobacco boxes, 148, 217
tongued handles, 120
touch marks, 56–60, 82, 100, 151–2, 176, 177, 204–5; plates, 20, 151
town marks (European), 210, 202, 204
Townsend, John, I (m), 52, 55, 177, 179, 182, 185, 186, 188, 194, 196; & Compton, 52, 139, 177, 180, 182, 185, 187, 188, 189, 194; & Giffen, 52, 177, 180, 182; & Reynolds, 52, 177
Townsend, John, II (m), 177, 180
Townsend, Mary (m), 177
toy(s), 17, 147
trade cards, 121–2, 124
Tregelles, I (m), 239
'trifle', 17
trophies, 140, 206; tankards as, 133
Tudric pewter (Liberty's of London), 3, 148
tulips, *see under* pots; tankards